First published by
Canonvela Publishing
26 Beech Road
Erdington
Birmingham
B23 5QN
2012
www.canonvela.com

ISBN: 978 0 9571749 0 0

A Cataloguing in Publication record for this title
is available from the British Library

Typeset in 'Baskerville', originally designed by
John Baskerville (1706-1775) Birmingham.
Printed in Great Britain by Copytech (UK) Limited.

Designed and Set by Tim Griffiths

To Birmingham's motoring pioneers.

Acknowledgments

I would like to thank:

Mike Worthington-Williams for his invaluable advice and input correcting my technical errors.
Janet and David Griffiths for proof reading and comma wrangling.

Ian Ferguson, Roger, Andy, Cosmo and Derry at the VSCC Library, Chipping Norton
Michael Gasking in Australia
Michael Curry in New Zealand
Merv Kroll in Australia - Merlin, Autocrat
The Archivists at Birmingham Central Library Local Archives Section
Geert Versleyen at Yesterday's Antique Motorcycles
David Moore at the Midland Automobile Club
Brian Slark at the Barber Museum, Birmingham, Alabama - Wall
Andrew Marfell of the SAHB
Bob Jones - Cycles and Cyclecars
Tony and Phil Smallbone - Smallbone
Edward Hickmott - Stellite
Peter Morris - Calthorpe
Norman Hills - Rover
Paul Cooper - Rollo
Bob Millington - Adcock
Sheila Lyons - Brockas
Anthony Prosser, Nigel Harrison - Morris Commercial
Bill Baker - Singer.
Martyn Wray - Singer.
Ian Lawes - Garrard-Blumfield
Johnny Thomas - Alldays and Onions
Margaret Till - Levetus
Bill Phelps - Quadrant
Jim Whorwood - BSA
John Spicer - West
Liz Ford - Traffic
Michael Cole - Garrard
Peter Richmond - Topham
Brian Hands - Hands
Peter Harper - Patrick Motors
William Morrison - Mulliner
Ian McKenzie - McKenzie
Norman Painting - Alldays and Onions, Wrigley and Morris Commercial
Phil Baildon and the Austin Seven Clubs Association archive.
Temple Press
Iliffe
Photographs from the Phyllis Nicklin Collection on pages 8 and 105 © University of Birmingham, UK. Reproduced with permission.

Preface

This book should have been written decades ago. Birmingham has a long history of involvement in the metal working trades so it was no surprise to find that it played an important part in the development of the motor car. The problem is that few people today seem to know this and those directly involved at the time didn't think to write an account of what happened.

When I started to research this book I was told that one of the problems would be that everyone who was there at the time is no longer with us. They were right. If the inspiration to write this book had appeared to someone fifty years ago there would at least have been some surviving manufacturers or employees to corroborate the evidence and steer the research. The lack of witnesses has meant that a great deal of detective work has had to be employed and information garnered from a wide range of sources, though this has proved an enjoyable exercise in itself for someone of a curious nature.

If that inspiration had happened sooner then I wouldn't have been ready to write this book so, for me, it has provided an unexpected opportunity to look at a fascinating period and discover some interesting people whose stories deserve to be told.

Also on the plus side, the delay in writing this book has, at least, allowed technology to develop to a point where the disparate scraps of surviving information can be pulled together relatively quickly. If it wasn't for the speed of keyword searches and the wealth of information sources now either accessible or indexed on the internet this book could have taken a decade to write.

Much information has disappeared over the years as companies failed, photographs were lost and records destroyed but what is still with us can now be recorded cheaply and easily and stands a better chance of staying with us for posterity. All that it needs is for someone to put the scattered pieces of the puzzle together and tell the forgotten stories. This is my attempt...

April 2012

A scattering of cars in Corporation Street in the twenties.

Contents

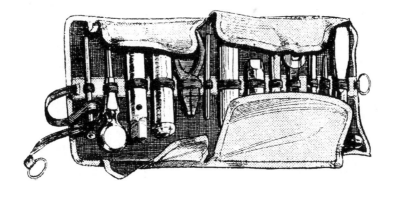

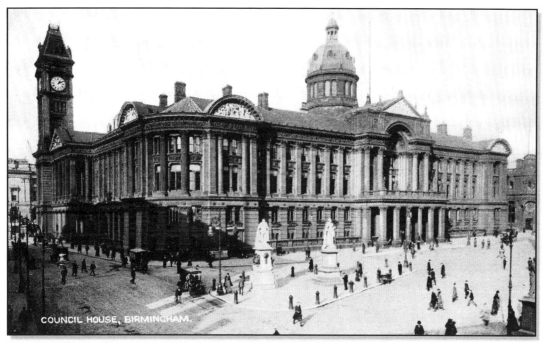

COUNCIL HOUSE, BIRMINGHAM.

Introduction - Discovering Birmingham's past.

A few years ago I started to trace my family tree, but at that stage genealogical research, as a popular pastime, was in its early stages. The internet existed, but little had been made available online and so the only way to progress research was in Records Offices and Libraries. I knew that all of the more recent generations of my family had come from Birmingham and spent some time in Birmingham Central Reference Library searching the shelves for clues.

Whilst researching in the Library I started to study the larger scale Ordnance Survey maps of the Hockley area, where many of the strands of my family came together, and was amazed at how dense the fabric of the inner city was in the 19th and early 20th century compared with today.

I am old enough to remember the rows of terraced houses in the city centre that gave way to the slum clearances of the 60s and 70s and have memories of wandering the streets with their blue brick pavements and a pub on every corner as a child. I had finished my Vimto and bag of crisps, given to me whilst the older males in the family occupied one of those pubs (The Duke of York in Duke Street) of a Sunday lunchtime, and started to explore.

What I don't remember is much about the industry that had existed in the inner city because, by then, the life of the areas had pretty much drained away into post-war housing estates and factories in the suburbs. But, looking at the old Ordnance Survey maps, I could see that in amongst the back-to-back houses were hundreds, if not thousands, of factories and workshops making everything from brass bed knobs to engines.

Today you need to resort to Google to find anything specific or obscure and it will probably be shipped in from China but, in those days, it was almost certainly being made in a workshop a few streets away.

As I have said, I am old enough to remember the last remnants of the old Birmingham, the 'City of a Thousand Trades', the 'Workshop of the World', but the generations that have followed me probably have no idea of what went before and probably have enough trouble coping with the city at present with the massive rate of change sweeping away landmarks and then sweeping away what replaced them.

One of the things that has disappeared in more recent times is the Museum of Science and Industry that used to be in Newhall Street, in the Jewellery Quarter. At the time of writing parts of the building are still there but their contents have migrated to the new 'Think Tank' in Curzon Street and an anonymous wrinkly tin shed in Nechells.

Think Tank is the 'modern' version of a science museum, a triumph of style over content, a mess of interpretive displays but very few of the artefacts that used to fill every space in the old museum.

The modern child can go and press buttons and manipulate touch screens but if he wanted to see the actual fabric of history he would have to search the sparse and badly-lit scattering of glass display cases or explore the horrors that are the ground floor displays. Tucked away on the ground floor is an early Austin Seven wedged into an alcove so that it can only be seen from one side through a forest of interpretive devices. A few steps away there is an Austin Ten that has been hung upside down from the ceiling at a jaunty angle for no obvious reason. This is a pale shadow of the 'cabinet of curiosities' that was the old Science and Industry Museum.

George Elkington patented the first commercial electroplating process and built a large factory in Newhall Street behind an elegant neo-classical facade. As industry vacated the city centre for industrial parks, more practically accessed by heavy vehicles, the factory was turned over to a new life as a museum celebrating the city's illustrious industrial and scientific heritage. Indeed, Alexander Parkes, the inventor of the first plastic, had worked in this very building.

Passing through its doors, the inquisitive child of fifty years ago would find displays of pen nibs, steam engines, mechanical musical instruments, button making machines, primitive draughts-playing computers and all manner of treasures. Most of these are still in the possession of the Museum but are only viewable now by appointment for a guided tour in the aforementioned wrinkly tin shed where they can just about be seen, stacked high on

Birmingham Museum of Science and Industry 1960 from the Phyllis Nicklin Collection.

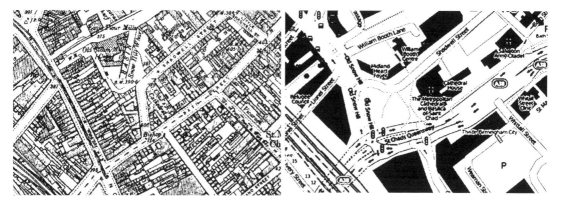

Typical 1905 Birmingham street pattern.   *The same area today.*

industrial racking, that is if you even know of the Museums Collection in the first place.

In this building are most of the remaining collection of historic vehicles that had accumulated in the old museum, parked in no particular order and gathering dust. No way to treat a city's industrial heritage.

Birmingham's near neighbour, Coventry, has a different approach. Possibly in reaction to the German wartime raids that devastated most of the historic, mediaeval centre in one night and the waves of planners that demolished most of what was left, Coventry, in more recent years, has developed an appreciation of its motoring heritage and has a modern transport museum to prove it.

There is nothing like having a few actual artefacts to put across a message and Coventry Transport Museum has plenty of them, rows of cars, most of which were built in the city, make for an interesting day out with a more low-key 'interpretive' content.

One particularly interesting display shows a map of the city centre with the old car factories, which have almost all gone now, picked out in red. What strikes you from this is what would strike you from looking at the old Ordnance Survey maps of Birmingham city centre - the sheer density of manufacturing workshops.

Coventry boasts that 100 makes of car were built in the city and the list of makes is impressive: Rover, Singer, Talbot and Triumph all came out of Coventry. But what about Birmingham? How many makes of car came from Birmingham's factories and workshops? When we try to answer this we encounter a problem. During the 70s and 80s British manufacturing was in its death throes; the major industries, mining, steel, car making, were mired in disastrous industrial disputes where powerful unions weighed in against management that had lost its way and, by their combined actions, managed to export all their jobs to the up and coming countries east of here.

Birmingham was tainted by this. The name that is probably most linked with Birmingham's motor manufacturing in this period is 'Red Robbo' - a union convenor with what could be considered a particularly destructive take on running a business.

Post war Birmingham's motor industry was dominated by a few big players; Austin/British Leyland/Rover at Longbridge, Jaguar at Castle Bromwich and Land Rover at Solihull. All have

The old museum transport section.

9

had their problems and share of bad press; but it wasn't always like that. Birmingham played a major part in the development of the modern motor car.

So, how many marques of motor car came from Birmingham?

The obvious one is Austin. Based in Longbridge, it was Austin's factories that became synonymous with British motor manufacture.

But what about Wolseley? Based, in more recent years, in Ward End it was taken over and phased out by bigger players to be replaced

BMSI, Newhall Street more recently.

by an ill-fated van making operation. What about BSA? Birmingham's motorbikes have become legend but the factory that produced the M20 and the Gold Star also made three and four wheeled cars for many years before WWII.

Prompted by the idea of gathering some pre-war, Birmingham made cars in the centre of the city of their birth to celebrate 'Drive It Day' in 2011 so, with assistance, I started to investigate just which cars would qualify and we were surprised to find how many contenders there were.

Most people could probably think of two or three (remember that Rover, Land Rover and Jaguar didn't appear until after the war), but the truth is that the number is over 114 (We haven't stopped looking). And this includes one or two names that many people would not associate with Birmingham.

Of course the obvious question has to be; what constitutes a Birmingham car? It is rare that all the components of a car are sourced from one place. Is a Toyota built at Burnaston from parts sourced all over the world British or Japanese? Is a Jaguar assembled in Birmingham, again from parts sourced all over the world and owned by an Indian steel magnate a Birmingham marque, or an Indian marque, or still a Coventry marque? Some of the simpler early cars were substantially fabricated locally but used engines sourced from the few manufacturers, like JAP in Tottenham, who could make them. Other cars, like the Austin Seven could be wholly made in Birmingham or sent as a rolling chassis to a coachbuilder in another town who would add the bodywork so that the most visible parts of the car were not actually built in Birmingham.

Inevitably we have had to make a broad value judgement here but, if the net were widened only a little, many more marques would have to be included. The basic rule is that the marque should have been based in what we now recognise as Birmingham or substantially built in the city - preferably both.

The marques are represented chronologically with Garrard and Blumfield, who were the developers of the first car in the city at the beginning and Atco who started production of their (very individual) vehicle in the city at the end. In between we have Lanchester who produced the first British four-wheeled, petrol engined car and Austin, one of the biggest car manufacturers the country ever had, but also we have the small car makers in their workshops trying to make their way in a new industry. But first we must look at the early experimenters...

The Beginnings - Steam Carriages and the Locomotive Acts.

Motoring in Britain got off to a difficult start. The will and invention was there but legislation got in the way. This allowed the continental countries to forge a lead, with France and Germany in particular becoming major motor producing nations, before Britain even got off the starting blocks.

It wasn't always that way, the early attempts at building road-going vehicles had been as evident here as abroad, but that was possibly part of the problem - the people who occupied positions of influence were not ready for them.

In 1759 a Dr. Robinson wrote a letter whilst a student at the University of Glasgow, to James Watt suggesting that the power of a steam engine could be applied to moving carriage wheels but abandoned the idea when he went abroad. Watt chose not to progress this line of thought for another 25 years.

In 1765 Benjamin Franklin and Lunar Society members Matthew Boulton and Erasmus Darwin were in correspondence about steam as a means of motive power and Boulton sent Franklin a model of a steam engine that could be turned to the task. Franklin was preoccupied with political matters at the time as the US and Britain were going through a period of difficult relations on the run up to the American War of Independance. Darwin, however was excited by the idea of a 'fiery chariot' and encouraged Boulton to build one. He identified that what was required were:

      1. A rotary motion
      2. The direction of the motion should be easily changed
      3. It should be able to start, accelerate, decelerate and stop easily
      4. The weight and cost of the machine should be as small as possible.

He went on to describe a three or four wheeled vehicle with a two cylinder steam engine, a steering wheel and steam cocks to control the speed, basically a steam car. Boulton didn't take to the idea so it was later dropped.

In 1769 Francis Moore, a linen draper from London proposed a vehicle "*constructed upon peculiar principles, and capable of being wrought or put in motion by fire, water, or air without being drawn by horses, or any other beast or cattle*". He sold his horses and advised his friends to do the same as their value would fall once his invention took hold and started trials of his steam carriage. The experiments grabbed the attention of the Lunar Society and William Small wrote to James Watt about Moore's patent applications. Watt replied saying that his carriage could only succeed using his (Watt's) patented steam engines and if Moore tried he would stop him. Moore didn't try, in fact he gave up the idea. Dr. Small continued to give the idea some thought and tried, but failed, to persuade Watt to experiment.

William Murdoch was born in Lugar, Ayrshire in 1754 and worked for his father at his Mill. He had an inventive mind and, attracted by the work of James Watt at his Soho works, he walked the 300 miles to Birmingham in 1777 wearing a wooden hat that he

Erasmus Darwin   *James Watt*   *Matthew Boulton*   *William Murdoch*

had turned on a lathe. It was the hat that attracted Watt's attention as it was elliptical in section and so he employed Murdoch for a trial period. Murdoch, probably inspired by the discussions going on between Watt and Boulton at the Works, set to work building a model of a possible steam carriage whilst living in Redruth and working on the Bolton and Watt steam engines being installed in the tin mines.

In 1784 the model steam carriage was demonstrated and was described as a *"hissing and fiery little monster"* but it did manage to move faster than Murdoch could, despite its size. This model was the first, recorded example in Britain of a man-made machine moving around, completely under its own power.

The model still exists having passed through the Murdoch family, via the Tangye brothers to the Birmingham Museum at Think Tank.

James Watt was still resistant to the idea of steam as a motive power and both he and Boulton put pressure on Murdoch to drop the idea so that he could concentrate on the increasing workload of the business. There is some speculation that he went on to build a full size version, but there is no real evidence to support this.

The first patent to appear for a road vehicle was in 1821 when Julius Griffiths of Brompton patented a steam carriage *"expressly for the conveyance of passengers on the highway"*. The

Murdoch's model steam carriage.

vehicle was built by the company founded by Joseph Bramah, (the inventor of the beer pump), in Pimlico and had a few trial runs in Bramah's yard. However the boiler wasn't up to the job, and it never made it out onto the roads.

Over the next few years, a number of experimental vehicles were developed by Samuel Brown in London and Burstall and Hill of Edinburgh and London, amongst others, but with little success.

William Henry James was born in Henley in Arden in 1796 and, by 1823, was patenting his developments in steam propulsion. He set himself up in Birmingham and built a series of experimental steam-driven road vehicles including his 'Steam Drag'.

A drag (or 'park drag') is a small private carriage usually driven by a team of four horses, (which lent its name to the street on which it rode, as in 'main drag' and then on to 'drag racing', an event originally held on

W H James's Steam locomotive.

the 'main drag') but on this occasion was powered by two, small, separate two-cylinder, steam engines.

In 1824 Walter Hancock of Marlborough in Wiltshire started to construct steam-driven vehicles at his Stratford works in London and the race to set up steam driven passenger services began. In 1827, he built a four seater, three-wheeled steam carriage and carried out a number of successful test runs and, at about the same time, Sir Goldsworthy Gurney ran trials up the hills of north London with a carriage that not only had wheels but also mechanical legs to push it along as he didn't consider that wheels would give enough grip to work!

In 1830 John, William, George and Reuben Heaton of Birmingham patented *"certain machinery, and the application thereof to steam engines, for the purpose of propelling and drawing carriages on turnpike roads, or other roads, and railways"*. The Heaton family later went on to found the Birmingham Mint, but the brothers were busy in the 1830s inventing, and patenting, their 'Steam Drag' with an engine which was a combination of the features of those found in both Watt's and Trevithick's.

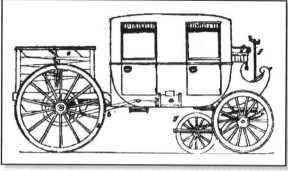

The Heatons' Steam Carriage.

In October 1830, their vehicle, now called 'Enterprise' made its first appearance on the streets of Birmingham pulling a large cast-iron press along Bath Street, Whittall Street, Steelhouse Lane, Bull Street, Temple Row, Waterloo Street and Ann Street and on to the premises of the button and medal maker John Hardman, where the load was detached. The recipients of the press would, as 'Hardman and Iliff', later go on to work with the neo-gothic architect, Pugin creating 'medieval metalwork' in Birmingham.

In 1832, the experimental vehicle made another trial run from Shadwell Street, up Great Charles Street and out along the road to Halesowen reaching speeds of 10mph and for part of the way carrying 30 of the Heaton's pupils. Further trips were made out to Dudley and Wolverhampton in 1833 and, in August of that year, the steam drag towed a coach with up to 25 passengers on a return journey to Bromsgrove via the Lickey Hills - quite a challenge.

Following further trials, the brothers advertised the formation of the 'Heatons' Steam Carriage Co' with the intent of providing a regular passenger service, but the later trials must have proved unsuccessful as, by November of 1848, they had abandoned all further trials and dissolved the Company.

Meanwhile, back at the Hancock works, in 1831, a small ten seater steam coach called the 'Infant' started making passenger trips into London and also made an experimental trip from London to Brighton.

In Southampton, William Alltoft Summers and Captain Nathaniel Ogle RN were also at work building their steam carriage. The first trial ended with a broken crank on the approach to Basingstoke but their improved design managed to travel from Southampton to Birmingham, Liverpool and London a number of times during 1932, entering the Inn Yard in Birmingham, dragged by passengers and bystanders, as it had run out of coke. Hancock continued to develop bigger and better vehicles and, in 1833, his strangely named 'Autopsy' appeared and his own 'Enterprise' started the first regular steam carriage service between London Wall and Paddington. In 1834, his 'Era' appeared and was shipped to Dublin where it ran around the streets at up to 18mph throughout 1835.

Birmingham's next contender was the

The Church Steam Carriage.

three-wheeled steam carriage designed and built by an American, Dr. William H Church, and backed by fellow American financier Henry Van Wart after 1832.

The carriage had a lightweight body, built using a method similar to those that re-appeared in 'Weymann' car bodies in the early twenties, and wheels with elastic rims that presented a flat area to the ground which increased grip on the soft road surfaces of the day.

Great claims were made for the vehicle and it raised a great deal of financial backing so that, in 1835, it was able to have its first public trial with forty passengers on board.

An 1831 satire on steam carriages.

The carriage travelled along the Coventry Road on, what was intended to be a 12 mile round trip and was claimed to have reached speeds of up to 15 mph; but this cannot be verified. The hoped for regular speeds of 15 to 20 mph proved unattainable on the roads of the time and the carriage finally broke down after striking the footpath and damaging the boiler, it must have been a difficult beast to control.

Church abandoned further development and was last heard of in 1861, sailing back to America.

In 1834, Messrs. Yates and Smith trialed their steam coach from the works in Colchester Street, Whitechapel, London and managed to achieve between 10 and 12 mph on the return run to the factory only to have an exhaust pipe joint break due to the roughness of the road and little more was heard of them.

Relations between Hancock and the Company that ran his buses, 'The London and Paddington Steam Carriage Company' became strained and, in 1837, their own engineer took the 'Enterprise' apart with the intent of building his own carriage. Hancock had the vehicle returned and broke off relations with the company entirely.

Hancock's final, and largest, vehicle, the 22 seater 'Automaton', appeared in 1839 and he demonstrated it at a number of events in London but the end of the steam carriage was approaching. Between 1840 and 1857 the attention of the more inventive engineers had turned to the railways with a few, like a Mr Bach of Birmingham, trying their hand at producing small passenger locomotives.

By 1861, the damage that locomotives could do to roads was worrying the government and the first of the Locomotive Acts appeared. This restricted vehicle weight to 12 tons and speeds to 10mph. The second Locomotive Act of 1865, known as the 'Red Flag Act' limited speeds to 4mph in the country and 2 mph in town and required that each vehicle should have a crew of three; a driver, a stoker and a man walking in front with a red flag or lantern warning horse riders and horse drawn traffic of the approach of a self propelled vehicle. The 1878 Act added the requirement to stop if a horse was sighted.

The big problem, as far as the development of the car was concerned, was that there was no distinction made between vehicles of different sizes. This meant that the requirement for a driver, stoker and flagman and a slow speed limit, though reasonable for a vehicle the size and weight of a traction engine, was applied to even the smallest of motorised carriages.

This, combined with the Tolls that had been applied under the Turnpike Acts, effectively killed the steam carriage and made the development and use of cars in Britain impossible for the next thirty years.

Cycle Manufacture

With the restrictions placed on motor driven road vehicles, the railways became the major means of long distance public transport with horse drawn vehicles competing in a poor second place.

In towns, the usual modes of transport were either horse drawn or pushed. What was missing was an affordable means of personal transportation and the only means that the law allowed had to be propelled by its rider. Thus the bicycle rose to fill this role.

A French 'Velocipede'.

The first bicycles appeared in Germany in 1817 and were little more than a length of wood with a wheel at each end, one of which was steerable, that was sat astride and pushed along with the feet. Better than nothing - but not much.

What was needed was a way of getting the rider's feet off the muddy ground and a number of methods were tried, including one by Kirkpatrick Macmillan, a Scottish blacksmith, who assembled a treadle system to drive the rear wheel in 1839.

The eventual solution was the introduction of pedals invented by Frenchman Pierre Lallement in 1862 but to get the pedals a comfortable distance from the seat the wheel had to be rather large and the rider had to sit on top of this large wheel. To balance this the other wheel became smaller. Thus was created the 'velocipede' or 'boneshaker' with its heavy wooden wheels with iron rims. It was better, but rather uncomfortable to ride.

Starley and Sutton's 'Ariel'.

In about 1870 Eugene Meyer on the continent and James Starley in England took the design of the French velocipede and made it lighter. The wooden wheels were replaced by lighter metal rims with wire spokes and the front wheel got progressively bigger, eventually evolving into the high-wheeler that eventually came to be called the penny-farthing.

More correctly called simply a 'bicycle' or later an 'ordinary', the 'Penny Farthing' as invented by Eugene Meyer wasn't able to be developed in France as the French were a little pre-occupied with the after effects of the Franco-Prussian War and so it was left open to the English to start manufacture. Birmingham, along with Coventry, London and Manchester became a centre of cycle manufacture in the 1870s.

James Starley was born in Sussex in 1830 and ran away from home as a teenager to Lewisham to work as a gardener. Inspired by industrial

An 'Ordinary' from 1886.

advances he spent his time devising gadgets and mechanisms and moved to Coventry with his friend William Hillman, and Hillman's brother in law, Thomas Brockas (see **Brockas**) where they manufactured sewing machines. The company's sales agent , Rowley Turner, had bought a 'Michaux' cycle back with him from a trip to France in 1868 and it inspired Starley to look at the possibility of producing an improved machine.

James Starley's design had wire spokes like Meyer's but they were tangential and his cycle, the 'Ariel' had a lighter, more elegant look than what had gone before. He introduced a step that allowed easier mounting and dismounting and created what was known as the 'Coventry Model'. His 'Penny-farthings' look impressive but were not particularly practical and, as anyone who has ever tried to ride one and dismounted unexpectedly over the handlebars will tell you, something else was needed.

That 'something' was a method of propelling the cycle along, linking the pedals by a drive to the back wheel and removing the rider from a position on top of the steered wheel so that it could be turned more freely.

It wasn't until Harry Lawson developed the chain drive to the rear wheel and James Starley's nephew, John Kemp Starley, in partnership with William Sutton, a Coventry cycling enthusiast developed their cycle with chain drive and similar sized wheels that the modern bicycle was born. Starley and Sutton's 'Rover Safety Bicycle' See Rover) of 1885 was ground-breaking.

The Rover Safety Bicycle from 1888.

It had a 'diamond' arrangement of tubes to form the frame and the wheels could now be closer to a similar size, though this did, initially, require a great deal of thought on suspension design to counter the effects of rough roads. All later bicycles, to this day, have followed its pattern and the cycle industry took off in the late 1880s as, at long last, a simple but effective means of transport for the masses became available.

To this point Birmingham had supplied the tubes and parts for others and had also been producing the earlier cycles, now termed 'ordinaries' to distinguish them from 'safety' cycle, but with the new design the workshops and factories of the city stepped up a gear and, literally, hundreds of cycle companies appeared. It was the 'Golden Age' of cycle production.

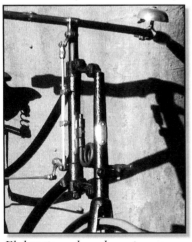

Birmingham became the centre of the cycle industry as further refinements appeared. Dunlop introduced the first practical pneumatic tyres to replace the hard, solid tyres previously used. A 'freewheel' was developed in 1898 allowing the pedals to be used as a foot rest when not propelling the cycle forward and improvements to brakes and gearing appeared over time.

The massive expansion in cycle manufacture had a downside - over production. The sheer number of cycle companies provided competition that was forcing the prices down and, as the century neared its end, a depression in the cycle trade loomed. The cycle companies needed a new product and new markets to survive. That new product was the motor vehicle and the simplest, most easily built, form of that was the motorcycle...

Elaborate early cycle suspension.

Motorcycle Manufacture

Cycles were all very well, they had at least given the common man a method of getting from A to B that he stood some chance of affording. The problem was that he would still be using his own muscle power to move and the alternatives; horses, carriages, canal boats and trains all moved under their own power. The obvious answer was to attach some sort of motor to a cycle and take some of the effort out of travel.

One candidate for the first motorcycle appeared in America in 1867, but it is arguable whether this qualified. Sylvester Howard Roper (1823-1896) built a cycle that moved under its own steam, literally, by attaching a steam engine to a primitive wooden bicycle. The only problem was that it needed stoking with coal at regular intervals and that was not easy to do on the move, straddling a cycle.

Roper Steam Cycle 1867.

The first, generally recognized, motorcycle was built by Gottlieb Daimler in 1885 when he took advantage of advances in design of the cycle made by Rover in that year and the petrol engine by Nicolaus Otto in 1876 and married the two together. Daimler had previously worked for Otto so he was in the right place at the right time.

Daimler may have built a 'motorcycle' but the term itself wasn't coined until 1893 when Edward Joel Pennington used the word to describe his motorised bicycles.

Daimler 1885.

Pennington was a notorious figure, an American who, in the early years of the motor industry, became involved in a number of enterprises that never made a penny for their backers. The patents for his machine were sold to Harry Lawson in England, another notorious figure who we will encounter later. The first production motorcycle was the 'Hildebrand & Wolfmüller' in Germany. This machine was built in Munich in 1894 the same year that Garrard and Blumfield were producing their electric phaeton (see **Garrard-Blumfield**).

The locomotive acts had applied to all motorised transport and so, as a consequence of the late-start in the UK, motorcycles and cars developed side-by-side. In 1899 a number of contenders for the first British motorcycle appeared, all of them in the Midlands. Colonel Sir Henry Capel Holden designed the world's first four-cylinder motorbike in Coventry, Quadrant (see **Quadrant**) started to produce their first motorbike in Sheepcote Street, Ernie Humphries

Hildebrand & Wolfmuller 1894.

and Charles Dawes built their first machine in Hall Green (Dawes cycles still exist as a company) and the Bard Cycle Company (see **Calthorpe**) built their motorised tricycle in Barn Street. Birmingham companies were to the fore and, throughout the period up to the Second World War covered by this book Birmingham's motorcycle manufacturers were the dominant force in the industry.

But two wheels and limited seating couldn't satisfy the market...

The Horseless Carriage

The motorcycle had liberated people but it had the disadvantages of having limited carrying capacity either in passengers or luggage, lack of protection from the elements and lack of comfort, particularly for the passengers. The answer was to take a carriage, remove the horses and add a motor - simple.

The restrictive legislation in Britain made development, or use, of such vehicles impossible before the Emancipation Act of 1896 but experimentation in this area was by no means dead. The steam vehicles developed in the early part of the century for public transport had not been forgotten and some brave souls continued with the work. In Birmingham one such person was John Inshaw.

John George Inshaw was born in 1855 in Birmingham. He came from an engineer-ing background; his father, another John, born in 1807 was an engineer and his uncle Joseph, who lived next door to them for a time in Morville Street, Ladywood, was also an engineer.

John the younger, with the assistance of his father, worked on a steam carriage that could seat ten people and travel at an average of eight to twelve mph.

The boiler was composed of steel tubes and took about twenty minutes to develop sufficient head of steam before it could move off. Between 180 and 200 psi of steam pressure drove two cylinders with a 4in bore and an 8in stroke with power transmitted to the wheels through a three-speed, plus reverse, gearbox with the option of disengaging the gears 'for downhill, etc.' It ran around the streets for several years and became *"well known in Birmingham and district"*. Unfortunately, the law eventually

John Inshaw Snr.

caught up with him and he was forced to abandon any further excursions.

Inshaw senior was quite a character. Besides being a mechanical engineer he was a paper maker and, from 1859, had run a pub in Ladywood on the corner of Morville Street (now Browning Street) and Sherborne Street that he filled with his working models and devices to attract customers to its rather out of the way location. One of the features of the pub was his amazing steam clock so he named it 'The Steam Clock Tavern'. The Pub became a success and in the early 1880s it became a popular Music Hall.

Inshaw's 1881 Steam Carriage.

The tavern and music hall have both long gone and the site is now covered with inner city housing. John Inshaw, the younger, appeared in one of the first editions of Autocar magazine in 1895 to tell the story of the steam carriage and say that he would be working on an updated version as soon as legislative changes were made.

He was true to his word and became involved in the formation of the 'Birmingham Motor and Supply Company' who would start car

The Steam Clock Tavern.

production in 1900 (see **Rex**) and probably used his engineering works in Cheston Road, Aston a few yards away from the factory that was to produce the Stellite from 1913 (see **Stellite**), for that purpose. He also appears to have carried on experimenting in his own right as he patented and constructed an 'autocar' in 1897 and an unidentified steam wagon was seen on the streets of Birmingham in 1899 bearing his name.

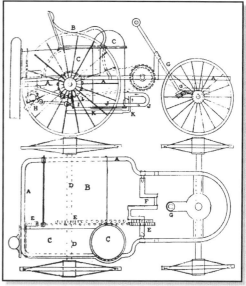

Wilkinson's 1865 Petrol Car.

The Inshaws were not alone, but not everyone had their degree of showmanship and developments tended to take place out of sight. In February 1896 Joseph Wilkinson wrote to the Birmingham Argus and laid claim to having constructed a 'road car' in about 1876. This was not '*one of the lumbering four-ton weight sort described in the mechanical papers and the Autocar but a light tube built car with engines driven by petroleum spirit.*'

The correspondent was Joseph Wilkinson born in 1837 in Lambeth. He had an engineering company in Smallbrook Street, Birmingham, from which he had retired in 1892 handing the business over to Edward Baker. Whilst still in Southwark, where he had grown up, he saw the steam car exhibited by Lee of Leicester at the Great Exhibition of 1862 and, thinking it too heavy, designed a lighter car and had it built by Joseph Clement and Co. This company had been started by Joseph Clement, the inventor of the metal planing lathe and builder of Charles Babbage's difference engine. Drawings of the car appeared in Autocar in April 1896. If this car was built, it predated all the currently accepted 'first cars'.

One of the companies that claimed to have been working on motor vehicles from an early date was Ralph Gilbert and Son, the coachbuilders in John Bright Street (see **Gilbert**). They unveiled their first vehicle, a motorised carriage that could carry twelve people, in 1899 but had been working on it for three years and had built what they termed a 'road motor' as early as 1887.

Even earlier were the efforts of the Tangye brothers at their Cornwall works in Clement Street in Birmingham who, in 1862, built a road going, steam driven vehicle that could seat up to 10 people.

Their 'Cornubia' weighed 27cwt and could travel at over 20mph. Richard Tangye, in his autobiography 'One and all' wrote that they travelled '*many hundreds of miles*' in the vehicle with it, rather unsurprisingly, generating great interest. The vehicle fell foul of the Locomotive Act and all further experimentation was abandoned.

The Tangye family came to Birmingham from the Camborne area of Cornwall, where Murdoch

The 'Cornubia' outside Yardley church.

had demonstrated his model steam carriage, hence the name of their works. Another native of that same area was William Ivy Rogers (see **Merlin**). They built a large business in Smethwick and founded both the Birmingham School of Art and the Museum and Art Gallery.

These were all early experimenters. There was no real possibility of any of their designs going into production and widespread use and, when the time finally did arrive when the legislative barriers would be lifted, there was another issue - patents.

The continental car manufacturers would not only build cars but also endeavour to patent as many of their innovations as they could to secure an ongoing income from licensing. This would have a restraining effect on the British manufacturers as they would either have to pay a licence fee every time they used a patented design or else design something sufficiently different to do the same job and be patentable in its own right.

Harry Lawson.

Frederick Lanchester (see **Lanchester**) took the latter route, wanting to design his cars from the ground up with little owed to any other designers. Garrard and Blumfield (see **Garrard-Blumfield**) also created a car of their own design which they didn't put into production, but rather sold the patent, which is where Harry Lawson enters the story...

1879 Lawson Bicyclette.

Lawson was a singular figure in the early years. His aim was to control the market for British built motor cars by buying up every available patent to drive competition from the market and set up a number of companies to further this aim, what would be known today as a 'patent troll'.

Henry John Lawson was born in London in 1852 the son of Thomas Lawson, a Calvinist Minister and mechanical model maker. He followed his father into model making and developed an interest in cycle design, inventing the chain-drive to the rear wheel on his 'Bicyclette' of 1879 that was to be such an important part of Starley's 'Safety Bicycle'.

As the century progressed he became more interested in motorised vehicles and set up

1896 Run Medal.

the British Motor Syndicate in 1895 in collaboration with Ernest Hoolley from Nottingham and Martin Rucker from London with the aim of acquiring motor car patents.

The first company that they took over was the 'Daimler Motor Syndicate' formed in 1893 by Frederick Simms, who was born in Hamburg to a family originally from Birmingham.

It was with Simms that Lawson set up the 'Motor Car Club' in 1895 to promote the use of the vehicles he intended to manufacture. The Motor Car Club organised the Motor Show at Olympia in the summer of 1896 and, in the November of that year, organised the London to Brighton Emancipation Run as the Club's first motoring event. This run is what is commemorated each year by the Veteran Car Club.

In the emancipation run, held to celebrate the liberation of the motorist from the restrictive Locomotive Acts, Lawson drove the 'pilot' vehicle. One of the others was driven by Charles McRobie Turrell who was involved in both the Club and Lawson's companies. He later teamed up with James Accles (see **Accles-Turrell**) and manufactured engines in Perry Barr for Lawson's vehicles.

In February 1896 Lawson joined forces with Gottleib Daimler and Frederick Lanchester (see **Lanchester**) and formed the Daimler Motor Company to take over the interests of the, earlier, Daimler Motor Syndicate. This company purchased a thirteen acre site in Coventry, complete with a newly-refurbished cotton mill building and sold on part of the site to the 'Great Horseless Carriage Company'.

This company was intended to take over all of the patent rights, including those of Garrard and Blumfield, held by the British Motor Syndicate and had Herbert H Mulliner, the Birmingham coachbuilder, as a one of its directors.

The building was christened the 'Motor Mills' and had the Beeston Tyre Syndicate on the top floor, the British Motor Syndicate on the second floor and the Humber Company on the ground floor, but the complicated web of companies that Lawson had created were viewed with great suspicion in the press and subscribers to their share issues were discouraged.

In December 1897 it was decided that a voluntary liquidation of the company would be needed to allow restructuring of the business. It was intended that a new company would be formed, to be known as the Motor Manufacturing Company (MMC) and it would take over the activities of the Great Horseless Carriage Company and the British Motor Syndicate both of which then became bankrupt in June 1898.

MMC continued for a short while producing cars and, until it liquidated in 1904, it carried on making engines only. The activities of these companies gave Coventry a head start in the motor industry by stifling competition and, in the early years at least, Birmingham trailed behind.

But Birmingham was making its own advances, as was evidenced by the activities of Garrard and Blumfield, Levetus, Lanchester, Anglo-French, Dunkley, Alldays and Onions, Accles-Turrell, Gilbert and Wolseley, all of whom had been engaged in car building since before the turn of the century.

Motor Mills, Coventry.

The First Motor Shows

The first British motor show was held on 13 October 1895 at Tunbridge Wells. It was organised by pioneer motorists David Salomons and Frederick Simms and featured a few French vehicles. The following month the Stanley Cycle Show exhibited two cars and had Charles Garrard (see **Garrard-Blumfield**) demonstrating the Gladiator Motor Tricycle (right). The 'Exhibition of Horseless Carriages' held at the Imperial Institute in London from May to August 1896 was a longer, and larger exhibition. Amongst the exhibits were the Garrard Blumfield Electric Phaeton (see **Garrard-Blumfield**) a Roger pattern vehicle from L'Hollier & Gascoign (see **Anglo-French**) and a carriage frame from Mulliners of Birmingham.

Veteran Cars 1894 - 1904

Due to legislation, Britain was slow to join the race to develop the motor car and the early laurels went to the French and German manufacturers. But once the Emancipation Act was passed in 1896 Britain's budding car makers were at last able to start work.

Birmingham, being a city founded on the metal trades with a large cycle industry and many parts and accessory makers, was in a good position to capitalise on car making and had even gained a head start on competitors like Coventry when Frederick Lanchester built Britain's first petrol driven four wheeled car in 1895 and Anglo-French started car production the following year.

The car manufacturers in this book appear chronologically and, therefore, they conform

The 1895 Lanchester - the first all-British, four-wheeled, petrol car - made in Birmingham.

to the age groupings that have become generally recognized. These are; Veteran, Edwardian, Vintage and Early Classic. These groupings have evolved over time and can seem a little arbitrary but they are the de facto standard. So... on to the manufacturers:

There are 100 manufacturers described here including as many of the smaller companies as we could find. The list is as exhaustive as we could make it and certainly more comprehensive than any book has managed before. We have included some examples of home-built cars because they were usually built with the intent, at least, of going into production rather than purely for the builder's use. Many of the smaller companies failed after building prototypes, some just got the timing wrong. Wars do have a habit of happening at inopportune moments.

The first manufacturer we have included came as a surprise. In the reference sources it is usually listed as a Coventry marque but, it turns out, the car was designed and instigated by two Birmingham manufacturers who subcontracted the assembly work to a Coventry company. If the individuals responsible for a car are based in Birmingham, then it qualifies. If they designed the car, then even better. If components in the car were sourced in Birmingham then better still. All of the above apply with **Garrard and Blumfield**...

Garrard and Blumfield/Clement-Garrard/Garrard

The Garrard Manufacturing Company Ltd. 101-111 Ryland Street, Birmingham. 1894-1908

Before the Emancipation Act of 1896 there was little incentive to become involved in motor car manufacturing. The market for cars didn't exist because the practical use of them was so restricted. There were, however, a few far-sighted individuals who could see the shift in public opinion and made their plans for the dawning motor age. Two of these individuals were Charles Garrard and Thomas Blumfield (see **Blumfield**)

As was commonly the case, the two partners came from outside the city. Charles Riley Garrard was born in London in 1855, the son of Charles Garrard, a pianoforte maker, and Barbara Ann Riley, a dressmaker. His father died when he was young so he was raised by his mother. When he was 23 he married Ellen Frances King in Camden whilst running an engineering and cycle part manufacturing business in Uxbridge. The business failed in 1879 and he moved, first to Balsall Heath and then The Avenue, Acocks Green in Birmingham

and it was there that he met Thomas Blumfield and Thomas met Ellen's sister Alice. In 1894 Thomas and Alice were married in Solihull.

Charles started as a foreman in a cycle factory while Thomas was a cycle examiner, turner and fitter at a works in Coventry. The two men aspired to better things and started working together on a means of personal transport that didn't involve muscle power and turned to electricity as a motive force. They worked on designs for an electric powered vehicle and arranged to have it produced by Taylor, Cooper and Bednell in Coventry.

The Garrard and Blumfield electric phaeton.

The Company was run by three men who all had links with some of the big names in Coventry manufacturing but it was these men that actually manufactured Coventry's first cars to the designs of Garrard and Blumfield.

The car had four wheels and two bench seats over ventilated compartments containing a quarter ton of batteries. The wheels were of small diameter and fitted with pneumatic tyres - the first to be fitted to a British car. The deck was supported on coil springs with the electric motor bolted onto the tubular steel undercarriage. When finished the 'electric phaeton' was test driven from Coventry to Birmingham at an average speed of 10mph and then driven around the streets of Birmingham. We can only guess what the good burghers of Birmingham thought. In July 1894 the 'Garrard and Blumfield' was the only British car to be entered in the world's first ever car race; The Paris-Rouen, organised by Le Petit Journal. Unfortunately, the car didn't make it to the start line.

Garrard established his manufacturing company in Ryland Street, off Broad Street, the 'Magneto Works' and produced cycle parts and accessories side-by-side with electrical devices. The partnership was not to

An early advert.

Charles Garrard.

last and the two men parted company as the turn of the century approached and set up separate manufacturing operations. Blumfield we will encounter again when the cyclecar craze took hold, but Garrard formed other alliances and produced further road vehicles.

The first alliance was with 'Gladiator', a French company that had produced cycles since 1891 under the control of its founders Alexandre Darracq and Paul Aucoq.

In 1896 Lord Charles Chetwynd-Talbot, the 20th Earl of Shrewsbury and Harry John Lawson, who gained a degree of notoriety in his attempts to take control of the fledgling British motor industry by buying up the controlling patents, bought into the company. Charles Garrard, who had sold his patents for the electric phaeton to Lawson, became involved with the company at the same time and contributed to the development of a motorised tricycle.

In 1897 Lawson's business collapsed and this left Clement and Talbot in control of the company. The company's motorised vehicles, motorcycles and tricycles, were introduced to the market in 1902. These had a 145cc single-cylinder, four-stroke engine with an atmospherically controlled inlet valve, overhead mechanical exhaust valve and external flywheel, the same engine as was used on the very first Norton motorcycle. This was no coincidence as James Lansdowne Norton had been subcontracted by Garrard to build the frames for the Clement-Garrard machines and had then used the engine in his 'Energette' motorcycle in 1902.

In 1904 Clement-Garrard suffered from energetic competition from companies like Rex, now based in Coventry, who were advertising heavily. James Norton decided it was time to concentrate on developing his own machines in his premises at 320 Bradford Street. Garrard started to produce vehicles in his

The Garrard Suspended Tricar.

own name with backing from Adolphe Clement and introduced The Garrard Suspended Tricar later in 1904. This was a forecar with a 4hp water-cooled engine driving the rear wheel via a clutch, three-speed gearbox and drive shaft. The suspension was by leaf-springs to the front and a sprung fork to the rear and the passenger sat in a seat mounted on the front of the machine - an arrangement not without its problems that meant that it would be a short-lived vehicle type. In fact the Tricar was only in production for less than a year as the company was voluntarily wound-up at the end of 1904.

In the later years of car production Garrard teamed up with Alfred Maxfield (see **Maxfield**) and patented a number of refinements to engine design. The motor that they developed out of this, the 'Garrard-Maxfield' was used to power the first aircraft to fly in the Midlands, the 'Maxfield Monoplane'. The plane took off from Castle Bromwich on 24th September 1909 and was later exhibited at the Royal Hotel and in the Masonic Hall in Birmingham. This interlinking of car and aircraft development was a feature of the Birmingham manufacturers with many of them being members of the Midland Aero Club.

The Maxfield Monoplane.

Levetus

The Midland Motor Carriage Syndicate, 47 Vittoria Street, Birmingham. 1895-1899

The choice of fuel most appropriate for the new road-going passenger vehicles was not clear-cut. There were four possibilities and each had their disadvantages.

As the Birmingham representative of Autocar magazine spelled out in December 1895; electricity was a non-starter for long journeys, steam had not fared well in the French vehicle trials, Benzoline was likely to 'receive its final banishment' and paraffin would only work if they could dispense with the need for a water jacket. With this in mind he interviewed a Mr H Levetus of Birmingham who had strong opinions about which fuel would win - electricity.

He had argued its case in the pages of the Electrical Review and claimed to have overcome

Celia Moss.

its shortcomings regarding range. He stated that he had devised a system whereby a car weighing one ton (as opposed to a steam carriage weighing nearly two tons) could travel for one hundred miles without a recharge and then after adding a quart of a 'slimy material' could go another hundred miles. On the face of it this sounds ridiculous until you discover that research is currently (no pun intended) being carried out into liquid based batteries which could be recharged in just such a way.

Mr Levetus said that three smaller vehicles each carrying four people and weighing three hundredweight were currently being built to use his 'Milner' batteries. The Milner batteries were, what is termed, primary batteries in that they are not rechargeable but are generally used once and discarded. The difference with these batteries was that the materials in the battery that developed the electrical potential were replaced when exhausted, a quick, if potentially (again, no pun intended) expensive, way of charging. The Mr Levetus in question was Hymen Levetus born in Birmingham in 1849 who later formed a company with his brother Edward Moses Levetus and nephew Arthur Levetus, to develop electric cars in the Jewellery Quarter.

The location of the company sprang out of their business background, as Hymen was a manufacturing jeweller who had developed an interest in batteries and, with his son-in-law Walter Rowbotham, had developed and patented a number of refinements to both batteries and motors in the early 1890s.

Arthur Levetus was the Secretary of their company and had an interest in motoring that was demonstrated by his motor racing exploits, usually in an Alldays machine.

Hymen and his brothers had wide experience in trading anything from jewellery to fire extinguishers and money boxes. They came from a background that was a mixture of commerce religion and art.

Their father, Lewis Levetus was a

The 47 Vittoria Street premises.

25

Romanian immigrant from Moldavia and a 'shohet' or Kosher butcher to the Hebrew congregation. When the brothers' mother died he had married Celia Moss, a prominent Jewish artist and poet who had become one of the leading artists of the Birmingham Group creating bookplates in a distinctive style. Other members of the family were active in poetry, writing and crafting jewellery.

The brothers traded from premises on the corner of Vittoria Street and Regent Place which they called the Canada Works, no doubt reflecting the fact that they travelled widely across the world from Australia to Canada buying and selling. The premises are still there and, though built originally as a jewellery works, would have adapted well to small scale car production calling upon the myriad of small engineering firms that were clustered in the Hockley area for components.

One of these engineering firms was that of the aforementioned Walter Rowbotham who had premises further down Vittoria Street at number 27 and later married Hymen's daughter Kate.

Walter was an inventor and was responsible for the 'primary batteries' used to power the Levetus four-wheeled dog-cart when it was demonstrated at the Midland Institute in January 1896. By this time the range capability claimed of the electric car had risen to 150 miles and the recharging method, using a mixture of paste and water, allowed a recharge in less than ten minutes.

The 7hp Rowbotham Engine No1.

Walter wasn't totally convinced about this as he considered the weight of the batteries made electric cars impractical, and worked in parallel on his version of the diesel engine designed to run on paraffin as it was less volatile and potentially less explosive than petrol.

Following an exchange of letters in 'Autocar' magazine photographs of his engines for autocars were published. The first, called Engine No. 1 had four cylinders in opposed pairs with an electric commutator to time the firing of the cylinders. It was 2ft 9in long by 1ft 8in wide, weighed 145 lbs and produced 7 horsepower. The second, Engine No 2 had two cylinders with four pistons, each pair sharing a combustion chamber. This engine was 3ft 8in long by 1ft

The 11hp Rowbotham Engine No 2.

6in wide, weighed 180lb and produced 11 horsepower. Both engines were claimed to be vibrationless.

Claims made about Rowbotham indicate that he was actually involved in a petrol engined car with electric starting in 1895 but no further details of this have, so far, been found.

Relations between Rowbotham and the Levetus family seem to have become strained and,

by 1901 he had left his wife and their young son Walter and moved to London to pursue his inventive career. His mind had turned to other things by this stage and his patents of this time are for acetylene generation and electric alarm clocks. In about 1905 he moved over to Canada and started working on designs for vacuum cleaners. His 'Vacuna' company produced portable turbine vacuum cleaners in Canada from about 1908.

Meanwhile, back in Birmingham, it is not known what happened to their prototype electric cars, or if they managed to get past the prototype stage as very little more was heard of them. Following the death of Edward at the Buxton Hydropathic (a spa hotel) the company was dissolved in 1898 and Hymen turned his attention to a new company The Ferrolite Electrical Syndicate. This business started in April 1899 with a share capital of £30000 but soon failed. His next venture was a laundry company; the Thornhill Laundries Company in Franklin Road, Bearwood with his brother Charles. This company failed in 1901 but the trading companies continued.

In 1905 Hyman Levetus bought a Wolseley, his motor-building aspirations spent, and this vehicle featured in Wolseley's press advertisements for that year.

Hyman and Charles and their families were frequent visitors to Canada in the early years of the 20th century, but by 1907 they, along with their brother Henry, had moved permanently to Canada and become Canadian Citizens.

Their sons carried on the family business and travelled widely around the world in the interests of trade.

In 1909, whilst on business in India, they witnessed the first flight by an Indian aircraft which had been designed and built by one of their clients. They were so impressed that they sent a picture of the event to Flight Magazine who then announced it to the world.

The Levetus car building venture was short lived but, being of such an early date, very important in the development of the fledgling British motor industry.

The first Indian-built aircraft.

But what will it run on?

At the dawn of the age of motoring nobody knew what sort of engine would be best. In the beginning there was the steam engine which had been used for motive power since 1769. It produced plenty of power and the raw materials to build and run them were easily available, but they took a long time to fire up and were heavy. Electricity could be stored, and used in motors that were relatively vibration free. It was cheap, but the storage, and therefore the range, was limited.

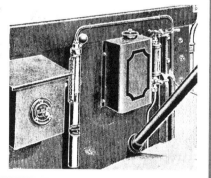

The internal combustion engine, often using petrol as its fuel, seemed to offer the best option as it was relatively compact and fired up quickly. Petrol won but, as the best option in a world where supplies are finite and progressively more expensive its days are numbered.

Lanchester
Armourer Mills, Montgomery Street, Sparkbrook, Birmingham.
1895-1931

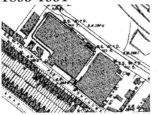

Lanchester is one of the most important marques to spring from Birmingham. Not only did they produce what was arguably the first true British car but they also contributed many innovations that were to shape the car's development.

The Lanchester story starts with the architect Henry Jones Lanchester who married Octavia Ward, a teacher of maths and Latin, in 1862. From this marriage there were eight children, three of whom went on to form the Lanchester Company. Frederick William Lanchester was the brother with inventive genius.

Born in 1868 in Lewisham, which was also the birthplace of William Hillman and home to James Starley and Thomas Brockas (see **Brockas**), he was the driving force behind the development of the first British, four-wheeled, petrol driven car. It is important to remember that other contenders existed for this title but only his bore any real resemblance to what we would today recognise as a car. Having been educated at the Royal College of Science he took a job as an engineer at the Forward Engine Company in Bloomsbury, between Aston and Saltley, at the low wage of £1 per week but made up his earnings by patenting a pendulum inertia governor that paid him a royalty of £3 every time one was fitted to an engine. Within a year his inventiveness earned him the position of Works Manager and Chief Designer and he was in a position to take on his younger brother George Herbert as an apprentice. Four years later George was promoted to works manager and this freed Frederick to carry on experimental work in a small wash-room converted into a workshop adjacent to the factory in Taylor Street. He worked on developing engines and patented a starter that could be used on existing engines that paid him a royalty of £3 each time one was fitted. His royalty income from the Manchester engine maker Crossley alone added up to over £1000 a year and so he was able to finance his experimentation. He had already fitted an engine to a boat, thereby building the country's first motor boat and was active in early aircraft design but

The 'Stanhope Phaeton' of 1895.

The 'Spirit Passenger Phaeton' of 1897.

in 1895 he worked with George and a third brother, Frank, on his first car.

This was a vehicle designed from the ground up avoiding existing patents and the need to pay license fees and called the 'Stanhope Phaeton'. It was, from the outset, a car rather than an adapted 'horseless' carriage and had its first official outing onto public roads in February 1896. This prototypical car had a 5 hp single-cylinder 1306cc engine with the lone cylinder having two connecting rods. The con rods each went to separate cranks each with their own flywheels and rotating in opposite directions. This made their operation very smooth, vibration being a widespread problem in early engine design. This car also featured the first set of air filled motor car tyres that Dunlop ever made and some of the first in the world.

Outgrowing their rented workshop in Taylor Street they acquired a galvanised steel shed at 33 Ladywood Road, just down from Five Ways in 1897 and the middle brother Frank joined the team. The skills of the three brothers interlocked with Fred as the inventor, George as the engineer and Frank as the administrator commonly continuing their development work on a Sunday and becoming known as the 'Unholy

Frederick Lanchester.

Archibald Millership.

Trinity'. They assembled a team of engineers around them at Ladywood Road to assist in the car development. Amongst these was Walter Frederick Thomas (see **Thomas**) who would later go on to build his own cars.

In 1897 the prototype chassis was used again but this time with a more powerful 8hp, two-cylinder, 3459cc engine to cope better with hills and a second car, the 'Spirit Passenger Phaeton' was built at the same time. These cars used a foot pedal to operate the governors on the engine, a feature that Frederick christened the 'accelerator'. Experimentation continued over the next two years until they were ready to set up a manufacturing company. The Lanchester Engine Company was registered in December 1899 with a share capital of £100,000. The first Directors were the brothers Charles and John Pugh of the Rudge Whitworth Cycle Company (see **Atco**), Joseph H Taylor of the same Company, James Whitfield who, with his brother Allan, had been a financial backer since 1894 and Thomas Hamilton Barnsley, another cycle manufacturer. The company, with its board of directors, was necessary if the cars were to be manufactured but from the beginning there was friction as the directors clashed with the brothers.

Thomas Hamilton Barnsley was born in Birmingham in 1868, the son of a building contractor who had set up his own cycle factory. He was later to become chairman of the Midland Automobile Club and was the principal shareholder, Chairman and Managing Director of Lanchester until his death in 1931 but the Lanchester brothers were in charge of design and manufacture.

The premises in which they had carried on their development work were not suitable for car production so they sought and found new premises in Montgomery Street in Sparkbrook which were bought from a defunct armaments manufacturer who had made weapons for the American Civil War there and were thus called Armourer Mills.

The Armourer Mills production line.

29

The first production vehicles of the new company appeared in 1900. There were six machines built and they were used to demonstrate the cars to the investors and public and one of these was entered into the 1000 Mile Trial with a body coachbuilt by Mulliners.

The cars had horizontal, air-cooled, two-cylinder engines of 4033cc still with the twin-crankshaft design of the first prototype and epicyclic gears that, though complex, offered a compact design and a high power

The Montgomery Street Works in 2011.

transmission efficiency. They were steered using a tiller rather than a steering wheel, a feature that would distinguish the Lanchester cars for many years.

In 1900 Archibald Millership joined the company as a tester and demonstrator. He had been living with the brothers in rooms at Lincolns Inn in Corporation Street and formed what was known as the 'colony of residents' there. Also numbered amongst the residents were the Pugh brothers who invested in the first company. A keen pioneer motorist he was well known in motoring circles and would later form an association with John Jarvis (see **Jarvis and Weekes**).

The first Lanchester cars were actually sold to the public in 1901 when, in August of that year the 10-12hp car took to the road.

Frederick Lanchester was an engineering genius and introduced a number of features

1902 Lanchester Tonneau.

that we still find on cars today. In 1902 Lanchester cars were the first to have disc brakes.

Up to this point the company had entrusted the body fabrication to outside coachbuilders but in 1903 they set up a body-shop at the Alpha Works in Liverpool Street (see **Revolette**) with Archie Millership as Manager and for the next decade built most of the bodies themselves. In 1904 the company produced cars with a 12hp, water-cooled, four-cylinder, overhead valve 2470cc engine which featured pressure lubrication. The engine and its epicyclic gearbox were mounted between the front seats rather than at the front of the car which gave the cars a somewhat odd, bonnetless appearance with only the radiator and the distinctive patent-leather, folding wind deflector between the driver and the road in front. Frederick Lanchester was constantly developing new ideas and patenting them. In this period he patented the world's first outboard motor and the first four-wheel drive system.

From the beginning the company had been under-capitalised, leading to disagreements between the brothers, with their particular ideas of the cars they wanted to build and the directors who wanted more 'conventional' vehicles that would be easily sold. The company was successful and had a full order book for its cars but, in 1904 it experienced cash flow problems and went into receivership. The company was reorganised and, later in 1904, became the Lanchester Motor Company Ltd. As part of the reorganisation Fredericks salary was cut nearly in half but he was, at least, allowed to do outside consultancy work. Also, as a consequence of the restructuring, Frank lost his position of Company Secretary and Archie Millership was forced to leave and joined Wolseley (see **Wolseley**).

In 1906 six-cylinder engines appeared and in 1908 tiller steering gave way to the more conventional steering wheel. Fred Lanchester had resisted this change since his experiments on the 8hp Stanhope Phaeton in 1897 had revealed tiller steering to be superior to the steering wheel. This year's cars were also the first in the world to feature forced lubrication of the gears, clutch and brakes. The cars produced in 1912 illustrated that Lanchester were always keen to adopt good ideas

The first Lanchesters fitted with steering wheels.

from elsewhere. The Delco Company in America introduced an electric self-starting and lighting set that was adopted by Lanchester in both their 25hp and 38hp models making it the first European car maker to offer a complete, integrated starter and generating system.

Frederick had a wide range of interests and, in common with many of the early car makers, became interested in aeronautics, publishing works on both natural and mechanical flight. In 1909 he became a consultant and technical advisor to the Daimler company in Coventry as his contract allowed. The company expanded operations at Montgomery Street in 1910 adding a new wing and bringing the coachbuilding department over from the Alpha Works. The Liverpool Street buildings were retained for storage.

By 1912 Archie Millership had returned from Wolseley and Austin (see **Austin**) but Frederick Lanchester was no longer associated with the company that bore his name though his patented inventions continued to be used. One of these, his worm drive, found wide spread use as a silent and efficient way of transmitting power to the rear axle. A cheaper but less refined alternative was developed and produced by E G Wrigley (see **Wrigley**) and found even further markets.

He continued his consultancy work with Daimler until 1927 and became a consultant with Wolseley in 1924 (see **Wolseley**). In 1925 he went into partnership with Daimler to form a new company, Lanchester Laboratories Ltd. to work on and develop his inventions but financial problems led to it being wound up in 1929. He used his own money to buy out Daimler's interests and continued experimenting and inventing until he was forced to retire due to ill health in 1934 but made little money and, ironically, couldn't even afford to run a car.

A 1911 25hp Lanchester.

Following Frederick's departure his brother George took the lead in design and, bending to the wishes of the Directors, the cars became more rounded and conventional in appearance. Despite protestations that bonnetless cars had a less 'crowded' appearance the company now started to produce cars with a bonnet.

The first of these was the six-cylinder 'Sporting 40' of 1914. It was this car that acted as the catalyst for Frederick's departure as many of its 'conventional' features merely aped those found on other cars. The car was disappointingly orthodox but stylistically successful, the results of George's efforts carving models out of cheese during the design phase. It is thought that only eight of these cars were made as production was halted for the First World War.

A Sporting 40 and a WWI tank side by side.

Frank Lanchester, now based in London, used his contacts to win an order to build the company's 25hp and 38hp vehicles as armoured cars. This was found to be a more appropriate use of the company's experience than the contracts for production of shells and guns previously awarded.

The armoured cars with their 7ft 6in high bullet-proof superstructures and Vickers-Maxim machine guns mounted in revolving turrets were a formidable sight.

WWI 25hp Covered Wagons.

As the war progressed the factory was turned over to the production of ambulances, covered wagons and aero-engines.

At the end of the war the company faced a problem common to many manufacturers - how to survive the transition back to peacetime production. The war had provided contracts that had kept the factory busy but, also, had taken their toll on the precision equipment with the sheer rate of production.

Despite the recommendation of George and Frank to pursue further aircraft-related orders the Directors were unconvinced that there would be any future in the peacetime air industry and decided to concentrate on car production and to continue development of more conventional looking models. The first car to be produced was a six-cylinder 40hp model, launched to critical acclaim.

The car was launched in 1920 as a direct attack on the luxury end of the market dominated by Rolls Royce. The cars appearances at subsequent Motor Shows and dramatic demonstrations of the car's abilities by Archie Millership won the praise of many and the factory ramped up production. The car had many of Frederick Lanchester's design features including epicyclic gears and the underslung worm-drive on the rear axle but many more of his ideas had been sacrificed in the interest of orthodoxy.

Immediately after the war coachbuilding operations were moved to the Alliance Works at Foremans Road, Greet to overcome the problems of having woodworking and precision

Archie Millership demonstrates a 40hp.

engineering taking place in adjacent spaces. The Alpha Works gained a paintshop and a pre-delivery storage area.

In 1921, Lanchester staged an export drive in the USA and became the first British car maker to export left-hand drive cars; however their efforts were undermined by Rolls Royce who entered negotiations to buy the American motor agency that had handled their sales there.

Lanchester cars became popular amongst the ruling classes in India and Maharajahs vied with each other to specify the most ostentatiously appointed vehicles. Some of these were the first to use tinted glass.

Today, electric driven vehicles are promoted as the eco-friendly, next generation of motor car despite having been present at the dawn of motoring but what about petrol-electric hybrids? Surely they are a modern invention? Actually... no.

The Maharaja of Alwar's State Landau 1924.

Lanchester built them in 1927 and gave them wooden bodies. The Mark 7 wooden car with its 'Petrelect' drive is on display at Think Tank in Birmingham.

Production of the 40hp car continued until 1929 with numerous refinements and variations appearing over the years but was phased out as sales diminished.

Prototypes of a smaller 21hp car were built in 1923 and launched at the Motor Show in that year and attracted a ready market amongst the car buying public who aspired to owning a Lanchester but couldn't afford the 40hp models; though, at £1250, this was still not cheap, at a time when the average wage for a skilled engineer was less than £4 per week.

40hp Chassis in production.

The men who headed the original company were now falling by the wayside. Charles Pugh died in 1921; Arthur Gibson, who had replaced him as Chairman; Joseph Taylor died in 1923 and James Whitfield, who had been with the company for nearly 30 years, died in 1924.

Hamilton Barnsley took control as Chairman and agreed to George and Frank becoming Directors. Their new status gave them increased influence and they were able to introduce changes to the car range. The 21hp car benefited from an increase in engine power and a new 16hp car was proposed but the financial situation of the company was at odds with his aspirations and the Board repeatedly refused to introduce the new car. The profits of the company were falling; difficult times lay ahead.

Having failed to gain approval for the 16hp car George turned to developing a twelve-cylinder engine but, in 1927, another direction was taken at the suggestion of Frederick Lanchester who was operating from the sidelines as a shareholder with an interest in the financial viability of the company.

He proposed a straight-eight of 30hp that would sit between the company's current 21hp and 40hp offerings. The resultant car was launched in 1928 and sold well despite the deepening economic recession, but not well enough and the company headed toward its end. Seeing the approaching difficulties and alienated by the Board many of the leading players left the company.

In June 1930 Frank Lanchester was appointed acting manager to take the place of Hamilton Barnsley who was suffering from ill-health, and started cost cutting. He persuaded the bank to provide further loans so that an order for armoured cars could be fulfilled, but it was all to no avail as the bank, in the way that banks do, ignored the long-term potential of the company for short-term remedies and pulled their overdraft.

On 28 December 1930, Hamilton Barnsley sold the entire company to BSA and, six months later he died. After the merger, production of the Lanchester cars was moved to Coventry and the brand was gradually diluted as more components were shared with BSA and Daimler models.

After the war, consolidations and mergers meant that Lanchester, as part of Daimler, became part of Jaguar in 1960 and Jaguar was bought by Ford in 1989. Since 2008 the rights to the Lanchester marque have been owned by Tata of India. *Plus ca change*.

There were a total of about 3000 Lanchester cars produced in the years before the company moved to Coventry and, of these, about 90 have survived. The Montgomery Road works is the only one that still stands and still looks remarkably as it does in the photographs taken of it in its heyday but containing a rather different type of car, as it now houses a BMW repair company.

The contribution that the Lanchester company made to the city's motor industry means that it is the only one that has its old works marked by a blue plaque, on the Armoury Mills. There is also a remarkably complete reproduction of the 'Stanhope Phaeton' by Tim Tolkein, grandson of the author JRR Tolkein, that now stands close to the site of Frederick Lanchester's original workshop in Bloomsbury Village.

The Lanchester Monument by Tim Tolkein.

What's in a name?

At the dawn of motoring even the name of the fuel used to power the vehicles wasn't yet standardised and a confusing array of terms were used. Based on the specific gravity of the fuels, Samuel Rodman, a chemist and explosives expert in Chicago in the United States defined them in 1895 as:

Gasoline	.660 to .669
Naptha	.690 to .700
Benzoline	.730 to .760
Paraffin	.820 to .860

But this is only the start because Gasoline was also known as Petroleum, Paraffin as Kerosene and Benzoline as Benzine - what's in a name?

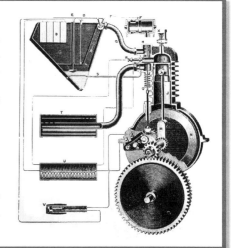

Anglo-French

The Anglo-French Motor Carriage Company, Digbeth, Birmingham. 1896-1898

At an early stage in the research for this book I had come to the conclusion that the 'Anglo-French' car was little more than an imported French model, reflecting the early lead that continental manufacturers had gained as a result of the restrictive motoring legislation in the UK. On deeper investigation I came to the conclusion that I may have underestimated Leon L'Hollier, the owner of the Company.

His was a very important role in the early years of the British motor industry, his manufacturing capacity was impressive and, what is more, relevant to production of the relatively conservative type of cars that appeared about that time.

Leon Francois L'Hollier was born in France in 1847 and married Margaret Sandford, the daughter and grand-daughter of basket makers from Worcester. It is very possible that he came to England from France as an apprentice to Margaret's father, as his later businesses involved basketry, and married the boss's daughter.

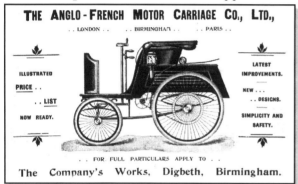

An early advertisement.

His main factory was sited in Bath Passage, in an area that is currently the Chinese district in the City centre.

The road that links the Hippodrome theatre to the market area is called Ladywell Walk after the Lady Well that used to stand under what is now an Ibis Hotel and the site in the late 18th century of *'the most extensive and complete set of baths in the kingdom'*. This, no doubt, contributed to Birmingham being *'one of the healthiest Towns in England'* despite the smoke from the metal industries! Striking off to the north-east, between two Chinese restaurants, is the ghost of one of Birmingham's lesser known roads, Bath Passage, that used to link the Ladywell with the also now defunct Smallbrook Street but is now little more than an oddly configured service access, lined, for part of its length, with cafes.

The Factory stood on the corner of this passage and produced perambulators, invalid carriages, delivery carts and all manner of vehicles that used wicker and wheels in their construction. In 1885 adverts boasted that the company had over 3000 prams and 3000 invalid carriages in stock at all times - these were serious players.

The Anglo-French Motor Carriage Company was floated in 1896 with the intent of buying the Emile Roger's company in France and taking over the manufacture of their cars. At the same time L'Hollier was to set up an English production base.

Not wishing to disrupt the output from his main factory L'Hollier acquired new premises at 80 Digbeth on the site now occupied by the Digbeth Institute nightclub and went into production of cars to the *Roger* design.

The premises had originally been the Birmingham Battery

The 5th Earl of Lonsdale.

and Metal Company's works and were 'familiar to local engineers'. Rather than making batteries, this company had used 'battery', or beating, to form their metal products and moved out to premises in Selly Oak that were a local landmark... until Sainsburys demolished them.

The new Company listed amongst its directors, Hugh Lowther, the 5th Earl of Lonsdale, famous for the Lonsdale Belt. He was known as the 'Yellow Earl' because he adopted it as his livery with cars,

The unfortunate Bridget Driscoll.

carriages, footmen and even his buttonhole Gardenia being yellow. He was a founder of the Automobile Association which is probably why yellow is the AA's corporate colour.

This was not L'Hollier's first experience in the car business. In 1896 he had bought the rights to import the cars actually built by 'Roger' and was, therefore, responsible for starting the motor trade in Britain.

His partner in this enterprise, Edmund Gascoine (commonly misspelled), an engineer born in Maidstone in 1862, joined him in the role of works manager at the Digbeth works.

Whilst on a promotional run in one of his cars, he was arrested for speeding at between 5 and 6 mph without a person preceding him on foot with a flag on the Bristol Road. Only one of a number of clashes with the authorities when trying to raise the profile of motoring.

This wasn't the end of his motoring misfortunes either, as it was one of his cars that knocked over and killed Bridget Driscoll in August 1896 at Crystal Palace, making her the first British, pedestrian motoring fatality. Quite an achievement at a time when there were only a handful of cars on the road.

The 1897 Anglo-French Motor Carriage.

It wasn't all bad though as another 'first' that he could lay claim to was providing the country's first wedding cars at the marriage of his daughter, Irma to Edward Day, the son of his Assistant Manager at the Anglo French works, at St Augustine's Church in Solihull in April 1897.

Leon had nine children with Margaret, one of whom, Lionel James L'Hollier, joined the Royal Artillery as a bombardier during the First World war and came back to start a cane furniture manufacturers in Newcastle upon Tyne that carried on the family's connection with basket making.

The company added a showroom to the front of the Digbeth premises and estab-

The 1897 Anglo-French Van.

lished a range of workshops to construct a variety of motorised vehicles including cars and delivery vans, with a workforce of about 70. They called upon the expertise of French engineer Daniel Courtois and Thomas Meacock, a mechanical engineer based in Birmingham to refine the 'Roger' cars.

The cars were 'spirit' or benzoline driven and had been the subject of a number of changes to the basic Roger-Benz design. The engine had two cylinders instead of one in an attempt to reduce vibration and the weight of the accumulators (batteries) that powered the ignition had been reduced in weight to 14lbs each, whilst improving their endurance from 60 hours to 180 hours. The usual drive of belts and chains had been replaced with a very early friction disc assembly and all of the working parts had been enclosed to protect them from dust and dirt. The bodies were coachbuilt as a separate unit in the 'English' rather than 'French' style and there were plans to fit a patented condenser that would reduce water loss and allow the vehicles to run for eight hours between top-ups. Some of their vehicles were fitted with tyres from the New Grappler Pneumatic Tyre Co in Corporation Street.

They had hoped to manufacture between ten and twenty cars a week but L'Hollier,

The Digbeth Works in 1897.

The Fitting Shop.

Courtois and Gascoigne's Company didn't last very long and ceased car production in 1897 with Leon returning to pram making.

The remaining stock of the company including *'sixteen finished and unfinished cars'* went under the hammer at auction in November 1998. Leon L'Hollier sold his premises on to Thomas Clyde Mckenzie (see **McKenzie**) in 1908 and died in 1914 in Kings Norton aged 59.

Edmund Gascoine moved to London in 1904 to join the Motor Car Department at Armstrong Whitworth and Co. but stepped down in 1912 and died in Brighton in 1921.

An attempt was made to save the company and the 'English Road Car and Manufacturing Company' was set up for this purpose, but it too failed.

The car factory was mostly demolished to make way for the Digbeth Institute, however a small section of the factory possibly still survives in the centre of the block.

None of the cars are known to have survived.

The Manager's Office.

Dunkley

The Dunkley Car Company, Alvechurch Works, Bradford Street, Birmingham.
1896-1924

It was 1896, the year that it became legal to drive a motor car on the public roads without having a minimum crew of three and a speed limit restricted to walking pace. The French and Germans had captured the market; so who would pioneer British manufacture? Another pram maker of course!

William Henry Dunkley was a visionary, if somewhat eccentric, figure in the very early days of motor manufacturing. He was born in Milcote, near Stratford upon Avon in Warwickshire in 1856. His father, William, was an agricultural labourer and carter (who was born and raised in Pillerton Hersey at the same time as my G G Grandfather - it's a small world) and young William would normally have been destined to follow in his father's footsteps, but he had bigger ideas and made the 30 mile journey to Birmingham and a career in manufacturing. William was one of eleven children and this may have influenced him as he went into pram manufacture, as did his brother Samuel.

At the age of twenty-two, after a brief period in Manchester working on his patents, he acquired premises in Jamaica Row in the centre of Birmingham, opposite the old Smithfield Market. From there, according to his 1880 catalogue, he would supply 'prams, rocking horses, see-saws, pedal tricycles, hobby-horse tricycles, mail carts, steam circuses & roundabouts with organ complete'. Quite a list, but his aspirations would not stop there, and in 1896 he acquired further premises in Bradford Street and started experimenting with car manufacture. Being William Dunkley these were to be no ordinary

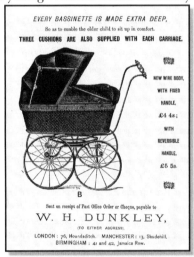

Dunkley Perambulators.

cars... For a start they ran on compressed coal gas. The idea was that they would be fitted with a hose that would connect to coin operated gas meters, fill their gas tank and compress it with an onboard compressor to give the car more range. This was only the beginning. One of the early cars was called the 'Moke' and had a wicker body with seating for four arranged back-to-back. This in itself was quite common but Dunkley then arranged the four

The 1897 Compressed Gas Car...

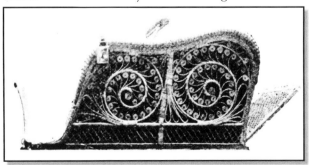

...and its improved wicker body design.

The 1897 Dunkley Moke.

wheels in a diamond formation with two large drive wheels to the side and two small wheels steered by a tiller and connected by linkages so that they acted in unison (on the first prototype the small wheels were not linked but only one would touch the ground at any one time, meaning that whoever was heaviest got to steer - his 'Galloping Horse' arrangement).

Amazingly, this isn't the only local example of this wheel formation, as Sunbeam in Wolverhampton produced a 'skid-proof' car called the Sunbeam-Mabley in 1901 with an even more peculiar seating arrangement.

The Moke had a half-horsepower engine, so there was no danger that it would go up hills, and the engine could be stopped and started easily so that it didn't need to idle as other cars had to, with the attendant unpleasant vibration. Dunkley calculated that the car would travel half the distance from Birmingham to London on one charge of gas and would attain a speed of 20mph.

He did work on other, slightly more conventional cars producing a three-wheeled tiller-steered, single -seater in 1897 and a four-wheeled, tiller-steered, four seater in 1901. All were gas powered.

In 1915 he produced another three-wheeler, second-hand examples of which found their way into the small-ads of Light Car and Cyclecar.

In the twenties he launched his 'Pramotor' an unlikely contraption that connected to the back of a pram allowing a child's nanny to take a motorised trip in the fresh air.

In tandem with his own efforts to manufacture cars he also started to import the American Oilmobile through another of his companies, The English Motor Co in Mill Lane, opposite the Digbeth Coach Station and his son later produced a light car probably from his 'Alvechurch Works' in Bradford Street. (see **Alvechurch**).

1901 Dunkley Gas Powered Car.

It is clear from the tone of contemporary articles about Dunkley that he was recognised as being somewhat odd. In 1923 the Light Car and Cycle car magazine took obvious glee in reporting his launch of a small motorised hearse propelled by his 'Pramotor' with the heading 'From Cradle to Grave'.

He died at home in 1928 at the age of 69 and his obituaries listed aviation as an early interest, with him reportedly building model aircraft at the turn of the century. What isn't mentioned is whether his last journey was made in one of his Pramotor driven hearses!

It is the world's loss that none of his vehicles survive and neither do any of the works in which he built them.

The Dunkley Pramotor.

Wolseley/Wolseley-Siddeley/Siddeley

Adderley Park Works, Vauxhall, Birmingham.
1896-1938

Frederick York Wolseley was born in Kingstown, Ireland, in 1837. He travelled to Australia and ran a number of sheep stations in the Melbourne area. After many years in development, in association with engineer Richard Pickup Parks, he acquired a patent in 1887 for the first mechanical sheep shearing device and set up a factory to manufacture it.

In 1889 he sold the company to a group of British businessmen and employed the young Herbert Austin (see **Austin**) as his works manager at the Melbourne workshops. Wolseley was having health problems and the firm had difficulty finding subcontractors to produce components for their machines so, in 1893, they moved production to a new factory in Broad Street, Birmingham and in May 1894 Wolseley was forced to resign the managing-directorship. He died in 1899 at the age of 62 and is buried in London.

Autocar Number 1.

1901 5hp Wolseley Voiturette.

Frederick York Wolseley.

In 1897 Austin moved the works to Alma Street in Aston, next door to the Ralph Martindale Works, where they produced machetes for use in colonial jungles (they still make 'Crocodile' machetes now, but from their works in Willenhall).

The sheep shearing trade was seasonal so Austin took up manufacturing bicycles in the quiet periods and experimented with a prototype car, based on a 'Leon Bollee' that he had seen in Paris, through the winter of 1895. Finding that the Leon Bollee rights had been acquired by another British company he designed his second car, the three-wheeled 'Wolseley Autocar Number One' in 1897. This car was the first that was offered for sale, but none were sold so he designed a four wheeled 'voiturette' which was revealed in 1899 and a further four-wheeled car in 1900. The first car actually sold by Wolseley, in 1901, was based on the 'voiturette' but had a steering wheel instead of a tiller.

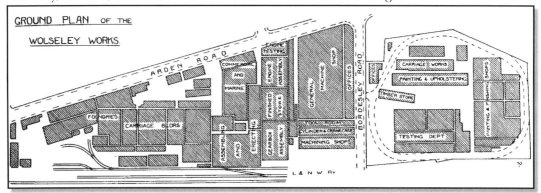

Adderley Park works.

A 1904 Wolseley in Victoria Square.

By this stage the car manufacturing part of the company had outgrown the resources of the parent company and more financial backing was needed. Austin approached Frank Kayser, a steel supplier from Sheffield, whose father Charles had a financial interest in Wolseley and a seat on the board, But a deal was soon arranged with Vickers Son and Maxim and the company established itself at the Adderley Park site. Herbert Austin was, at this time, living at Berwood Grove on the Chester Road in Erdington and was manager of the company but he was dissatisfied with the direction the company was taking and left to set up car making in his own right in 1905 (see Austin). He did continue however in a part-time capacity with Wolseley and, between 1911 and 1933 was chairman of the Board of Directors.

In 1905 Vickers purchased the Siddeley Autocar Company. The founder of this company John Siddeley took charge of the Wolseley car making operation.

John Davenport Siddeley was born in Chorlton on Medlock, Cheshire in 1866, the son of William Siddeley, a hosiery manufacturer from Altringham and Elizabeth Davenport from Canada. After studying at Beaumaris Grammar School in Wales he started his working life as a shirt cutter in his father's business. In the mid 1890s he married Sarah Goodier and moved to Coventry where he started a family and started working for the Humber Cycle Company as a draughtsman. In 1893 he joined the Pneumatic Tyre Company (who later changed their name to Dunlop) at their Alma Street works in Coventry and, by 1901, had become the managing director. Though working in Coventry, he had moved to Birmingham and was living with his family at 150 Heathfield Road, Handsworth by the time of the 1901 census so he was already forging links with the city.

In 1902 he formed the Siddeley Autocar Company assembling cars in Coventry from parts imported from Peugeot in France. By about

1906 Wolseley-Siddeley.

1904 he started to design his own parts and had them manufactured by Wolseley at the Adderley Park works and assembled by Vickers in Kent. The 1905 purchase by Vickers

John Davenport Siddeley.

created the merged Wolseley-Siddeley Motor Company with Siddeley as sales manager, moving into the role of Managing Director vacated by Austin during 1906.

John Siddeley was an excellent self-publicist and Vickers found that their Wolseley marque was gradually being eroded by the public perception of them being 'Siddeley' cars, particularly when they became associated with motor sport and foreign adventures orchestrated by Siddeley. The financial stability of the company was also being undermined during this period and so, when Thomas (Colonel Tom) Vickers died in 1908, it was time for change. His brother Albert took over as MD of Vickers and wanted to pay a dividend to shareholders, but the Company finances were weak so he looked to cost cutting measures including; closing their Crayford works, stopping taxi and commercial production and moving the Head Office back to Bimingham. Siddeley, and his main ally Lionel de Rothschild, disagreed with the changes but were outnumbered and so, in 1909, they both resigned.

John Siddeley moved to the Deasy Motor Company in Coventry in 1910 changing the name of the Company to Siddeley-Deasy and would eventually later merge with Armstrong-Whitworth to become Armstrong-Siddeley then Hawker Aircraft to become Hawker-Siddeley. He

The main machine shop at Adderley Park.

was knighted in 1932, purchased Kenilworth Castle and became Baron Kenilworth. He died in 1953.

Meanwhile, back at Wolseley, in 1910 the Company took over the adjacent Britannia Works previously occupied by Brown, Marshall and Company who had built railway carriages and wagons there. The Company introduced a new range of four and six-cylinder models for 1910 and continued in production of these until WWI.

During this period the company became involved in building some more unusual vehicles. The ill-fated Scott 'Terra Nova' Antarctic expedition of 1910-1913 took three Wolseley built motor sledges, but their performance was less than impressive. The first fell through the ice whilst being unloaded from the ship and the other two broke down part way through the expedition.

Another vehicle was unusual and impressive but suffered a sad end - the Gyrocar.

Scott Expedition Motor Sled.

In 1912 the Russian Count Peter Schilovski visited Wolseley and gave them the drawings for a gyro-stabilized two-wheeled car. Wolseley built the car, a 2.75 ton monster powered by a 20hp Wolseley engine and kept upright by an electric driven gyro. The car worked but when WWI broke out the Count disappeared and the car gathered dust in a corner of the works. Needing the space but, mindful that the Count could reappear at any time, they buried the car, only to dig it up again in 1938 and destroy it - a tragic loss.

By 1913 Wolseley was the biggest manufacturer in the country producing 3000 cars per year at the Adderley Park works and with 4000 employees.

In 1914 Vickers decided that they should enter the booming light car market. Wolseley

The Gyrocar.

disagreed, though they did design the car that would later be produced by another Vickers business in Birmingham - the Stellite. (see **Stellite**)

During WWI the Wolseley factories were turned to war production and, when they returned to car production after the war, business was good. They had formed a joint venture with a Japanese company to produce Wolseleys in Japan, (a company which was later to change its name to Isuzu) and in 1919 they took over the Ward End works, halted production of the Stellite and launched their own 10hp car.

1924 Wolseley.

Before the war Wolseley had resisted producing a light car because it would compromise their brand values, which is why the Stellite was produced by another Vickers Company, but in the new circumstances after the war they launched a 7hp car into the more affordable end of the market.

Over 12000 cars were produced in 1921 and, in the same year, the company commissioned prestigious neo-classical showrooms in Piccadilly, London where its cars were displayed on marble floors. The venture folded in 1926 but the building survives, now housing a refined and exclusive cafe-restaurant called, naturally, 'The Wolseley'.

Despite selling well at the luxury end of the market the company's finances were strained and, in 1926, they faced receivership with debts mounting up to over £2,000,000, a massive amount of money for 1926.

In 1927, following bids from Austin and General Motors, the company was bought by William Morris (see **Morris Commercial**) for £730,000 out of his own funds. Wolseley became a subsidiary Company of Morris Motors and Wolseley production was confined to the old Stellite plant in Drews Lane. The Wolseley models produced after the takeover were basically Morris designs and sometimes mere re-badged versions.

In 1938 The Nuffield Organisation, named from William Morris's title of Lord Nuffield, was formed when Morris, Wolseley, Riley and MG were merged into one company.

The original Wolseley Company still exists but has not had any involvement in the car industry since 1901 when Vickers bought the motor-building arm. The present day Wolseley company is the biggest supplier of heating and plumbing products to the professional market in the world with 'Plumbcentre' and 'Bathstore' among its brands and, ironically, has one of its outlets on the site of the old Stellite works in Cheston Road, Aston.

Nothing remains of either the Adderley Park or Ward End works but Wolseley cars can be seen at classic car events and some very early cars take part in the London to Brighton Veteran Car Run each year.

1926 Wolseley.

Alldays and Onions

The Alldays & Onions Pneumatic Engineering Co., Sydenham Rd., Birmingham.
1898-1918

A number of Birmingham marques were produced by long established companies that returned to their core business and, as a result, still exist today, with their excursion into car production a distant memory. One such is Alldays and Onions.

Birmingham has had a metalworking industry since the Middle Ages. Long ago Deritend workshops and forges turned out tools and implements to service a wide area. With the need for forges came the need for bellows and, in about 1650, William Allday and Sons started in business to manufacture them.

In 1720 another engineering company, which was later called John C Onions Ltd. (pronounced Oh-nions by the family) was founded and, in 1885, the companies joined forces, registering as a limited company in 1889 under the title of the Alldays and Onions Pneumatic Engineering Co.

The first directors of the new company were; Edwin Ludlow, Joseph Wilson, Edward Tailby, Simon Onions, William Allday and Edmund Allday.

The company produced bellows, hearths, forges, cranes and all manner of tools from their individual premises but they needed to rationalise and so, in 1888, acquired premises in Sydenham Road, Small Heath, previously used by the Midland Joinery Company.

At this time the premises were on the very edge of the growing city, bordered to the north-east by the Grand Union Canal and surrounded by fields, but this would soon change.

In 1889 they renamed the site the 'Great Western Works' and started to extend but found that their relatively remote location meant that finding staff was difficult, so they built an estate of 39 houses on land the other side of Sydenham Road, a row of which still survive.

As the company developed, new product lines were sought and, with the boom in the cycle industry, a move into cycle production was almost inevitable. They built a new self-contained, cycle factory in Fallows Road called the 'Matchless Works' in 1895, even as the road itself was under construction, and added more houses to their works estate along with a two-storey mess room.

The company produced a wide range of cycles including delivery bikes, tricycles, rickshaws & handcarts and received orders from government as well as the retail trade.

The Alldays and Onion works today.

The 1899 Alldays and Onions Sporting Car.

A 1902 'Traveller' Voiturette.

They were well established and capable of fabricating most things so, when the motor car came along, they were in a good position to produce them.

Their first car was the 'Traveller' Voiturette, which appeared on a separate stand from their large cycle display, at the 1899 Stanley Cycle Show. It was a quadricycle available as a car or a delivery vehicle with a single-cylinder, 2.5hp De Dion engine and steered by a wheel rather than the tiller which was common amongst the early cars. It had an unsprung rear and the passenger sat in front of, but slightly lower down than, the driver. Production was limited but the company started to produce the car in numbers by 1903 with an increase in engine size to 4hp and the addition of an optional reversing gear.

The 500cc engine had an air-cooled cylinder but a water-cooled cylinder head and was produced at the Great Western Works for assembly at the Matchless Works.

In 1900 the company exhibited a four seater with a choice of 7hp or 8hp, flat-twin engine at the National Show, Crystal Palace in the November. The engine was mounted at the rear of the car and had a transmission that was a mix of shaft, gears and belt. It too didn't go into production until 1903.

Their first, really successful, car was their 10-12hp, 1611cc, vertical twin-cylinder model of 1905 with a three speed gearbox which saw some success in hill-climbing events and was popular amongst commercial drivers. This car later had a four speed gearbox available.

By 1906 their vehicle range comprised of 7hp, 8hp, 10hp and 16hp models and 5cwt 8hp and 10cwt 10hp vans in response to demand from a public more used to the idea of motorised transport.

An unusual car type appeared in their catalogues in 1907 - railway inspection cars. Designed to run on rails, they were aimed at the colonial market and could be used to pull small carriages if necessary.

Despite a general fall in car sales, 1908 saw the company acquire Enfield (see **Enfield**) and their Redditch production

Great Western Works, Sydenham Road.

Matchless Works, Fallows Road.

The chassis assembly shop in about 1909.

facilities, but the works there were found to be unsuitable and production of the Enfield vehicles was transferred to the Matchless works. After acquiring Enfield most of the models produced were sold under both the 'Alldays' and 'Enfield Autocar' marques with Alldays producing two-cylinder 14hp and four-cylinder 20hp engines.

A market identified by many manufacturers as having potential was the car for the General Practitioner. Through the early years of the century the Doctor's Coupe featured in model ranges. Doctors needed a vehicle that could transport them cheaply and reliably on their rounds in any weather, usually unaccompanied and with their bag as the only cargo. Companies vied for this market because they were also, generally, affluent individuals and more interested in practicality than status, qualities that appealed to engineers. Alldays responded to this market by producing their 'Alldays Doctor's Victoria' in 1909.

Another niche market was taxis and Alldays added two models of cab, each of which seated four passengers, in the same year.

1910 saw the introduction of a completely new 30-35hp, six-cylinder engined car with a 10ft 6in wheelbase. To rationalise the range the other cars were now designated 10-12hp, 14-18hp and 20-25hp with only a few other changes.

The Alldays Light Four.

In 1912 The Alldays Midget was launched. A light car aimed at competing with the cyclecar market, it had an 8-10hp two-cylinder engine with water cooling via a gilled-tube radiator. Its Best and Lloyd semi-automatic drip-feed lubricator was mounted on the dashboard and a

The Alldays 8hp Light car.

Zenith carburettor was operated by a steering column mounted throttle. The leather cone clutch delivered power to a three speed plus reverse gearbox and via a shaft with worm drive to the rear axle. The car sold for £195 complete with two side lamps, rear lamp and horn with a hood as standard, with screens available for an extra £8.

The new market for light delivery vans was also exploited with a light 'Midget' delivery van launching at the same time as the car.

In 1914 a four-cylinder 10hp version of the car became available with an increased body width but the war stopped production of all of the car models. Also, in 1912, the company aimed at an even lower market, adding a three-wheeler called the 'Autorette' to their range. This had two steer able wheels at the front and a single-cylinder engine-driven

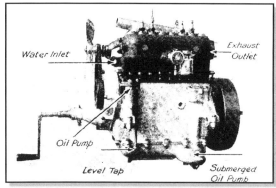

The 1914 Midget four-cylinder engine.

wheel at the back as patented in 1911 by Charles Edward Simms.

As the years progressed, the number of models produced grew until, by 1913, there were eleven cars in the range, but 1914 saw a shake-down and only five models were offered; 8hp Midget three-seater, 8-10hp Midget three-seater, 12-14hp four-seater, 16-20hp six-seater and 25-30hp six-seater. All of the cars had a three-speed and reverse gearbox.

During WWI car production was moved to the Waverley Works on Waverley Road, Small Heath to allow the Matchless works to concentrate on commercial vehicles and the Great Western Works to produce munitions. The war years also saw a shift in management as William Allday, who had steered the company since the merger, died in September 1916 following an operation. Control of the company passed to his younger brother Edmund, who became managing director, and his son, Percy William Allday.

After the war had ended in 1919, Alldays and Onions merged their car making brand with Enfield, which they also owned, and set up a new company called Enfield Allday (see **Enfield-Allday**) with Percy William Allday and Edward Tailby in control.

Production of both cars and the 'Allon' range of motorcycles was rationalised and concentrated in the Waverley Works.

The amazing thing about the Alldays company is that it still exists and, after over 350 years, is still manufacturing air handling equipment, though not bellows

A surviving 1909 Alldays and Onions.

anymore and, as with many old British Companies, they are now in foreign ownership.

A number of Alldays cars have survived and appear at runs and events both in this country and abroad. The facade of the works fronting Sydenham Road is, surprisingly, still there, though in a poor state. The Great Western mess building also survives along with some of the works housing, but the Matchless and Waverley Works have both met their fate.

Edward Mantle Tailby, who steered the company through the car making years, died in August 1832 aged 63 and the last car-making members of the Alldays family, Edmund and Percy William, died in October 1935 and April 1937 respectively.

Birmingham can be very big and very small at the same time. Edward Tailby, it turns out, was my 2nd cousin. Though four times removed.

The Waverley Works.

Regent

The Regent Engineering and Cycle Co., 6 Regent Parade, Birmingham.
1899-1900

Cycle manufacturers proliferated in Birmingham in the final years of the 19th century and were having a difficult time financially in a market both saturated and shrinking.

One of these cycle companies was run by Joseph Reece who had set up originally at 52 Moseley Street before settling in premises at 26 Pershore Street on a site now occupied by the south eastern corner of the Arcadian Centre.

Typical of the majority of cycle manufacturers his premises were not large, being one of a terrace of brick buildings facing onto Pershore Street with small yards behind. His next door neighbour were Barber and Co. who were tea importers established in 1797, and responsible for the 'Little Miss Barber' signs fading from walls all over the city as I write.

Little Miss Barber advert.

Joseph Harry Reece was born in 1869, the son of Joseph Reece, an engine and machine fitter from Tipton, who had married a girl called Sarah from Lichfield and lived in Yardley.

His background may have had an influence on his son who, probably in an effort to diversify, experimented with engines and car production at the turn of the century. He set up a second company, The Regent Engineering and Cycle Co. operating from premises at 6 Regent Parade, around the corner from the premises of Walter Davies (see **Traffic**), in the Jewellery Quarter and, from 1899 to 1901 tried to get the '*Regent*' car off the ground. The premises had previously been occupied by John Wall, an engineer who was born in Solihull in 1866, to John Wall, another engineer. John Wall Jnr. was also a cycle maker and car building was possibly a joint venture between the two engineers.

The car was a three-wheeler with a frame similar to the contemporary De Dion tricycles and a motor manufactured by Accles-Turrell. The carburettor and ignition were also made by Accles-Turrell (see **Accles-Turrell**).

Autocar, when they reviewed it at the 1899 Stanley Cycle Show, said that the machine was 'well-guarded and had strong wheels' - evidently a weak point in some of the machines

that had evolved from cycles.

Alas, the public response was muted and his foray into car making was not successful, so he returned to cycle making. He continued making cycles under his own name, the *Regent* and *Astoria* brands until at least 1908 but, despite being in business for over 15 years none of his cycles or cars are known to have survived. His premises in Pershore street were demolished some time ago and have been replaced with, rather fittingly, a car park.

The site of the Regent Cycle Works today.

Accles-Turrell

Accles-Turrell Autocars Ltd., Perry Barr, Birmingham.
1899-1901

James George Accles was an Australian entrepreneur. Born in 1850 in Bendigo in South Australia. He trained in the manufacture of small arms and ammunition and then emigrated to England where he established a factory in Ward End to produce percussion caps.

In about 1873 he started working for the Gatling Gun Company and named his short-lived son, born in 1895, William Gatling Quintard Accles! He established the business in premises at Holford Mill in Witton on what was later to become part of the IMI Kynoch Works but, in 1890, it was wound up due to debts and Accles took over the Company.

The 1899 Turrell Quadricycle.

The 1899 Turrell Light Car.

Turrell 1899 Two Seater Light Car.

He established a new Company called Grenfell and Accles producing tubes for the ever-growing bicycle market but this also ran into financial difficulties and was wound up.

In 1896 another new Company, Accles Ltd. was floated on the Stock Market with The Earl of Verulam, John Harvey, Charles Bedford and John Sugden (of Lu-Mi-Num manufacturing) listed as Directors. Accles himself was noted as due to join the Board once shares were allocated. At this stage the Company Prospectus claimed that their increased capacity would be 1000/1200 cycles per week but that it was not reliant upon the cycle trade to survive. Indeed, one of the products that the company manufactured was a 1.75hp engine for 'motorcycle propulsion' which powered the 'Lady's Motor Safety Bicycle' designed by Harry Lawson for the British Motor Syndicate in 1897. The company went through a number of changes until, in 1899, Turrell left The British Motor Co and joined the Accles' Company.

Charles McRobie Turrell was born in Coventry in 1875 and served his apprenticeship with engineering companies in the city eventually becoming the works manager at the Coventry Motor Company where he developed a motor tricycle called the 'Coventry Motette' in 1898.

Turrell was a pioneer motorist who, when working for the British Motor Syndicate, had helped to organise the 1896 Emancipation Run, now commemorated each year as the London to Brighton Run and drove the lead car with Harry Lawson as a passenger.

The first product of their association was the Turrell Quadricar in 1899. This was a (at first) tiller-steered, four-wheeled vehicle with a vertical, 3hp, single-cylinder engine designed to seat two people. Power was transmitted to the rear wheel by a flexible belt, running at 1400ft per minute, that could be shifted to one of three pulleys. The centre one ran free to act as a neutral, the other two powered the high and low gears on the rear axle. Testing of this vehicle, and a tricycle also developed as a test-bed for the new technology, was carried out on a mile long test circuit which ran around the workshops at the Holford factory. The trials went well so they prepared a production model, now with a steering wheel.

The Quadricycle was built to Turrell's design for The British Motor Syndicate of which he was Company Secretary but, with both men excited by their progress, he joined forces with Accles to create an 'autocar' and a joint patent was taken out. The Accles-Turrell Autocar Company was formed in 1900 to produce the cars.

The J G Accles Motor.

The Accles Turrell Autocar produced in 1900 was a light carriage with two seats and a water-cooled, 3 1/2 hp engine. The engine was manufactured by Accles and had a single cylinder located under the seat aligned front-to-back. The bodywork was coachbuilt in mahogany by Mulliners of Northampton. It had a three-speed and reverse gearbox driven by a belt from the driving axle which projected out from both sides of the crankcase. The three gear speeds were 4, 10 and 20mph with an average speed attained of 15mph.

In 1901 Accles produced a larger four-seater car, the 'New Turrell', which was described as *"vibrationless, very simple, quiet and efficient"* The car had a flat twin 10-15 hp engine under the front seat driving the rear wheels through a two-speed, constant mesh gearbox. One of the original directors of the Company, Thomas Pollock, bought the rights to the car and, after 1902 produced it at his works in Ashton-under-Lyne, which, at that time, was in Lancashire.

Accles Turrell Tricycle.

From 1903 the Turrell was produced by the Autocar Construction Company of Openshaw, Manchester and badged as a 'Hermes'. The collaborations didn't finish there. The Accles Tube Syndicate was backed financially by Thomas Pollock and moved out of Holford Mill to works at Oldbury under the new company name of Accles and Pollock. This company went on to be a major player in tube manufacture and also produced the world's first all metal aircraft, the 'Mayfly', from the Oldbury Works.

After the collapse of his companies in 1902, J. G. Accles engaged in consulting and experimentation with small-arms and ammunition. He joined Birmingham Small Arms Co Ltd, as a consultant to advance his experimentation and also advised Christopher Cash (of J. and J. Cash) on the development of a humane killing device for animals.

Since 1898 Accles had also worked with Frederick Henry de Veulle, an associate of Charles

Turrell on a number of patents for refinements to the fuel and cooling systems on cars. In 1903 Accles, De Veulle and William Starley, the son of James Starley and cousin of John Kemp Starley (see **Rover**) designed and patented a motorcycle together. Accles and De Veulle were both listed as residing at Holford House, Perry Barr at the time and Starley was in Coventry, his adopted home town. William Starley went on to patent a large number of car related inventions and, during WWI, moved to live at 9 Wood End Road, Erdington which was his base till the thirties.

In 1903 Accles joined forces with a number of backers and formed 'Bennett's Successors Ltd'. to take over a long standing business based in St Pauls Square, run by the Bennett family, making meat jacks and stair rods and moved the business to Aston Lower Grounds.

In the late 1800s the Lower Grounds, part of the park around Aston Hall, were an amusement park, complete with skating rink, aquarium and a polar bear house, but the land was sold off for housing at the turn of the century with the fish pond filled in to create Villa Park.

He convinced his fellow directors that they should take up manufacturing his design of humane killing device in collaboration with George Edwin Shelvoke (whose brother formed Shelvoke and Drewry, a company that built fire engines and dustcarts until 1991) and so, in 1913, Accles and Shelvoke Ltd was formed. The company still exists and make captive bolt killing devices to this day.

Accles continued with the company until his death in Newquay in 1939. As for the cars...

1900 Accles-Turrell Autocar.

The 1901 New Turrell.

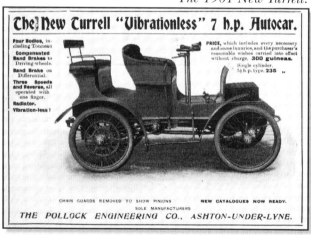

A contemporary advert for the New Turrell.

Unfortunately no examples are known to exist - we have only the photographs to remind us. Holford House and the extensive manufacturing facilities at Holford have been replaced by more recent industrial and warehouse buildings, a similar fate to that which befell the Kynoch, Lion Works next door.

Gilbert

Ralph Gilbert and Son, John Bright Street, Birmingham.
1899-1901

Ralph Benjamin Gilbert was born in Birmingham in 1852 the son of Isiah Gilbert, a master silver chaser, and Maria his wife. By 1881 he was living in Colchester with his wife Charlotte and two children, Frederick and Harold, working as a machinist and toolmaker but returned to Birmingham and joined forces with George Frederick Chutter of Handsworth, an electrical engineer, to form Chutter and Gilbert.

The company were based at 54 Buckingham Street and traded as mechanical engineers. The business was not to last though and, in 1889, the partnership was dissolved with Ralph 'retiring'. What he actually did was become a furniture dealer in Summer Lane and start a coachbuilding business with his son, Frederick Ralph Gilbert.

In 1890 they set up in John Bright Street, in an area called Green's Village, a rabbit warren of small dwellings and businesses that for decades had been the site of an Irish immigrant community. The area was named after Beau Green who lived in Hinkley Hall, otherwise known as 'Rag Castle', a rather dilapidated house in its own grounds that had been swallowed up as Birmingham grew around it to form a, less than salubrious area, called the 'Inkleys'. The only thing that remains today to remind of its existence is Hinkley Street behind the Centre City building on Smallbrook Queensway.

It was not only the surroundings that could be difficult but also some of their clients. In September 1899 Frederick Gilbert

Longuemare Carb.

appeared in court in Birmingham charged with assault on John Thomas Wrides who lived on the Moseley Road. The facts of the case made it clear that Wrides, who had designed and built a 'motor car that did not vibrate or smell' and had asked the Gilberts to build a body for it, had difficulty paying their bill. Whilst still having a balance outstanding he took the car and Fred Gilbert and his workmen took off in hot pursuit. When they caught up with him they mounted the car and took possession of it. The court heard the pleas and found for Fred Gilbert as it was clear that no excessive force had been used in repossessing the car.

The Gilberts were early experimenters with car building, claiming to have built their first 'road motor' in 1887.

The first vehicle for which we have any evidence was the twelve seater motorised carriage that appeared in October 1899. It was designed as a char-a-banc (French for 'carriage with wooden benches), with four removable benches mounted on a flat deck and access flaps to get at the running gear. It had a 10hp engine mounted at the front with two horizontal cylinders of 5in bore and 8in stroke operating a double

The 1899 Gilbert.

crankshaft. The engine was fitted with a Longuemare carburettor made by the Holley Company in Bradford, Pennsylvania and had electric ignition with separate coils and accumulators for each cylinder. The transmission consisted of belts and jockey pulleys with two forward speeds and one reverse. The speed between gears was adjusted by 'adjusting the firing time' and steering was effected with a wheel which operated via rack and pinion to levers on the front swivel axles.

The Gilbert Heavy Oil Car.

The Gilberts said that this was the first car that they had built throughout and it had taken them four months to complete. They hoped to be producing another two seater carriage with a single cylinder engine of their own design and in 1901 they were true to their word unveiling just such a car.

This 'heavy oil' car had a single-cylinder 3.5hp valveless two stroke engine with a chain drive to the rear wheels. The engine was to Gilbert's design and could run on either paraffin or petrol. The Motor Car Journal sent a correspondent to look at the car in 1901 and he reported that it was undergoing street trials but was in an unfinished state as regard bodywork, mudguards etc. Gilbert said that a 6hp engine had been installed at their premises two years previously and was working perfectly. The partnership of Ralph Gilbert and his son, however, was not working as well and in 1901 their partnership was officially dissolved. In 1903 Gilbert teamed up with Walter Thomas to produce cars under the Thomas name (see **Thomas**).

Ralph Gilbert died on 30th April 1931 at 9 Church Street, Rhyl though, by that time, he was still listed as living at 22 Hampton Road, off Trinity Road in Aston. None of the cars that the Gilberts built has survived and neither has their premises. The part of Station Road where their workshop was located was redeveloped in the 1960s and is now little more than a vestigial passageway linking John Bright Street with the Suffolk Street Queensway. On the site of their workshop there is now a car hire company.

Tube Manufacturers

Birmingham was a centre of tube making - a vital element in cycle, motocycle and early car manufacture. Birmingham's early tube manufacturers included Tubes Ltd., New Credenda Tube and Accles and Pollock.

In 1919 these companies were merged into one huge conglomerate, Tube Investments, who had their headquarters at Abingdon but, following a merger in 2000 with the London based Smiths Group plc., the name disappeared.

It is indicative of the shift of focus away from manufacturing that if you were to use a locally made tube today there is only one small, specialist tube maker left, Reynolds Technology Ltd (Est. 1841). in Shaftmoor Lane.

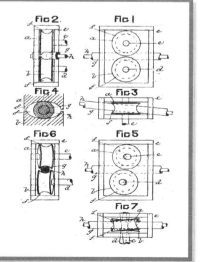

Buckingham and Adams

Buckingham and Adams Cycle & Motor Co., Coventry Works, Arthur St., B'ham. 1899-1902

Frederick Samuel Buckingham and Joseph Adams were keen and accomplished cyclists who started selling cycles in London with Buckingham's half brother, Francis Henry Fearns.

By the late 1880s they were manufacturing cycles from premises in Arthur Street, Small Heath. In 1889 the company was incorporated and sold to Joseph Gothard, Harry Percy Cook and George James Eveson, retaining Buckingham as manager, Adams as a Director and Fearns as a travelling salesman. The money received in the sale was, presumably, not enough for Buckingham so, with his half-brother he hatched a scheme to defraud the company. Setting up a string of bogus companies, they sold machinery to themselves and made an estimated £112 before being discovered. They were found guilty of fraud and sentenced to 9 months hard labour. Buckingham went on to manage the Elswick Cycle Company in Newcastle upon Tyne, a company which still exists today.

The Works in their heyday.

The new owner of the company, Joseph Gothard, had wide business interests being a director of Henry Boys Ltd. a brick maker, Griffiths and Browett, iron and tin workers, Perks bedstead makers and a member of the board of the Birmingham and Liverpool Ship Canal. Like everyone else in the business they were forced to restructure and change direction in the late 1890s. In 1899 the 'Buckingham and Adams Cycle and Motor Company' was registered to carry on the business of manufacturers of and dealers in bicycles, tricycles, velocipedes and motor cars with John Joseph Shannessy (born in Kildare, Ireland in 1869) as Managing Director. The Company had existed for ten years previously as cycle manufacturers but recognised the opportunities in branching into motor driven vehicles.

These were still troubling times for the cycle industry with over-production driving down prices and causing the cycle businesses to lose money.

In 1900 a group of cycle manufacturers met under the title of the 'Cycle Manufacturers Trade Protection Association' at the Grand Hotel in Colmore Row to discuss the situation. The meeting ended with the formation of a committee to look into ways of coordinating rises in prices to a more sustainable level. However, not all of the invited manufacturers agreed with this strategy and an amount of infighting broke out. Buckingham and Adams, meanwhile had problems of their own - a winding-up order had been applied for at Court by J Leadbetter and Sons, the Sheffield steel company in January 1900.

By February, the order had been withdrawn and the pressure was off for a time but things were not to get easier, the company was restructured in 1901 and wound-up in 1903 without producing a single car.

It had been a troubled company and, despite having large manufacturing facilities spanning between Arthur Street and Herbert Road only a small, run-down part of their works in Small Heath remains to mark their passing.

The Coventry Works in Arthur Street.

Sanspareil

The Sanspareil Cycle Co Ltd., Victoria Road and 91 Bracebridge St, Birmingham. 1900

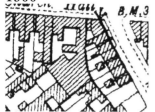

William Andrews produced sewing machines, cycles and, for a short time, motor driven quadricycles from his Sanspareil works in Aston.

Born in 1839 in Hulme, Manchester, William Andrews travelled to America as an engineer, worked on the automation of ammunition production for the Gatling Gun Company and allegedly designed the power take-off for Massey Ferguson Tractors. He was then employed as a construction engineer on the Civil War ship 'The Monitor' before finally working for the Singer Sewing Machine Company.

By 1871 he had returned to the UK and set himself up as a sewing machine maker in Steelhouse Lane. He spent the next few years building the business and developing patents.

In 1874 he married Fanny Elizabeth Parkes the daughter of a Birmingham spectacle maker, and raised a family. In 1880 he relocated to premises further along Steelhouse Lane and was by now, producing sewing machines under the 'Sanspareil' and 'Wheeler and Wilson' brands amongst others.

1881 saw him branching into the manufacture of 'ordinary' cycles, a line of business that expanded and took over from the sewing machines by 1884, when he moved cycle production into the Victoria Road, and later, the Brace-bridge Street, premises. The company was registered in 1896 with Frank Powell of 'Powell and Hanmer' the carriage

William Andrews.

lamp makers and Frederick Warwick of the companies that were to become 'Ariel' and 'Dunlop' as directors, and Ralph Gilbert (see **Gilbert**) and William Allday (see **Alldays and Onions**) amongst the shareholders. At the Birmingham Cycle and Motor Show in 1900, the company exhibited a range of cycles but also had a motorized quadricycle tandem on show. The quadricycle was a bridge between cycles and cars. Generally it was built in the same way that cycles were but it had four wheels and a motor. The quadricycle was convertible into a tricycle as was usual at that time and had a De Dion pattern motor probably made by Accles-Turrell at Perry Barr.

Since 1884 Andrews had been building cycles for Siegfried Bettmann's company of London under the 'Triumph' name and, in 1902 Triumph bought Andrew's business. William Andrews went on to found a new business, the United Steel Wire Mill, with a

partner called Riley to make wheel spokes for cycles and motorcycles. This business was still trading as late as the 1970s.

In 1910 William Andrews moved to his summer retreat in Bournmouth and enjoyed a long retirement however, in 1932 he caught flu and died.

None of the works, or their motorized output survive.

The Sanspareil Company Letterheading.

Automobile Supply Co

The Automobile Supply Company, 56 Broad Street, Birmingham.
1900-1903

In 1900 the slump in the cycle industry was being offset, to some degree, by the growing motor car market and, at the end of January, the 4th Annual Midland Cycle and Motor Show was held at Bingley Hall.

The Birmingham Post commented that *"thanks to the excellence of the English workmanship this country is beginning to make up the leeway which it lost by allowing the foreigner to get ahead in motor propulsion"*. The exhibition included a three day trial of cycles, motorised tricycles and light cars that were designed to test reliability and expose the industry to a wider public. The light car trial had five entries. Four vehicles lasted the course but two of those had to take a detour along Moor Street because they couldn't manage the Bull Ring hill.

1900 also marked the appearance of The Automobile Supply Company on a site that wrapped around the back of the blue-brick Presbyterian Church of England in Broad Street and reappeared with a frontage in Oozells Street.

The Church, built in 1849 and designed by J R Botham still stands, though now pressed into use as a nightclub - whatever would the Church Elders have thought?

The Company was managed by John Thomas Scarborough, born in Market Harborough in 1859. John Scarborough's parents, Thomas and Mary, were haberdashers. Whilst he started as an assistant in their shop a wanderlust set in. By the time he was 24 he was a leather factor in Kettering and, by the age of 30, was working as a Tanners Agent in Knighton, Leicestershire.

The Presbyterian Church.

By 1901 he was in Birmingham boarding in Edgbaston and was describing himself as a motor car engineer. At the Stanley Show in 1900 he exhibited *"a two and a quarter horsepower tricycle, two and a quarter horse-power quad, "De Dion" engines, and a small voiturette, but whether their own or another make was not decided at the time we called"*. The 'Horseless Carriage' a magazine of the time, reported that he had on show a Locomobile manufactured in Bridgport Connecticut in the USA and a frame with a 4hp gasoline motor which was intended for supply to carriage builders. The former was obviously not of Birmingham manufacture, the latter was built by the Birmingham toolmaking firm Thomas Chatwins.

At the exhibitions held the following year their exhibits were both the more tried and tested Darracqs built in France. In 1903 the Company was being managed by William Spiller and in 1905 by Edgar Harris. Thomas Scarborough had moved to Westcotes, Leicester and continued to generate car related patents.

Chatwin continued production at his Great Tindal Street Works. (see **British Peerless**).

The 'Peerless' before coachbuilding.

Ariel/Ariel-Simplex

Ariel Automotive Works, Dale Road, Bournbrook, Birmingham.
1900-1911

These days it is generally accepted that the pneumatic tyre was invented by John Dunlop in 1888 but, over 40 years earlier, another Scot by the name of Robert William Thomson, had patented what were actually the first pneumatic tyres, in France and the USA, for use on horse-drawn carriages. He called these 'Aerial (*sic*) Wheels'.

In 1870 James Starley and William Hillman, (of cars fame), revived the name when they invented wire spoked wheels allowing them to build a cycle that was much lighter than those that had gone before and so was appropriately named after the 'spirit of the air'. Their 'penny farthing' bicycle (a name only applied to them in more recent times, they should be more correctly called an 'ordinary') revolutionised the industry.

The Ariel name disappeared for more than twenty years before being, again, revived by Charles Sangster who acquired the rights to use it in 1896.

Charles Thomas Brock Sangster was born in Aberdeen in 1872. He was named after his grandfather Charles Thomas Brock of fireworks fame. After initially working in the City of London he joined Linley and Biggs who made 'Whippet' cycles and found his interest in mechanical engineering.

Over the next few years he moved from the New Howe Machine Company in Glasgow via the Rudge Company in Coventry to the Coventry Machinists Company and designed their 'Swift' model cycles in 1895. This put him on the map, revolutionising

Charles Sangster.

cycle design and, riding this wave, he found financial backing and acquired the site for a new factory at Bournbrook.

In January 1894 in collaboration with, amongst others, pioneer motorist S.F. Edge of Napier and Harvey du Cros (see **Austin**), Irish founder of Dunlop Tyres, he formed Cycle Components Manufacturing Ltd. and made cycle parts for the trade at 'Componentsville' in Bournbrook, claimed, at the time, to be the largest manufacturing facility for cycle components in the world.

In 1896 Dunlop started manufacturing cycles under the 'Dunlop Cycles' brand but met with resistance from other cycle manufacturers, who, having to fit the Dunlop patent tyres, were concerned that the word 'Dunlop' appearing on their tyres would give the new cycle company free advertising. In 1898 they set up an adjoining manufacturing facility for 'Ariel' cycles and found great commercial success in a difficult market.

CTB Sangster was a prolific inventor, devising the method for manufacturing the 'endless rim' and setting up a company to manufacture it. He was also a keen pioneer motorist and, soon after

The Ariel Works in their heyday.

the Locomotive Act was repealed, he imported a French De Dion motor tricycle to familiarise himself with the technology.

By 1898 he had designed his first 'Ariel' motor tricycle and, three years later, produced his first motorcycle with a 211cc Minerva engine.

Ariel exhibited a quad cycle with a De Dion type engine at the Birmingham Bicycle and Motor Show, but it was 1902 before car production started with a 10hp two-cylinder engine, followed in 1903 by their first four-cylinder 16hp model.

Up until 1906, manufacture of Ariel cars was carried out at the Dale Road works in Bournbrook in conjunction with other manufacturers. Ariel Motors (1906) Ltd was floated as a public company to acquire the freehold of the Dale Road works for manufacture of Ariel Motor Cars, and the goodwill and assets of the retail business, the Ariel Motor Co. at Long Acre in London, together with the rights to use the Ariel and Ariel-Simplex names.

The Ariel Quadricycle of 1900.   *The Aerial Voiturette of 1900.*

Charles Sangster joined the Army in May 1908 becoming a Captain in the 4th Warwickshire Howitzer Battery before moving to the 4th South Midland Ammunition Column in October of the same year. Also in 1908, the Ariel Motor Company was bought by Lorraine-Dietrich to produce their 20hp model exhibited at the 1908 Motor Show (see **Lorraine-Dietrich**). This was a commercial failure and production lasted for little more than a year. Ariel production continued under the 'Ariel' name only as 'Ariel-Simplex' had trade mark difficulties.

The demise of Ariel as a Birmingham car marque came in 1911 when production was moved to Coventry.

As of 2011 the Ariel factory no longer exists. The last remaining part of the building was demolished to make way for the Selly Oak New Road which passes through the site of the factory. The same fate as its near neighbour the Patrick Motor coachbuilding works (see **Patrick Motors**).

The name, though, lives on with the Ariel Motor Company now based in Crewkerne in Somerset makers of the, rather distinctively styled, Ariel Atom sports car.

The last piece of the factory before demolition.

British Ideal

Montague Hawnt & Co., 98 Bradford St., and 56-58 Dudley St., Birmingham. 1901

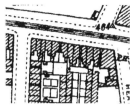

The name suggests that this was a British product and the company that marketed it was Birmingham based with another base in London but the product was, at least to begin with, another early example of badge engineering; the cars themselves were initially sourced in France with minimal adaptation for the British market. British motor companies needed time to develop their cars, as a design brought to market before it was ready could destroy a brand before it had time to establish itself, with breakdowns and unreliability taking their toll. They had to take a measured approach. The continental companies had already gone through the prototype design phase and developed models which could satisfy the early demand in Britain following the Emancipation Act. William Montague Hawnt took the easy route.

The car he chose to import was the Schaudel, a French car manufactured in Bordeaux by a gunsmith who had made bicycles from the mid 1890s and turned to car making - a familiar story. The 1900 car had a two cylinder engine mounted transversely with the gearbox in the sump - an arrangement adopted by Sir Alec Issigonis when he designed the Mini. The engine and gearbox were all made as one unit and the cylinders, rather than being made separately as was common at the time, had the cylinders cast in a single unit as they tend to be today - a forward looking design. Charles Schaudel described the design as a Motobloc, a name that was adopted as its marque in France when the company was bought out by Schaudel's brother in law Emile Dombret in 1904.

The British Ideal.

In 'The Autocar' in 1901 the 'British Ideal' is reviewed and Montague Hawnt states that he will eventually build the car in Birmingham, but it is not known if he actually did.

William Hawnt was born in Birmingham in 1874. He was actually christened William John Hawnt but adopted the Montague, an old family name, when he went into business. By the time he was 25 years old he had established Montague Hawnt and Co as a hardware business at 98 Bradford Street and had further premises in Dudley Street to manufacture cycle accessories so he had the facilities to build the cars but it is difficult to prove as none of the vehicles have survived. His driving offences do survive, however, and he wasn't beyond driving unregistered cars. He had further business interests in London where he began a cycle manufacturing business in partnership with a Joseph Mason (which was dissolved in 1903) and later with Warren Percy Cook. The London business at 140-146 Clerkenwell Road and the Birmingham premises at 56-58 Dudley Street were both pressed into service as car showrooms. The partnership with Warren Cook was also short lived and ended in 1907 to be replaced with another company, W Montague Hawnt Ltd. which survived, in name at least, until 1916. Meanwhile, by 1910 William Montague Hawnt himself had been declared bankrupt.

Interestingly, his son, Frederick Montague Hawnt became an accountant and spent much of his career as a liquidator of companies. Carrying on the family business?

Richmond

H S Richmond, 174 Great Lister Street, Birmingham.

1901

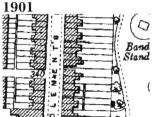

The car built in Birmingham by Henry Richmond in 1901 was one of the first cars to have been built by an amateur.

Henry S Richmond was born in Birmingham in 1877, the son of Howard and Bertha Richmond who lived in a small terraced house in St Clement's Road, Nechells under the shadow of the Saltley Gas Works... and close enough to have had their windows blown out by the 1904 explosion. Howard worked on the railway and was raising five daughters and one, treasured son, Henry. He trained as a carpenter but, as he entered his twenties was inspired by the new motor cars that he saw in the magazines and occasionally on the roads of Birmingham, and he decided to build one of his own, in the front room of his mother's house.

Unfortunately, things were not going to go well and in the summer of 1901 he was made unemployed. About a week later, close to completing his car, he caught the middle finger of his left hand in the chain wheel when operating the motor and took the end clean off. This story and his other domestic woes touched the hearts of the readers of Autocar and

a Mr. Joseph Holdsworth of Bradford sent him £6 to finish the car. With another half a guinea donated by Autocar he was set to complete it.

The car was fitted with a 2.25hp De Dion engine mounted very low to 'catch the wind' and with the power transmitted to a countershaft, then by two chains to the rear wheels. The steering wheel was attached to two rods which ran under the floor connected at each end to a short length of chain. Each of the chains were wrapped around chain

Henry Richmond's 1901 car, part finished.

rings, one fixed horizontally on the centre of the front axle and the other on the bottom end of the steering column. Next to the steering wheel was another wheel that operated the friction clutch and a lever fixed to the steering column controlled the electric ignition. The carburettor was of the 'ordinary surface type', presumably one of the few items not built from scratch. The exhaust, however, was noted as Richmond's own construction. The engine was lubricated by sight-feed into the crank chamber and fed from a one gallon petrol tank mounted on the side of the frame. The 26in wheels were made wholly by him, even to the hub castings and the 2 1/2in tyres. He used standard bicycle tubing and fittings to build the frame and constructed it in such a way that the wheelbase could be altered to anywhere between 6ft and 3ft 6in by adjusting telescopic tubes. The car was 2ft 6in wide and designed to go through a typical door opening, a vital point when you are building it in your mother's front parlour!

The car, with a seat over the back wheel for the driver and a forecar seat for a passenger was capable of speeds up to 16mph and was, as the reviewer commented, *'constructed in a workmanlike manner'*. Unfortunately the car hasn't survived.

Universal

The Universal Trading Company Ltd., 55 Dale End and Moor Street, Birmingham. 1901-1902

The Universal Trading Company was set up by Harold Tanner and George Bennett to build and sell cycles, motorcycles and cars but probably did more selling than building.

Harold Thomas Tanner was an engineer who had previously set up a company called The Redditch Engineering Co in 1899 with the intent of manufacturing, amongst other things, 'motors, horseless and other carriages'. George Augustus Albert Bennett joined forces with him to set up a business called the Universal Trading Company in premises at 55 Dale End, (which now lie beneath one of the teaching blocks of Aston University), to further those aims. With a name like 'Universal', they were obviously ready for anything and in 1901, that was motorcycles. He imported a motor bicycle called the 'Merkel' from the United States, but his ambitions didn't end there. He listed himself as a motor manufacturer. His dreams were short lived, however, and the company got into financial difficulties culminating in a meeting of creditors held in September 1902.

Things didn't go smoothly. At the meeting Bennett and his solicitor objected to the presence of a representative of one of the trade papers, himself a creditor, and refused to continue as long as he remained. After Bennett departed, the creditors had a whip round to pay for the room and decided to have the company's affairs thoroughly investigated.

Moving on, he teamed up with Sydney Slater Guy, a talented engineer who was born in Wolverhampton in 1885, though raised in Kings Norton, and had served his apprenticeship with the Birmingham marine engineers Bellis and Moorcom. Together, they made their first patent application in 1908 for contact breakers. This was to be the first of many patents held by Guy who went on to become works manager for Sunbeam motors in 1909 and formed his own company Guy Motors, with its distinctive Indian Chief figurehead, in 1913.

55 Dale End.

The Midland Automobile Club

At a meeting in the Grand Hotel, on 11th January 1901, the Midland Automobile Club was formed. Many of the leading lights in the Birmingham motor industry were present including Fred and Frank Lanchester, Herbert Austin and J D Siddeley as was Alfred Bird of custard fame.

The first sporting event that they held was a hill-climb later in 1901 on Gorcott Hill near Alcester, which was won by an Ariel Quadricycle. In 1903 they held an event on Sun Rising Hill, one of the toughest hill climbs in the country, (adopted in their logo) and soon after, were offered Shelsley Walsh as an alternative to running events on public roads which were considered dangerous following the disastrous Paris-Madrid race of that year. Shelsley Walsh is still owned by the Club and is therefore the oldest operational motorsport venue in the world.

Rex

Birmingham Motor Manufacturing & Supply Co. Ltd., Broad Street, Birmingham. 1901-1902

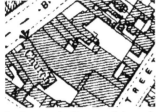

The origins of the Rex marque, now more often identified with Coventry, lie with a interesting group of businessmen most of whom lived in the Erdington/Wylde Green area of the city.

The individuals involved were the Pilkington brothers; William, George, Arthur and Alfred, John Inshaw, Charles Bishop and Anderson Brownsword.

Though having a surname usually identified with the glass industry in Lancashire, the four brothers were born in Birmingham to George Pilkington, a shoemaker from Hampton in Arden and his Birmingham-born wife Elizabeth.

George died early so Elizabeth turned to shoe binding to support the family and the four boys worked as tool and tube makers. At this time they were living at their uncle's house in Icknield Port Road, who was, ironically, a glass cutter.

Two of the brothers, William and Arthur, joined forces in 1890 with Charles Bishop and Anderson Brownsword to form the Birmingham Climax Steel Tube Company, with offices in Martineau Street and the main works on the banks of the Birmingham and Fazeley Canal in Catherine Street, Aston.

Charles Thomas Bishop was born in

The 1901 Rex Chassis.

Belper, Derbyshire in 1833 and started his working life as a coal merchant in Edgbaston and, later, formed the Arrow Cycle Company at 34 and 35 Lower Loveday Street.

Anderson Henry Brownsword was a lace manufacturer from Nottingham who had held the posts of Sheriff of Nottingham and Mayor of Nottingham in the early 1890s and championed the women's suffrage movement. The four men built up their tube business, filing patents for improvements to the manufacturing process over the next five years.

On the other side of the canal was the Aston Paper Works owned by John Inshaw.

We have already encountered John George Inshaw, in 1881, when he built a very early steam driven road vehicle with his father, the owner of the Steam Clock Tavern.

In November 1895 he spoke of his intent to build another carriage as soon as the restrictive legislation was repealed. Three years later he joined with the others to form the Brazeless and General Cycle Fittings Company in a restructured Arrow Cycles business.

At the beginning of the new century the Birmingham Motor Manufacturing and Supply Company Limited was formed

THE REX, King of British Cars.

6¼ h.p. Balanced Motor.
3 Speeds and Reverse.

Immediate delivery of

REX Double Phaeton & Tonneau, 195 Gns.

COMPONENTS TO THE TRADE.

BIRMINGHAM MOTOR MANUFACTURING & SUPPLY CO., LTD., 189, Broad St., Birmingham.
Works Coventry.   W. Williams, Manager.

By 1902 production had moved to Coventry.

acquiring depot premises at 189 Broad Street Birmingham. In 1900 they unveiled their first motorised vehicle, a forward sloping four stroke engine within the frame of a safety cycle at the National Show in Crystal Palace. The company had William Williamson (born in Coventry in 1872) as its Managing Director and his brother Harold Williamson also on the board.

In 1901 they announced that the company would be producing both a belt-driven and gear driven car with a 6hp single cylinder engine and a range of parts, including gears, clutches, axles, engines, coolers and complete chassis for supply thorough parts dealers. There were to be complete coachbuilt cars with the coachwork fitted by 'people who are thoroughly conversant with automobile requirements'. The car was to be called the 'Rex' and would be of British manufacture throughout.

By this point another of the Pilkington brothers' interests, Allard, had become involved. Allard was a cycle company that had been founded in Coventry in 1889 by Frederick William Allard, a professional bicyclist from Northampton who had been active in racing circles throughout the 1880s, and George Pilkington. They had a manufacturing base in Moor Street, Earlsdon which was left in the control of two

Frederick Allard.

of Arthur Pilkington's sons whilst Fred Allard left the partnership a year later to concentrate on professional cycling. In 1901 Charles Bishop retired and the Arrow Cycle Co, by this time based in Rocky Lane, Aston, was dissolved. A fatal accident had occurred in Kenilworth involving an Allard built light car the previous year and Fred Allard decided to sell his interest in the business, following in his mother's footsteps by becoming a publican. Circumstances had changed and the facility in Birmingham was no longer going to be viable.

In 1902 the Allard Company of Coventry merged with the Birmingham Motor Manufacturing and Supply Company and the new company was called the Rex Motor Manufacturing Company. Its base moved from Birmingham to Coventry and, at the same time, Arthur and William Pilkington temporarily focused their attention on the new facility. Back in Birmingham, the tubes company, now called, simply, Tubes Ltd. was still in operation in Catherine Street and would be for a number of years.

Arthur Pilkington retired to his home, Wylde Green House, of which only the lodge now survives on the Birmingham Road in Sutton Coldfield and bought 32 acres of land around it from Emmanuel College creating Pilkington Avenue when it was developed for housing. John Inshaw moved up to Glasgow and became involved in the tubes industry up there. Anderson Brownsword continued as a lace manufacturer until his death in 1920.

William Pilkington moved to Coventry to follow the company and Alfred Pilkington picked up the baton from his brothers for Birmingham car manufacturing by setting up the Premier Motor Company (see **Premier/PMC**) in Aston.

Frederick Allard went on to work for Armstrong-Siddeley and died in 1943.

William Williamson.

Bailey

George Bailey, Motor Manufacturer, 79 Staniforth Street, Birmingham. 1901-1903

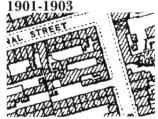

Bailey is a tantalisingly obscure marque that appeared at the dawn of motoring, of which very little is known. The company that produced it is sometimes quoted in, usually reliable, reference works as S R Bailey and Co. and their premises are reputed to have been at 160 Hartfield Road but as neither the company or the road seem to have existed, or at least, left any traces in the records, this remains a bit of a mystery.

The only S R Bailey connected with car manufacture appears to be the one who teamed up with L Lambert but they appear to have been dealers rather than manufacturers and, anyway, were based in London. There is always the possibility, of course that they had their cars built in Birmingham.

There was a George Bailey in Birmingham who could have been responsible for making the cars but whether he did or not cannot be firmly established.

George Bailey was born in 1869 in Aston the son of George Bailey, a police constable, and Hannah Bailey and started his working life as a machine maker.

In 1893 he married Mary Bayliss and started a family at their home in Ashford Street, a road that used to link Moorsom Street with St Stephen's Street in Aston. By the time of the 1901 census he was listed as a Gas Engine Maker and had three children Wilfrid, Doris and Clara who were joined by a fourth child, Desamond in 1902.

At about this time he may have turned his attention to car manufacture and established a motor manufacturing business in Staniforth Street in premises that had been occupied by a firm of drysalters. By 1908 George Bailey had ceased operating from 79 Staniforth Street and, in his place were Robert Thomas Shelley, who manufactured motors, a manufacturing chemist, a brass finisher and a currier who dressed and finished leather. Such was the density and diversity of manufacturing activity in Birmingham at that time. He moved to Whitehead Road in Aston where he was joined by his son Wilfrid building engines.

There is nothing surviving of their efforts, no engines or vehicles, and the premises have long since been demolished. Some manufacturers left no traces of their work, choosing not to register patents of form limited companies. There are a handful of these that we will encounter in this book but there is always the hope that something will turn up, eventually.

Engine Manufacturers

Many of the Birmingham cars used engines built by other, specialist, manufacturers. JAP engines were built by J A Prestwich Industries in Tottenham, Stevens were built by the Stevens Motor Manufacturing Company in Wolverhampton and Aster engines were built by the Aster Engineering Company of Wembley but Birmingham had its own manufacturers.

Blumfield built by Thomas Blumfield in Lower Essex Street, Ixion, built by the Ixion Motor Manufacturing Co in Great Tindall Street and Precision built by F E Baker were prominent makes.

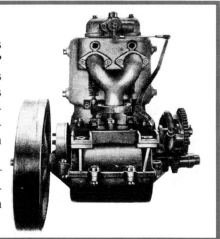

Abingdon/Meredith

John Child Meredith Ltd., 1-4 Hampton St. and 395 Summer Ln., Birmingham. 1902-1903

This company's founder died five years before it produced its first car but his efforts were recognised by later company adverts in which he was featured as a pioneer of the cycle and motor trades.

John Child Meredith was born in Birmingham in 1831 and was raised by his mother, Eleanor, at her draper, hosiery and haberdashery shop at 21 Cheapside in Digbeth where he helped behind the counter. He built a business on the corner of Summer Lane and Hampton Street at the bottom of Snow Hill selling bicycles and later ventured into motorised vehicles. His life was not without its excitements as he found himself involved in the controversy surrounding the Tichbourn Claimant, an event that was to inspire a number of books and dramas. He was also responsible for an illegal street! Walter Street in Aston was laid out by him without consultation with or permission from the Council - they were not pleased!

In 1848 he was baptised into the Mormon church and, in 1855, he joined the Mormon migration to the USA where five of his thirteen children were born in Council Bluffs, Iowa. He had to return to England due to ill health in 1864.

When he died on 20 February 1898 leaving his wife Ellen £1847, (worth over £100,000 today) she, and sons Hubert and Ralph, carried on the business becoming particularly known for carburettors and ignition systems. He was buried in Key Hill Cemetery in the Jewellery Quarter and

The Company Founder.

his grave was marked by a column surmounted by a miniature copy of the Statue of Liberty, possibly a reminder of their American excursion, which has since disappeared. (Efforts are being made by friends of the cemetery to replace it).

Hubert Augustus Meredith was born in 1874 and lived in Slade Road, Erdington in the early part of the century with his wife Leah. His brother Ralph Child Meredith was born in 1876

In 1900 the Company was registered as a going concern with a share capital of £4000 and the intent to make and sell, cycles, carriages and cars. In 1902, the Company started to manufacture two models of car. One had a two cylinder engine with a four seater tonneau body called the 'Meredith' and the other was a 3.5hp single cylinder two seater called the Abingdon.

The 'Meredith' had the two cylinders of its 8hp engine horizontally arranged and, rather unusually, offset to one side of the car. The

The Meredith Works and Showroom, Summer Lane.

flywheel formed part of a friction clutch which drove a three speed and reverse gearbox on the other side of the car which then had an offset, square section, drive shaft to the rear live axle. A De Dion carburettor was mounted beneath the steering pillar and the engines were cooled by water circulating through a combined tank and radiator mounted to form the sides and front of the bonnet in a similar form to that used by Wolseley.

The chassis had double elliptical springs front and rear and a wheelbase of 6ft 6in.

The 'Abingdon' was sold by Coxeter and Sons who were a long established engineering company managed by the great grandson of the Duke of Wellington and were responsible for, amongst other things, perfecting the equipment necessary to use laughing gas as a dental anaesthetic. They were based in Abingdon and so the car became known by this name. This has caused more than a

The chassis of the Meredith.

little confusion about the origins of the two Birmingham 'Abingdon' marques. Coxeter themselves realised that this was going to be a problem so they called it the 'Peerless'. The problem was there was another 'Peerless' already produced in America which is why another Birmingham car, produced about this time was called the 'British Peerless'. Life does get complicated sometimes. This car also weighed about 11 cwt. and was considered *'a smart little car that was quiet and vibration-free even while the car was standing'*.

The company was finally wound up in 1910. The premises used to produce the cars still exist at the corner of Hampton Street and Summer Lane, book-ended by two very different towers, but have suffered from neglect and have had their neo-gothic piers boarded over in a fit of modernisation of which Barry Bucknell would be proud. The upper storeys of the building were originally built to house a hotel but now await a sympathetic owner.

Hubert Meredith went on to form a motor accessories dealership in partnership with John Harry Daniel at 7 Gothic Arcade in the city but this business too foundered in 1920. The younger brother Ralph Meredith died in 1932 and Hubert died in 1953. There are no known surviving examples of the cars that they built.

The Abingdon, or should that be a Peerless?

Howles and Perry

Howles and Perry, 183 Spring Hill, Birmingham.
1902-1903

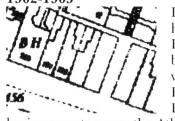

In the years around the turn of the century, Birmingham had literally hundreds of companies producing cycles. Frank Howles and Albert Perry both had cycle making businesses before they decided to join forces and produce motor vehicles.

Frank Howles was born in 1864 in Birmingham, married Emma Squires and became a steam engine turner. His first business venture was the Athlete Cycle and Engineering Company, which he started with Walter Joseph Ginder, but this partnership dissolved in 1896. In that same year he went into partnership with Arthur Phineas Berens, the son of a German Jewish immigrant, who was a dealer in precious stones in Birmingham's jewellery quarter. The partners took out a seven year lease on premises in Lionel Street to manufacture bicycles and the business developed.

By the turn of the century, he had a cycle making business at 183 Spring Hill and by 1901 had turned to manufacturing 'motors, motor parts, motor cars and all kinds of undercarriage work and general engineering'. Meanwhile, Albert Perry was also running a cycle business in Handsworth. Albert Thornton Perry was born in Aston in 1876 to Henry Perry, a jeweller, and his wife Louise. He moved swiftly into motor cycle manufacture and, in 1902, met Frank Howles. The two formed a new company called Howles and Perry to produce motors and motor fittings from the Spring Hill premises and described themselves as 'motor car builders'. Unfortunately, evidence of their car building is very scant and no photographs of their vehicles have yet come to light.

Two patents were filed in 1903 for improvements to internal combustion engines and for the improvement and simplification of clutch mechanisms for motorcycles. The patents were applied for by Frank Howles and W. A Lloyds Cycle Fittings Ltd. another Birmingham company that turned briefly to car production in 1905 (see **Walco**). Frank Howles didn't stay on the scene for very long and, by the following year, Albert was in business on his own at the Spring Hill premises and also at 5 College Street.

By 1909 Frank Howles was working on the production of engines and motorcycles with the brothers Charles William and James Harry Dalman at the Chunk Foundry backing on to the River Rea in River Street, Birmingham. The partnership produced engines that were aimed at the motorcycle, light car and cyclecar market and, for a short time. Immediately prior to the Great War, they produced the two-stroke, 'Dalm' motorcycle.

Although production of the Dalm motorcycle ceased in 1915 engine production continued until the company, J.C. Dalman and Sons, was dissolved in 1924. None of the vehicles produced by Howles and Perry are known to survive and the premises, along with most of the others in Spring Hill, have been demolished.

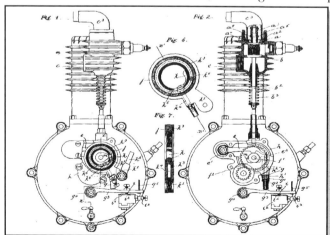

Engine drawings in collaboration with WA Lloyd 1903.

Dickinson Morette

B.E.Dickinson, Toledo Works, Aston Brook Street, Birmingham.
1902-1905

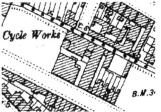

In the early years of the century there was a perceived need for a vehicle that bridged the gap between the motorcycle and the light car. Sometimes called the 'motorette'; this is the market that Benjamin Dickinson wanted to satisfy.

Benjamin Edward Dickinson was born in Pimlico in 1862. His father, also called Benjamin, was a boilermaker from Lancashire. He started his working life as an employee in a number of engineering companies and, in 1896, he took up a position as General Manager at the Kynoch Lion Works, staying there for three years. In 1899 the cycle side of the business at Kynoch was suffering from the downturn so he resigned his position to go into business in his own right manufacturing a vehicle called the 'Dickinson Morette'.

To do this he needed premises and found them in Aston Brook Street. The Toledo Works had hosted a number of businesses starting with Snell and Co, a company producing lamps and cycle accessories under the management of Samuel Snell

Refuelling the Dickinson Morette.

and John Parker. After this company was dissolved in 1892, the works were taken over by John Parker and Thomas Sanders, who continued to manufacture the same products as 'Parker and Sanders' before they too dissolved their partnership in 1895. The Toledo Works then played host to a company formed through the partnership of John William Phillips, Alexander Lamont Dugon and Richard Hine who produced a wide range of stamped ironmongery and, from 1902, the Dickinson Morette.

The Morette was a two-seater, three-wheeled car driven by an engine mounted above the single front wheel with a tiller for steering. It had a tubular steel frame and steel seat with a floor of 'wood-fibre' carried on cross tubes. There were two engine options; 2.5hp and 4hp, either of which would be hinged on a strong bracket that allowed the tiller to engage or disengage the drive. It would run at up to 15mph and was suitable 'for the use of ladies, doctors, clergymen and others who require a light handy vehicle capable of travelling at a moderate pace.'

In 1905 Benjamin Dickinson died in Wandsworth, London, bringing an early end to his car making ambitions.

Only one example of this improbable machine still exists, unfortunately not in the UK. It has been painstakingly restored and resides in New England in full working order. The premises in Aston Brook Street disappeared in the redevelopment of the area long ago.

The Dickinson Morette.

Quadrant/Carette

The Quadrant Cycle Company, Sheepcote Street, Birmingham.
1902-1908

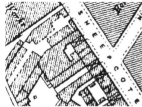

Another example of a vehicle that bridged the gap between motorcycle and car was the 'Carette' produced by the Quadrant Cycle Company.

Walter John Lloyd and his brother Albert were machinists trading as 'Lloyd Brothers' and making safety pins and other metal goods at the back of 93 High Street, Harborne in the early 1880s.

The brothers were both born in Harborne, Walter in 1853 and Albert in 1856. In about 1882 they were joined by William Alexander Priest, born in 1870 the son of an optician , also from Harborne, who had, up to then, been a commercial clerk in the hardware trade. They formed a partnership, but it was not to last and in 1883 Albert Lloyd left Walter and William to go it alone.

During the late 1880s they experimented with cycle production and, in 1889 and 1900, exhibited at the Stanley Exhibition of Cycles at Crystal Palace. By 1891 they were styling themselves as 'cycle manufacturers'; business took off and they needed larger premises closer to the centre of the City.

William Martin had built some splendid factory premises in Sheepcote Street that presented a symmetrical facade to the street with two arched openings into twin courtyards for waggon access, and had leased the left hand section to Edmunds Hudson tube makers (see **New Hudson**). They leased the right hand half of the premises and started trading as The 'Quadrant Cycle Co'.

The bicycle trade suffered a downturn in the 1890s, despite their introduction of a 'chainless cycle' in 1897 so they were on the lookout for the next big thing. This was motorcycle production. So, in 1895, they floated the Company on the Stock Market to raise share capital and, with this backing, they developed a motorcycle and launched it in 1899.

William Priest and Walter Lloyd on a Carette.

In 1902 their motorcycle range included a motorised tricycle. Motorcycles were one thing, but you couldn't really expect a woman in the clothing of the period to get her leg over a motorcycle saddle, so what do you do?

The Emancipation Act of 1896 had kick started the car industry but Priest and Lloyd were more familiar with motorcycle technology, so the answer? Put a seat onto the front of a motorcycle and call it a 'small car' or 'carette'.

Their Carette of 1903 was an unusual machine for a number of reasons; The

Tom Silver with a Quadrant motorcycle.

passenger sat in front of the driver in an upholstered single seat and between the driver and passenger there were not one but two engines. one of 2.5hp and one of 3hp. The theory was that two small engines would be easier to cool than one big one, as either could be disengaged and turned off, and it was possible to link the controls together for ease of operation. What you do end up with is a serious number of chains and a very complex piece of engineering.

The Quadrant Works, Sheepcote Street today.

Power was transmitted via v-belts from each motor to either side of the rear wheel. It had a 'surface' carburettor made by Quadrant which relied upon evaporation from the surface of the fuel in the reservoir to provide an explosive mixture that could be drawn into the cylinder. Braking was by band brakes acting on the rear wheel operated by 'Bowden wires' and a 'back-pedalling' brake to Quadrant's design.

To raise the profile of the business they contracted the long-distance motorcyclist Tom Silver and he undertook an attempt to break the speed record from Lands End to John'O'Groats in 1903 achieving the record in a time of 64 hours and 29 minutes. The company benefitted from the exposure that Silver had given them and he joined the company.

In 1906 they experimented with the production of four-wheeled cars. Their car had either a 14-16hp or a 20-22hp four-cylinder engine made by Coventry based White and Poppe, but was a short-lived venture.

In 1907 the company encountered financial difficulties and was restructured with William Priest and Tom Silver in control. The company was renamed the 'Quadrant Motor Co'. and, in 1908, production moved to Earlsdon, Coventry where the range of cycles and motorcycles expanded.

In 1911 the motorcycle arm of the business returned to premises in Lawley Street, Birmingham and the company continued manufacturing motorcycles until 1927.

After the Quadrant Cycle Company finished Walter Lloyd went on to form the Lloyd Motor and Engineering Company at 132 Monument Road and died in Birmingham on 14 September 1934.

William Priest died in Brighton in 1942. There are examples of the 'Carette' still surviving, as the photograph to the left testifies, and the premises in Sheepcote Street are still there, though converted to office and residential use, as are so many of Birmingham's old 'factories'.

A surviving Quadrant Carette.

Holdsworth

The Light Car and Motor Engineering Co., Dale End, Birmingham.
1903-1904

Location of works unknown.

The Holdsworth Light Car first appeared at the Stanley Show, the national cycle and motor show held at Crystal Palace in 1903.

It was a chain-driven car with two seats and came with either a 6hp air-cooled v-twin or a single-cylinder 4.5hp engine driving through a leather faced clutch and two-speed gearbox.

The car sold for 99 guineas and had a 'strongly built' body finished and upholstered in the best carriage style to produce a 'rakish-looking' vehicle. The seat was raised high and built for two people with deep buttoned upholstery. It had an ash framework, typical of coach-built cars, flitched with steel. This was a method for strengthening the framing members by sandwiching steel between sections of ash so that the wood braced the steel when it was in compression. The springs were semi-elliptical and hung by shackles to scroll irons attached to the frame to strengthen the corners. The engine had a two speed gearbox and was fixed to a frame made up of channel section steel. The controls for gear changing, throttle, ignition and choke were placed under the steering wheel as was common at the time The back axle was considered to be very strong by a contemporary review and both axles were fitted with tangentially spoked wheels. The petrol tank was located under the seat and a combined water and oil tank was attached to the full width of the dashboard. The oil compartment had a sight-feed cylindrical oil pump which worked on the pressure principal. The radiators had an extra large cooling area and the bonnet, which was of a Mors pattern, was carried on an extension of the frame in front of the dashboard.

No examples have survived and the company is a bit of a mystery.

The Holdsworth.

Sprags

There are many familiar features of a modern car that have been slowly added over the years but, before the handbrake was invented, how did they stop a parked car rolling away?

The answer is, they used a sprag. This little known element of early car design was a hinged length of wood that was lowered to the ground to act as a prop. They disappeared decades ago but in the early 1900s the length and design of the sprag was debated in the journals. The design illustrated to the right had a chain to stop the car from 'pole-vaulting' away.

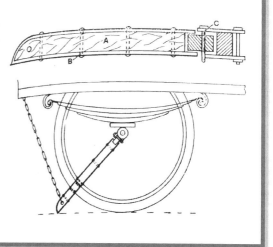

Mobile

**The Mobile Motor and Engineering Co. Ltd., John Bright Street, Birmingham.
1903-1907**

The Mobile Motor and Engineering Co started by selling a light car called the 'Waddington', manufactured in Middlesborough, from their then newly built premises, The Roseberry Building, in John Bright Street.

The Company had been started in May 1903 by Louis Antweiler and the brothers Mark and David Fridlander Lintine. It was registered with a share capital of £3000.

Mark, born in 1866 and David, born in 1875 were the sons of Morrice Lintine, a German Jewish pawnbroker, and his wife Rebecca. The family had emigrated to England in the 1830s and Morrice had been born in Birmingham. Mark had a cycle business based at 28 and 29 Wrottesley Street and the brothers, together, had another cycle components and accessories company at 4 Great Charles Street on a site now occupied by the Central Library, and a retail outlet in great Eastern Street, London. This same retail outlet was pressed into service as a car showroom when they started producing their cars, as was the John Bright Street building.

Louis Auguste Mourice Antweiler was born in 1874 and emigrated to England from the Netherlands. In 1914 he married Eva Jacob in Kings Norton and, in March 1915, became a naturalised British citizen. Louis was a pioneer motorist and participated in the infamous Paris-Madrid race of 1903.

The Company produced a range of cars starting with their light car, a 6hp Voiturette. This was a two seater with a De Dion engine and three speed gearbox. The bonnet and radiator were described as being to the 'Mercedes pattern', coachbuilt by a 'leading French body maker' and it aimed at being a 'luxury car in miniature'. It was claimed that the car would

The Mobile 6hp Voiturette.

attain a speed of 28 mph on flat ground. A cane basket was fixed at the rear and, at the front, there was the choice of car basket or umbrella. They also produced a 12hp car with an Aster engine and a landaulette with an open drivers section and enclosed rear cabin.

In 1907 the company was taken over by Calthorpe Motors (see **Calthorpe**) with Louis Antweiler retained as a Director. The Mobile Motor Company as an entity was wound-up but the owners of Mobile cars were assured that parts would still be available through Calthorpe.

After the sale the Lintine brothers moved to London to become agents and importers. David died in London in 1941 and Mark died in 1955 in Worthing, Sussex. Louis Antweiler stayed with Calthorpe for eighteen years before moving to Mulliners, their coachbuilding arm, as Managing Director. He died in Birmingham in 1965. No examples of Mobile cars are known to have survived.

The Mobile Landaulette.

Heron

The Heron Motor Company, Roseberry Buildings, John Bright St., Birmingham. 1903-1908

The Heron was produced by J J Horne, Louise Stamford Fenn, Frederick Goodhall and J S Arter who traded as the Heron Motor Company.

John James Horne was born in 1865 in Bootle, Lancashire the son of James Horne, a hardware merchant from Scotland, and his wife Catherine.

He had an early interest in motoring having set up a company called the 'Motor Touring Company' in the mid 1890s and then moved into pneumatic tyre manufacture with John Wild as the Fleetwood Tyre Company based at the Union Works, Coventry. In 1896 his company attempted to join with others to form the 'Midland Cycle and Tyre Company' with the stated aim to, eventually, go into car manufacture, but the enterprise failed in 1898.

James Sidney Arter was born in Moseley in 1885 to Frederick Arter the manager of an electroplating works. He was educated at King Edwards and went into business as an estate agent. He was, however, a keen motorist and engaged in motor sport so, a car company would have been an excellent forum for his business talents. The two directors, Horne and Arter, had lived three doors away from

The Heron.

each other in Cotton Lane, Moseley at the turn of the century. This may be where their paths first crossed.

Frederick Goodhall was an engineer from Bedford who became foreman in John Horne's tyre works in Coventry. He teamed up with John Horne in patenting a couple of tyre-related patents. The cars were produced under the Heron name (it being an anagram of John Horne's name), and ranged in power from 10hp, two-cylinder models to 22hp four-cylinder models, fitted with Aster engines with mechanically operated inlet valves made in St Denis, Paris. The chassis of the cars were produced by E J West while he was still in Coventry and the bodywork was constructed in ash with steel flitch plates.

The power from the engine was transmitted through a cone clutch to the gearbox which had three forward gears plus reverse. In 1907 Heron encountered difficulties and 'ceased all active business' in July 1908. The death of Louis Fenn, the firms' backer, in 1908 may have had some bearing on this.

After the company was dissolved, James Arter moved to Malaysia in January 1910 to become an assistant on the Sungei Way Estate before joining the Batu Tiger Rubber Company in 1911. He visited the UK in 1915 but had the misfortune to return to Malaya on the Lusitania. He survived being torpedoed by the German submarine on 7 May 1915 and lived in Malaysia until his death in 1932. John Horne died in 1937 in Birmingham.

There are no known surviving examples of the Heron but the splendid premises in John Bright Street still exist, having been home at various times to Heron, Mobile (see **Mobile**) and PJ Evans.

Traffic

The Traffic Automobile Manufacturing Company, 16 Regent Parade, Birmingham. 1903-1909

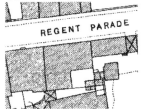

Traffic is a little-known marque founded by Walter Davies, an affluent hardware merchant in the City centre, who had an international business generating the capital necessary to start a car building venture.

Walter William Davies was born in Birmingham in 1855 to William Davies and his wife Sarah. He spent some time as a child at his maternal grandparents' place - a toll house on the Shropshire Turnpike, before establishing himself as a hardware merchant in Birmingham with a vigorous export business.

He lived, with his wife Amelia from Pimlico in London, his son and two daughters at the Grange in Tyseley which used to stand where the Colliers car showroom now stands on the Warwick Road.

At this time Tyseley was a small hamlet; none of the car manufacturers that characterised the area had yet appeared and he had space to pursue one of his big passions - motoring. It may be possible that he was the first person to establish a car building facility in Tyseley but he had other premises in the city centre that would allow him to scale up production, notably his premises in Regent Parade in the heart of the Jewellery Quarter.

Walter Davies Jnr. & Snr. at Sun Rising.

The first recorded appearance of one of his cars was at the Sun Rising Hill Climb organised by the Midland Automobile Club in July 1903, when his son Walter B Davies drove a Traffic in competition with cars driven by Lanchester, Austin, Crowdy, Pugh, Rolls, Deasy and Millership amongst others. They didn't make it onto the leader board but they were certainly in the right company.

The 1903 Traffic.

The business continued making and dealing in cars until at least 1909 but Walter Davies's business interests were wide ranging and he was often required to travel. In 1919 he was in Cairo in Egypt at just the wrong time in history as this was the summer of the Egyptian revolution against British occupation and Walter fell victim, as did many other Europeans living there at the time. He was buried in the Abbasyeh Cemetery and his wife Amelia took over the reins of the business.

Life didn't get any better for Amelia; she died just over a year later in November 1920. By this time the business had premises in Lionel Street, Birmingham, Valetta on Malta and Antikhana in Cairo.

None of the cars is known to have survived but the premises in Regent Parade are still there, though under threat.

The Regent Parade Works.

Lion

The Lion Motor Works, 239 Soho Road, Handsworth, Birmingham.
1903-1910

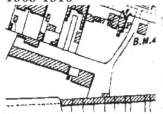

John Milbrowe Smith was a cycle maker, engineer and inventor who started making motorcycles at his Soho Road premises in 1902 and went on to build cars of which little is known.

He was born in Birmingham in 1854, the son of a pianoforte and organ tuner, Frederick Smith. In his twenties, he described himself as a 'velocipede maker' and ran a cycle making business called the Midland Bicycle Works in West Bromwich.

He was an inventive man and accumulated patents for such things as tyre pumps with pressure gauges and flexible mandrels for bending light gauge metal tubes without buckling. At the turn of the century he directed his spirit of invention to building motorcycles and tricycles becoming one of the founder members of the Birmingham Motorcycle Club and experimenting with methods of reducing chain noise.

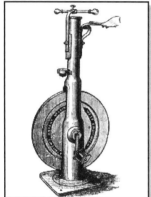

From his premises behind the shops at 239 Soho Road in Handsworth he started to produce motorcycles; the first in the area. He wasn't going to stop there and, the following year he started to experiment with car production. From 1903 to 1910 he described himself as a 'motor car builder'.

The Home Trainer.

The first motorcycle in Handsworth.

He didn't confine himself to car making he also designed and built an early piece of gym equipment - a cycle exercise machine. Called the Home Trainer, it was a sturdy iron device with pedals that was sometimes used competitively at cycle clubs. None of Smith's cars survive and neither do the premises which used to sit behind the shops on the Soho Road near to the rather splendid Billiard Hall.

Speed Limits and Speed Traps

The original 4mph limit imposed by the Locomotive Act of 1865, the 14mph limit of the 1896 Act and the 20mph limit of the 1903 Motor Car Act were always going to be challenged as cars became faster. The authorities responded with speed traps that involved timing cars as they passed. In response the Automobile Association was formed in 1905 to warn members of speed traps ahead.

In 1930 the Road Traffic Act abolished the 20mph limit replacing it with a variety of limits based upon vehicle type. Vehicles carrying under 7 people had no speed limit.

Despite the resulting drop in fatalities Leslie Hore-Belisha reintroduced a 30mph limit for cars in built-up areas in 1935 only to see the annual fatalities rise.

For some, the speed they were travelling was a guessing game, as speedometers were only made compulsory for new cars in 1937.

Premier/PMC

The Premier Motor Car Ltd., Aston Road, Birmingham.
1903-1913

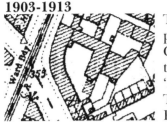

The Premier Motor Works occupied a prominent site approximately where the beam engine now stands on Dartmouth Circus. The works played host to a number of marques over the years starting with the 'Alexandra' and finishing with the 'Motorette'.

The Premier Motor Company was started by Arthur Pilkington, one of the four Pilkington Brothers who started the 'Birmingham Motor Manufacturing and Supply Company' (see **Rex**) that, by 1902, had moved its operations to Coventry.

Alfred Henry Pilkington was born in Birmingham in 1865 and worked with his brothers, William, George and Arthur in their tube making business. When their car manufac-

The Premier showroom at their Motor Works.

turing venture moved out of the city under the control of brother George, Alfred moved back to the city from his job as a foreman machinist at the Cycle works in Earlsdon, Coventry and, in 1906, became manager of the Premier Motor Car Ltd. Alfred's brother William was Chairman of the company and his nephew, also William, joined as Company Secretary.

Initially, the company occupied premises in the Cornwall buildings in Cornwall Street and established itself by selling the Italian built Marchand vehicles under the 'Premier' name before starting to produce brand-engineered lightcars in their own right in 1906 from the workshops at Aston Road previously occupied by the 'Phoenix Carriage Company' (see **Alexandra**).

The first Premier, actually an Italian Marchand.

The light car they built made a number of appearances at racing and trials events and in contemporary journals but it was not a success and production soon ceased.

Premier always had two sides to its business, acting as both car builders and dealers for other makes. In 1908 they became sole agents for Talbot cars and in 1909 started to produce the 'Premo' motorcycle but were forced to change the name of their vehicles to PMC due to confusion with the products of the 'Coventry Premier Cycle Company' who served an injunction on them barring its use. The only option was a new name and so they chose PMC from the initials of the company.

In 1912 they started production of a PMC three-wheeler with a single cylinder water-cooled engine, tubular steel frame and chain drive to an epicyclic gear in the rear wheel. The car had two seats in the 'sociable' side-by-side arrangement and a hood. The total weight of the car was 6 1/2 hundredweight.

After a number of years producing only three wheeled vehicles the company decided to produce a four-wheeled model in 1914. It had a four-cylinder 9.5hp engine produced by the SAB Engine Company based a few doors away at 180 Aston Road. This was located behind the driver's seat and drove the solid back axle via a roller chain and two-speed and reverse gearbox. Two band brakes were fitted, one operated by hand and the other by a foot pedal. The frame was tubular steel with hard wood strips bolted to it to prevent 'crystallisation of the metal' and the suspension was by quarter elliptics at the back and cantilevered semi-elliptics at the front. It had a V-shaped radiator at the front with plain tubes feeding the cooling water to the engine with a pump. Unusually, the engine could be started from the drivers seat by a lever and the gears were foot operated. It sold for £140 complete with hood, lamps, screen and detachable wheels. The four-wheeled prototype didn't make it into production as the company was liquidated in 1914 and wound up in 1915 probably as a result of the war.

The premises continued in use as a motor garage and was eventually taken over by Patrick Motors in the 1960s (see **Patrick Motors**). In the late sixties the building was demolished to make way for the Aston Expressway.

Alfred Pilkington died at the Burton on Trent Infirmary in December 1934.

There are no known surviving cars produced by Premier; we only have a photographic record.

The PMC three wheeler with hood down.

A PMC climbs Sudeley Hill.

The SAB engine.

Motoring can be dangerous.

An extract from the Lichfield Mercury, 23 May 1903:

'*Dr. Forbes Winslow, the eminent specialist on brain disorders, is of the opinion that the racing motor has outdistanced the powers of the man who drives it*'. Having been told that racing cars could reach 80mph, he said that they would have to drive themselves because the human brain wasn't fast enough. '*The human animal was not designed to travel at eighty miles an hour. The human brain and the human eye cannot keep pace with it*'. We had better be careful, then.

In 1888 L.Forbes Winslow used his crime solving skills and claimed to know the identity of Jack the Ripper. He agitated the police so much that, for a time, they had him listed as a suspect. It takes all sorts.

Perry

The Perry Motor Company Ltd., Rushey Lane, Tyseley, Birmingham.
1903 and 1913-1916

From stationery to cars in just under a century, Perry had a diverse manufacturing background and had two brief forays into motor car building.

The Perry family were prominent in Banbury in the nineteenth century employing a large number of workers in their nursery business. Stephen Perry was born in Banbury in 1801 and in 1824, with his father James, started a business in Manchester that, amongst other things, made pens sold under the 'Perryan' name.

The business moved to London and, in 1843, James died, so his son continued with the business. Stephen was interested in marketing a range of stationery products and formed business partnerships with Josiah Mason in Birmingham, to exclusively produce his steel pens, and a number of other companies that produced pencil cases, etc.

Always on the lookout for new stationery product lines, in 1845 Stephen Perry invented and patented a ground-breaking, new device for holding bundles of letters together - the elastic band.

The family business was based in north London and it was there that Stephen's sons Joseph John Perry and Lewis Henry Perry were born in 1838 and 1840. His sons joined him in the business as general manager and book keeper and the business prospered.

In 1876 they took over Wiley and Co. in Birmingham and started to produce steel chains and parts for bicycles from Wiley's Lancaster Street works. Shortly after, the interconnected businesses of Josiah Mason and A. Sommerville

The Perry Light Car.

and Co. amalgamated with Wiley and Perry to form Perry and Co Ltd.

By 1896 the company was experiencing financial problems and was taken over by Thomas Bayliss, a part owner of the Bayliss Thomas Company (see **Bayliss-Thomas**). Thomas Bayliss's son, James William Bayliss, was handed control of the cycle parts department and given three years to make it pay. He must have succeeded because by 1898 they were

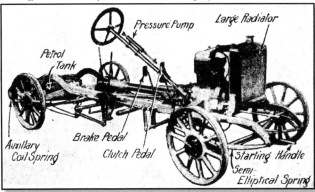

The Perry Chassis.

extending the Lancaster Street works and bought out their first motorised vehicle, a tricycle, in 1899.

In 1903 the company's first car appeared, a motorised forecar. The forecar was a short lived vehicle type, probably because of the vulnerability of having a passenger sat in front of the driver but also because it made conversation difficult, so production never really got going.

The company continued to grow and diversify and, in 1907, an 11 acre production facility was established in Rushey Lane, Tyseley.

In 1912 the 'Perry Motor Company Ltd' was registered with Josiah Martyn Smith and his son Oliver, Edmund Stephen Perry, Charles James Hampton and Arthur Edward Wiley as the Directors and James William Bayliss installed as a director and Works Manager.

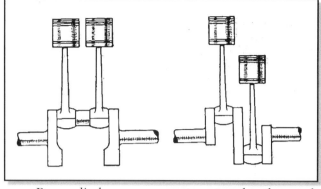

Perry cylinder arrangement compared to the usual.

1913 saw the introduction of the next Perry vehicle - a light car. Designed by Cecil Bayliss the son of the Works Manager, the Perry car had an 8hp twin cylinder engine but it wasn't a success. The company made a loss in 1913 and, despite introducing a heavier, four-cylinder, 11.9hp to bolster the range, repeated the loss in 1914. By 1916 the company was in financial difficulties and ceased production with less than 700 cars of each type having been built.

When the company closed and its assets sold the spare parts were sold to R H Collier, of the car dealership still existing today, who was buying up the inventory of a number of defunct car makers including Clyno, Crouch and Swift so that he could offer servicing and maintenance to their owners.

The jigs and tools were sold, through the agency of P J Evans, (who made a very handsome fee from the transaction), to 'A Harper, Sons and Bean' in Wolverhampton. The company had decided to enter the car market and make a mass-market car. They used the equipment to build a few cars that were 'Perrys' by any other name but soon made their own modifications and the Perry influence was rapidly diluted.

The Bean project was, itself, doomed to fail with the anticipated 'market-leading' car failing to materialise.

The works in Rushey Lane, Tyseley are no longer there and just three Perry cars are thought to have survived. Of these cars only one, found in a barn in Scotland and carefully restored, is still in the UK.

The Perry.

A Perry on the open road.

Revolette

The New Revolution Cycle Company, Liverpool Street, Birmingham.
1904-1905

Birmingham's links with Ireland run deep and the Irish community in the city hosts a St Patrick's Day parade that is reputedly only beaten in scale by those held in Dublin and New York. These links are demonstrated by a Birmingham company that had Irish roots.

Liverpool Street winds its way around the back of the Great Western Railway Company viaduct that runs parallel with Digbeth. It was in this Street that The New Revolution Cycle Company opened its works in 1900.

The Company had a rocky existence. Starting in Ireland as the Revolution Cycle Company in 1896 with exclusively Irish backing, the Company had promoted its 'Revolution' cycle very successfully and generated a great deal of interest amongst the public. Unfortunately it generated a level of demand that they could not satisfy despite the purpose built

facilities that had been set up in Digbeth to build the cycles. The problem was that advertising had begun before the cycle was ready for the market and so, when interest was at its peak, no cycles were available for sale. The inevitable result was that the company collapsed and out of the wreckage sprang the New Revolution Cycle Company.

The restructured Company started manufacturing cycles and accessories from the Liverpool Street works and moved into motorcycle manufacture in 1904 with their own, conventional, 2.5hp engine and belt drive. By 1905 they had added a forecar to the range - the 'Revolette'. Probably designed by Charles Ralph Townsend, this had a Stevens water

The New Revolution Works.

cooled engine (made by the Stevens Brothers of Wolverhampton who later went on to produce the AJS motorcycle), a two speed gearbox and chain drive. The frame of the Revolette was built from steel channel and the engine was mounted in its own cradle. The gearing was protected from the weather by a metal apron and it had three brakes acting on grooved drums. The car was put on sale for the princely sum of £70.

In January 1905 the Colossal Cycle Corporation of Loveday Street petitioned for the winding up of the New Revolution Company. When the company folded later that year the works were sold to Lanchester who started to build their cars bodies there (see

The 1904 Revolette.

Lanchester) calling it their 'Alpha Works'. William Clayton Lloyd who was the Managing Director of the company, went on to write a song called 'My Old Push Bike' with C.M and G.A. Woodrow in 1930. Charles Townsend went on to work with George Townsend Jnr. and Reginald Townsend of the Redditch needle and cyclemaking family (see **Enfield**) and started his own business, Townsend and Company. In the 1920s he produced the 'Autoglider' scooter.

Thomas

The Thomas Motor and Engineering Co., Inkerman St., Birmingham.
1904-1905

Walter Frederick Thomas was born in Birmingham in 1872 and started his working life whilst living with his mother, Elizabeth, a milliner, on the Coventry Road.

In 1884 he started an apprenticeship at the Tangye Company, the famous steam engine manufacturer, at their Cornwall Works in Smethwick just as they started production of gas engines and, in 1889, left to work on a number of projects in other countries, something common at that time with the being a heavy demand for engineers in the colonies.

In 1892 he got his big break when he joined Frederick Lanchester in his experimental workshops in Ladywood Road working on early prototypical cars including the first ever British built car, and, in 1895, became the foreman of the Lanchester workshop. He worked for Lanchester for five years before deciding to go it alone to develop his own inventions. Over the next few years he was granted patents for gas, oil and spirit engines and piston valves and honed his engineering design skills.

By 1900 he had moved into 98 Inkerman Street, Vauxhall, boarding with Annie Stuckfield, and started business as a motor manufacturer at premises a little further along the road at 110 Inkerman Street, the site now occupied by the Birmingham Museums Collection.

In 1903 he formed the Thomas Motor and Engineering Company in partnership with Ralph Gilbert, who had

The Thomas.

produced cars under his own name twelve years earlier (see **Gilbert**). The Company was registered with a capital of £5000 and, in 1905, they took premises in the same building as Ralph Gilbert at 104 Station Road on the corner of John Bright Street for his works. Development of the friction-driven 'Thomas' was reported on by The Motor Car magazine who were given a test drive in the experimental car in 1903. They described the car as running well with a load of four passengers and able to make 'good speed' on hills. The car had a two cylinder engine developing about 8hp lying transversely at an angle of about 16 degrees from horizontal. The piston rods of each cylinder were connected to a separate crankshaft under the breach of the opposite cylinder and each had their own flywheels which overlapped and travelled in opposite directions. With the success of his prototype he started work on a larger 10hp voiturette but the business failed to get the backing necessary to go into full production and the company was wound up in late 1905. Walter Thomas later moved to Taylor Road in Kings Heath and died in 1931 at the Ear, Nose and Throat Hospital in Birmingham.

The Thomas engine.

British Peerless

The Peerless Motor Company, Great Tindall St. and Bradford St., Birmingham. 1904-1913

After a short-lived and unsuccessful joint-venture with the Automotive Supply Company (see **Automobile Supply Co.**) Thomas Chatwin carried on production of cars under the British Peerless marque.

Thomas Chatwin was not a man, but a company run by the Chatwin family taking it's name from the man who started it; Thomas Chatwin born in 1825 in Birmingham. When he started the company, in the 1850s, he had 4 men with him; by 1871 the company was employing over 200 men producing cutters, dies, taps and a wide range of other tools. When he died, in September 1889, the business was taken over by his sons Alfred, James and Thomas, under who's control the company moved into car production. The company had a large factory called the Victoria Works on Great Tindall Street in Ladywood with a manufactory and a forge.

From these, the new 'Peerless Motor Company' produced a tonneau car with a vertical, 8 1/2 hp single cylinder engine running between 1200 and 1300 rpm. The crank case and its girder support spanned the full width of the chassis and were cast as one piece.

In June 1913 a new registered company was formed, 'The Peerless Motor Company Ltd.' with James Warren as Managing Director and Valentine Watkins, Charles Collett (the architect) and William Wray, an estate agent, as Directors.

The company was intended to continue production of the Peerless but things would not work out that way. They

The British Peerless.

acquired new premises at 314 Bradford Street which had become vacant following the winding up of J. Richardson Jeffreys and Co 'India rubber factors and merchants', and these became their registered offices.

There was a change of plan in 1913. Car production had ceased and James Warren, the Managing Director announced that he would be establishing a large manufacturing facility near to Montreal in Canada to produce British Peerless cars. The plans, however, were never realised, probably due to the outbreak of the First World War.

Meanwhile, the premises in Bradford Street were used to manufacture sidecars and the 'VAL' cyclecar (see **VAL**) under the aegis of Valentine Watkins following the winding up of the Peerless Company in August 1913. The other Directors, Collett and Wray, resigned their interests in the same year.

But what about Chatwin's? At the end of the twenties the firm looked into producing milk cartons using thin, waxed cardboard and patented a number of processes. If they had only continued this line of research they could have made a great deal of money and given 'Tetra Pak' a little competition. In the event, they carried on tool making and remained in business in Birmingham up until the 1950s.

Medea/Media

Mead and Deakin Ltd., Blytheswood Road, Tyseley, Birmingham.
1904-1908, 1912-1916

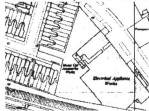

Frederick William Mead was born in 1879 in Aston the son of Samuel Mead, a school furniture manufacturer and his wife Jane. Frederick trained as a joiner in his father's business and when Samuel died in 1892, Frederick carried on the business.

In 1904 Fred Mead started to build his first car in Ladypool Road, Sparkbrook whilst trading as the Como Company, carriage body builders. The car was finished in 1907 and sold to a doctor in 1909. In 1910 he was joined by Thomas William Deakin, a boatbuilder born in Moseley in 1881, and they went into business together making sidecars. Their 'Canoelet' was a popular model and financed their forays into car building.

In April 1912, Roald Amundsen had just beaten Scott to the Antarctic and the Titanic had just struck an iceberg and was heading towards the bottom of the Atlantic. Meanwhile Fred Mead and Thomas Deakin were in their workshops in Tyseley working on the transmission of their prototype cyclecar. The 'Light Car and Cyclecar' magazine would visit their works in a few months and describe their transmission as "ingenious" and be quite taken with the suspension arrangement but, for now, it would mean a few more nights overtime to avoid disrupting sidecar production as this was their bread-and-butter trade.

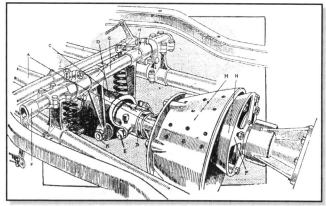

The Media Friction Cone Drive.

The first Medea (or Media) light car launched in December 1912 had a single cylinder 5hp Fafnir engine made in Germany and a friction cone drive. Later Medeas came in two versions, one fitted with a four-cylinder, 750cc engine made by the Salmon Motor Company of Burton-on-Trent and the other fitted with a French, 10hp, four-cylinder 1244cc Chapuis-Dornier engine, both with a three-speed and reverse gearbox but only one each of these is thought to have been built.

The Medea, like so many others, disappeared when WWI broke out. Their car making aspirations surfaced again when they produced the Rhode in 1921 (see **Rhode**).

The Canoelet accompanying a BSA.

The Medea/Media.

Calthorpe

The Calthorpe Motor Co., Cherrywood Road, Bordesley Green, Birmingham. 1904-1928

Calthorpe Motor Works

Calthorpe, one of the longest running car businesses in Birmingham is a name unfamiliar to many, probably because it didn't survive past WWII, but the first car produced by the company appeared in 1904 and the last nearly 30 years later.

George William Hands came from a Birmingham family but was born in Bridport in the USA in 1872. His father, John was an engine fitter and later an engine maker and, in common with many engineers at that time would have travelled for his work. In the late 1880s the job took him to Bethnall Green in London with the family but George, then a tool turner, and his older brother Harry, a professor of music, stayed behind in Birmingham.

With the increasing popularity of cycling George set up a business making cycles with Arthur Cake, the son of a baker and confectioner (you really couldn't make this up) from Portland in Dorset, and gave it the rather splendid name of 'Hands and Cake'.

Following the dissolution of that partnership Hands set up another company called the 'Bard Cycle Manufacturing Company' at premises at 16/17 Barn Street, Digbeth. The business grew and by 1898 had diversified into motorcycle manufacture starting with a 2.25hp De Dion engined, motorized tricycle - one of the first made.

The first car made by Calthorpe was their 10hp car of 1904. It had a two-cylinder, water-cooled, 1530cc engine and had a shaft drive. This was followed in 1905 by a 16hp model with a four-cylinder, water-cooled 2383cc engine.

In 1906 the company was registered as the 'Calthorpe Motor Company Ltd'. with George Hands, Thomas

The first factory in Barn Street.

Fletcher and Arthur Stamps as 'permanent Directors'. Thomas Russell Fletcher was born in 1885 in Walmley and had a military career before he became the Manager of the works. Arthur Lionel Stamps came from a family of brass founders and had lived, with his wife Agnes and their family, opposite Herbert Austin (see **Austin**) in Berwood House on the Chester Road until 1905.

The company took over the Mobile Motor and Engineering Company (see **Mobile**) in 1907, a business that had been based in John Bright Street and produced their cars from the Bordesley Green premises. The first product of the new company was the 12-14hp car with a four-cylinder, water cooled 1810cc engine. This was followed by 28-40hp, 25hp, 12-14hp, 16-20hp, 15hp, 20hp and 12-15hp models over the next half-dozen years. Alongside these the company also produced motorcycles starting with a

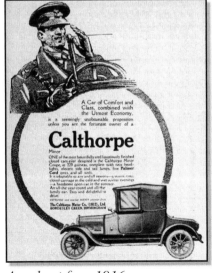

An advert from 1916.

211cc, two-stroke machine in 1911.

In early 1913 the company put a cyclecar, the 'Calthorpe Minor,' on the market. The car was described at the time as a 'car in miniature'. It had a radiator similar to that found on the other Calthorpe cars, a four cylinder 10hp engine, three-speed gearbox and shaft drive, so it was rather more substantial than many of the other cyclecars on the market and well suited to racing.

In May 1913 George Hands entered the car into the

A 'merry party' onboard a Calthorpe Minor in 1914.

BMCRC races at Brooklands, one of only four cyclecars to be entered. Despite putting up a good show it came in second to the Singer, though running on a flat tyre. In 1914 the company consolidated and became the Calthorpe Motor Company (1912) Ltd. just as the War broke out and car production ceased. Calthorpe were in a better position than many at the start of the war having been in the midst of preparing for the new seasons model they had run their stocks of the 1914 model down and had taken delivery of enough steel from Belgium to make over 700 cars.

The first post-war coupe to leave the works.

In 1917 the company took over the Birmingham coachbuilding company H H Mulliners and their Managing Director Louis Antweiler, who had previously run the 'Mobile' company taken over by Calthorpe in 1907, joined the board. From this point Mulliners made all of Calthorpe's bodies.

After the War the company built on the success of the 'Minor' and concentrated on 10hp models and by 1921 the company had a workforce at the Cherrywood Road site of over 1200 and was producing between 25 and 30 cars a week. The company continued to have a high-profile involvement with motorsport counting Woolf Barnato (see **Reaba**) amongst their drivers.

In 1921 George Hands was becoming dissatisfied with the direction of the company and broke away to produce cars under his own name from the Barn Street motorcycle works still owned and operated by the company. (see **Hands**). This venture resulted in

A Calthorpe racer.

A week's export output of 22 cars outside the works.

failure and in 1924 George Hands returned to Calthorpe bringing two of his models with him, but Calthorpe had financial problems of its own. The light cars they were producing were too expensive in a declining marketplace and the launch of the Austin Seven had given them the sort of competition to which they couldn't respond.

In 1924, with William Hill as the Chairman of the Board, the company went into voluntary liquidation and receivers were called in, a situation that was to persist until beyond 1932.

The last Calthorpe to be produced was the 1925 15-45 six-cylinder, 2 litre car. Its production was short lived and in the last few years of the Company. It appeared in show guides up until 1928 but the cars were generally made with whichever parts came to hand to use up stock. Calthorpe did, however, continue to produce motorcycles until 1939 when, despite a rescue attempt by Bruce Douglas (of the Bristol motorcycle building family), the company finally folded.

In 1926 the company bought out the failed Autocrat Company (see **Autocrat**) and attempted to sell their stock of cars but with little effect on the liquidity of the business.

Following the failure of the car business Louis Antweiler, being on the board of both Calthorpe and Mulliner arranged to buy the coachbuilding arm of the company and renamed it Mulliners Ltd.

With the demise of the Calthorpe Motor Company George Hands went, full time, into the hotel business. In 1920 he had bought a large, old, Italianate style, building in Torquay

George and wife, Fanny, in Torquay.

called 'Bishopstowe' from Sir Arthur Havelock the former Governor of Tasmania and turned it into a hotel - The Palace. The hotel was equipped with a gymnasium, bowling green, golf course, tennis courts and a cinema. By 1938 it had acquired an enviable reputation but, in that year, George Hands died at Fern Lodge, Bracknell in Berkshire leaving it to his wife Fanny and two spinster daughters.

One of the last surviving Calthorpes.

During the war the hotel was used as a military hospital but was hit by a bomb which demolished the east wing and killed 63 patients. Following another raid the hotel was abandoned but reopened in 1948. It has been estimated that at least 5000 Calthorpe cars were built in the post-war period of which fewer than ten are thought to have survived. The premises in Barn Street still, partially, survive but the Bordesley Green works that stood alongside the railway embankment have gone as have the ornate gates that used to grace the entrance.

Edwardian Cars 1905 - 1918

Motoring was still very much the province of the rich through the Edwardian era (known as the 'Brass Era' in the USA) but the sudden flush of light cars and cyclecars that appeared just before the First World War indicated that it wouldn't stay that way for much longer.

The chassis and the bodywork on cars were still considered separate elements with many cars leaving the factory without bodies ready for the attention of specialist coachbuilders. Petrol became the de facto fuel of choice with steam and electric powered vehicles being increasingly sidelined. Technical innovations like electric starting and all-steel bodies appeared and production line techniques, developed in America, were beginning to attract the attention of the car manufacturers here in Britain.

The motoring world was maturing as legislation appeared that both liberated and recorded the use of motor vehicles. The Motor Car Act of 1903 had raised the speed limits on British roads to 20mph and also introduced driving licenses and registration numbers, though driving tests were not introduced until 1935. An Order under the Act appeared in 1904 that defined 'light motor cars' and heavy motor cars' separately so that cars and commercial vehicles could be treated differently under the law for the first time, shaking off the last vestiges of the 'Locomotive Acts'.

Cars were improving and getting faster and were more able to breach the speed limits then in force so police forces around the country responded by stepping up speed traps leading to accusations of persecution. Nothing changes.

The Automobile Club had been founded in 1897 as a 'Gentleman's club' and had 2500 members by the dawn of the Edwardian era in 1904 but its members represented a wide range of opinions. Those opinions were becoming more polarised with the moderates, for whom the club was a social and sporting organisation on the one side and the militants on the other who saw its role as protecting the motorist from persecution by the authorities. The Club followed the moderate route so a new, more campaigning Club, the 'Automobile Association' was formed in June 1905 by the disenfranchised to combat the speed traps that were being set up around the country.

The response from the Automobile Club was to form its 'Associate Member Section' which performed much the same function as the AA for a wider membership allowing the main club to carry on as usual. In 1907 the Club was awarded its 'Royal' status by King Edward VII and both the AA and RAC then steadily grew as car ownership increased. The RAC that we know today is the 'Associates Section' and is a totally separate business from the Royal Automobile Club which is still a private members club with a grand clubhouse in Pall Mall and another at Woodcote Park near Epsom.

In 1907 the very first, purpose-built motor racing circuit in the world opened at Brooklands in Surrey. It had a 2.75 mile concrete track with steeply banked curves and was in use until 1939. The track was seriously damaged during the War and it only exists now as a Museum.

In the same year, 1907, the Caravan Club was formed to 'bring together those interested in van life as a pastime' and still does, operating 200 main sites and 2500 'five-van' sites.

The increase in car ownership meant that more people needed instruction in how to drive and, in 1910, the 'British School of Motoring' was formed in Peckham by Stanley Roberts, an engineering apprentice working for aviation pioneer Thomas Sopwith.

Just after the company celebrated its centenary year it went into administration and was bought by the AA for £1.

The Edwardian motorist.

Pioneer

GE Tovey, 58 High Street, Erdington, Birmingham.
1905

Anyone with a workshop facility and a mechanical bent would have had their interest piqued by the possibilities offered by the new motorised vehicles. 'Pioneer' was the marque used by George and Stephen Tovey in Erdington whilst they experimented with motorised vehicles.

The Tovey brothers started in business manufacturing cycles from their premises next to the bank and facing onto the village green in the heart of Erdington, then more of a village than a suburb.

George Edwin Tovey was born in Birmingham in 1872 and started his working life as a carpenter. His brother, Stephen Thomas Tovey, was born in 1874 and started out as a toolmaker. They were both brought up at their father, Stephen's, fruit and vegetable shop 'the Cozy Cottage' in Oughton Place (now Oughton Road), Highgate.

In the early 1890s they directed their attention to cycle making and acquired their premises in Erdington High Street, premises which still stand today between the HSBC bank and the Co-op supermarket. They were dealers in cycles made by other companies but also made their own incorporating fittings produced by W. A. Lloyd (see Walco) and, to demonstrate their wider engineering abilities, they repaired guns.

As with many small engineering based companies in the city,

they flirted with car making and listed themselves in the Kellys Directory for 1905 under Motor Manufacturers.

Unfortunately there are no surviving examples of the output from their works.

Tovey letterheading from 1903.

The Tovey shop and works.

This Motoring.

In June 1905 the 'Automobile Association' or AA, was formed with one employee, (its secretary, Stenson Cooke), a single office and a typewriter.

Needing a telegraphic address they found that all the obvious names had gone, so Cook opted for 'Fanum' meaning 'Temple' a name still used for their offices to this day. The club set up a network of scouts whose main purpose was to warn its members of the presence of speed traps, the first being deployed on the London to Brighton road.

The AA introduced a string of innovations to aid the motorist and grew rapidly as a result. The story of its early years is described in idiosyncratic style and with heavy use of exclamation marks!!! in 'This Motoring', Stenson Cooke's 1931 book.

Walco

The WA Lloyd Cycle Co., Clyde Works, Park St. and Monument Rd., Birmingham. 1905

William Arthur Lloyd was born in Birmingham in 1855 and raised in a furniture shop in Bridge St West by his father John, a furniture 'broker' and his mother Elizabeth who was an immigrant to Birmingham from Dorset.

His father made a career change in the 1860s becoming a gun finisher, a trade that he was to pass on to his son. By 1879 William had set himself up in the heart of the gun quarter at 5 Court, Bath Street, a little way down from St Chad's Cathedral, as a gun maker but, within a few years, had acquired a new house at 77 Anderton Road and a new trade; cycle making.

At that time the cycle trade in Birmingham was expanding rapidly, though still waiting for John Starley's invention of what we would recognize as the modern bicycle in Coventry in 1885. The bicycle was the only affordable, personal means of transport available to city dwellers in the late 1800s and business was good for William Lloyd and his partner John Blyth, (also from Birmingham), who took on further premises at 2 Lionel Street and, at the turn of the century, the Clyde Works in Park Street, Birmingham.

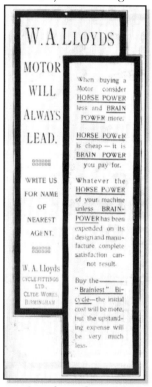

His company had specialised in cycle fittings in the beginning, with Lloyd and Blyth patenting improvements to pedals, spoke grips and dress guards for lady cyclists. As the company expanded and evolved, he moved into cycle manufacture and, by 1903, into motorcycle manufacture. During this period William Lloyd was moving house every few years, patenting refinements in the construction of cycles and, occasionally, falling foul of other companies in patent disputes. One of these, 'Waterson v WA Lloyd's Cycle Fittings', having made its way into case law as an example of 'actual user' (ask a lawyer!). During this period he was assisted in devising some of his patents by Frank Howles who had recently made his own excursions into car production (see **Howles and Perry**).

1902 marked the launch of the company's first motor cycle at the Stanley Show. It had a 2hp engine and patented contact breaker design. In 1905, following development work on a tri-car the previous year, William Lloyd made a foray into car manufacture. The car he developed was a three-wheeler powered by a 4hp engine made by A J Stevens Ltd in

An advert from 1905.

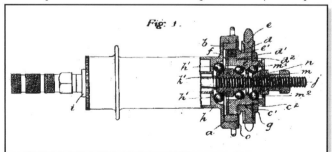

Drawing from Clutch Hub patent of 1902.

Wolverhampton who themselves later went into car production under the AJS marque. Lloyd was probably a little old to be branching into new fields and so the exercise came to nothing.

William Lloyd died on 22nd February 1922 in Birmingham. There are no surviving examples of his three-wheeler and the works have been demolished.

Jarvis and Weekes

Jarvis and Weekes, 71 Broad Street, Birmingham.
1905-1906

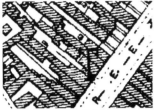 Planning zones were not part of the urban landscape in the early 20th century and so, unlike today, it wasn't unusual to have houses, factories, shops and theatres densely mixed together. Broad Street at his time had any number of industrial concerns scattered amongst the shops and offices. There were a number of car showrooms fronting the road and some of these had car making workshops attached. Jarvis and Weekes, motor car builders, were at number 71.

The company was formed when Frank Weekes, who had a cycle parts business on the corner of Steelhouse Lane and Whittall Street, joined forces with John Baxter Jarvis.

Frank Weekes was born in Birmingham in 1877 and was in business with Jarvis for only a short period between 1904 and 1906 but, during that period kept his cycle business going. After the break-up he set up his own motor engineering business, Weekes and Co, in Highgate Square off the Moseley Road in premises that still exist (if rather extensively modified). He died aged 71 in 1948.

John Baxter Jarvis was born in Wandsworth in 1879 and travelled across the world to Australia and back before settling in Birmingham to start a motor business with Weekes. The product of this partnership, the 'Jarvis and Weekes', was raced by him in the 1904 Sun Rising Hill Climb against cars built by Napier, Daimler, Wolseley, Lanchester and Rover. The winner was the famous pioneer motorist S F Edge in a Napier; Jarvis came second from last just ahead of a Wolseley.

After this partnership came to an end in 1906 Jarvis joined forces with Archibald Millership, an associate of Frederick Lanchester (see **Lanchester**) and Herbert Austin (see **Austin**), to form Jarvis Millership and Co at the Broad Street premises to sell cars and undertake motor car repairs. This was a short-lived venture; they dissolved the partnership in 1907 and Jarvis headed back to London. In February 1915 he joined the Army and became a Captain in the Army Ordnance Department, fought and was wounded in France. He was returned, ironically, to the Third General Hospital in Wandsworth near to where he had been born and died of his injuries on 10th April 1919.

Archibald James Walton Millership was born in Ashby de La Zouch in 1878 the son of a mining engineer. He was a pioneer motorist having driven his first car, a French Bollee, in about 1895 and having won the Mucklow Hill Trial of 1900 on an Ariel Tricycle. Archie Millership was not only a close associate of the Lanchesters but also one of Ernest W Beeston's circle of friends.

Beeston lived at Fernwood House on the Chester Road, now alas gone with only its gate lodge remaining. He was a gambler who had invented the 'Palladium' system to beat the roulette wheel and self published his 'Black Book' containing an illustration of a roulette wheel with each number occupied by a friend of his. In position number 30 was Archie Millership. In 1906 Millership took over the special repair department for Austin Motors (see **Austin**) but moved on to join Jarvis in 1907.

Millership later ran a car dealership on the Stratford Road and died in Bromsgrove Hospital in July 1958 aged 80.

The Fernwood Wheel.

Alexandra

The Phoenix Carriage Company, Aston Road, Birmingham.
1905-1909

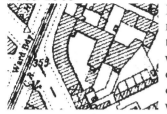

Electric cars are becoming more popular as oil becomes a more scarce resource and environmental considerations come to the fore but in the early years of car development petrol wasn't the only option being considered. Electric cars, steam cars and, even electric/petrol hybrids were being produced and competed vigorously. The steam cars were efficient but it took a while to get a head of steam to allow the car to be used. Electric cars were weighty due to their batteries and had restricted range and so petrol became the convenient line of least resistance.

The Alexandra was a rather old fashioned looking car developed by the Phoenix Carriage Company of Aston Road in the premises later taken over by the Premier Car Company (see **Premier/PMC/Motorette**). It had a wooden Brougham body similar to those found on the light, four wheeled, horse-drawn carriages which first appeared in 1838 and were popularised by Henry Brougham, the Lord Chancellor. The Company offered two models; one petrol driven and another electric. The car had safety doors fitted to the passenger cab similar to those found in Hansom Cabs (designed by Joseph Hansom, who also designed Birmingham Town Hall) to stop passengers falling out in the event of having to brake sharply.

The Company was started by the brothers Percy and John Creed and Samuel Groves Whitehouse. Percy Redfern Creed left Cambridge University to join the army and served in India and South Africa, leaving with the rank of Captain seven years later. He worked at the House of Commons, the Times newspaper and then for Lord Cromer who was mounting an opposition to the suffragette movement. He then spent some time working with Lord Roberts who was pushing to introduce national service in readiness for the impending Great War before

The Alexandra Brougham.

rejoining his regiment, the Rifle Brigade, in time for the war. He worked with Kitchener streamlining the production of munitions, and later, after the war, moved to the USA founding the 'Sportsmanship Brotherhood' who adopted the motto: "*Not that you won or lost—but how you played the game*". He was also the author of 'How to Get Things Done' in 1938.

His brother, the Rev. John Charles Creed, had an altogether quieter life as the Vicar of Killaliathan at Cashel in Limerick.

The Creed brothers were essentially the backers while Sam Whitehouse was the engineer. He started as a cab proprietor in Maida Vale in London but moved up to Birmingham in 1904 to set up a coachbuilding operation on the corner of Aston Road and Dartmouth Street, joined shortly after by the Creeds. The company itself was finally dissolved in 1912. There are no surviving examples of the car.

Maxfield

Alfred P Maxfield, Maxfield and Co., 5 Aston Road, Birmingham.
1905-1914

In July 1877 'Pericles', an iron, full-rigged ship was launched from the dockyard of Walter Wood and Co and three months later was on its maiden voyage from Plymouth to Sydney. On its return journey, in 1878, a child was born on board as the ship sailed the Indian Ocean. That child was Alfred Pericles Maxfield.

It was an interesting start to his life and it continued in that vein. In 1901 he was listed in the census as an engineers toolmaker but, soon after, he went into the cycle business with premises at 128 Vauxhall Road and added to that a motor business at 5 and 6 Aston Road just up from Gosta Green in a collaborative venture with pioneer car builder Charles Riley Garrard (see **Garrard**). He had formed this partnership in about 1901 and started, at first, to work on retro-fitted improvements (such as the Gar-

rard-Maxfield contact), to existing engines. In 1908 he formed Maxfield and Co Motor Manufacturers at 156 Victoria Road, Aston with William Henry Ireland who had patented a novel pneumatic wheel hub. Just before the First World War he moved operations around the corner to 175 Clifton Road into what used to be the Holte Arms public house, and which would in 1933 be the same premises used to build another Birmingham car, the Barclay (see **Barclay**).

A full-rigged iron ship of the time.

Maxfield was a member of the North Birmingham Automobile Club which used to meet at the Acorn Hotel in Erdington, and served as its Trials Secretary in 1913. He was an inventor, and since 1902 had a particular interest in aviation, building models of aircraft that he exhibited at the aeromodellers exhibition at Olympia.

His flying ambitions were not to end there though. In September 1909 he flew the first aircraft to fly in the Birmingham area from a patch of grassland in Castle Bromwich which later became the first Birmingham Aerodrome under the control of the Midland Aero Club; the same Club for which William Ivy Rogers, responsible for the Merlin (see **Merlin**) and Autocrat (see **Autocrat**) was Hon. Secretary. In 1914 the field was requisitioned by the Royal Flying Corps and the airfield was properly established.

After the war he continued inventing and patenting, working on wrench design and improvements in artificial respiration apparatus.

Alfred Maxfield lived to the ripe old age of 87. He died in Rugby in 1964.

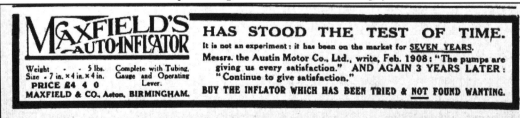

A motor parts advertisement.

Abingdon (King Dick)

Abingdon Works Ltd., Bath Street & Kings Road, Birmingham.
1905/6 and 1922/3

King Dick spanners are a well known Birmingham make, but did you know that the company that made them also ventured into car production?

The story of King Dick starts with Thomas Mabbutt. Born in Abingdon (then in Berkshire) in 1830, he moved to Birmingham in 1849 and had a child 'out of wedlock'; George Joseph Prosser Mabbutt.

The mother of the child was Miriam Prosser from Lichfield and on 27th October the following year they were married at Aston Church. Thomas settled down in the city and started a company building parts for guns at 21 New John Street West that, by 1861, was employing 25 men and 10 boys.

The company was called The Abingdon Works Co Ltd. after his home town, and acquired premises in Shadwell Street, and then Bath Street, from William Read the coachbuilders. The business expanded and produced guns, rifles, pistols and cases. The buildings still exist, adjacent to The Gunmakers Arms, and are now listed though used for residential rather than manufacturing purposes.

In the early 1860s bulldog breeding was a popular pastime in Birmingham and in 1864 a hairdresser called Jacob Lamphier of Soho Street, Handsworth, had defined the recognised characteristics of a dog breed for the first time when he bred his bulldog as a benchmark. To demonstrate this he showed his bulldog 'King Dick' at dog shows in 1860 and 1864 in Birmingham, and it was a puppy sired by this dog that Thomas Mabbutt owned and called 'Abingdon King Dick'.

A logo featuring a bulldogs head appears on King Dick tools.

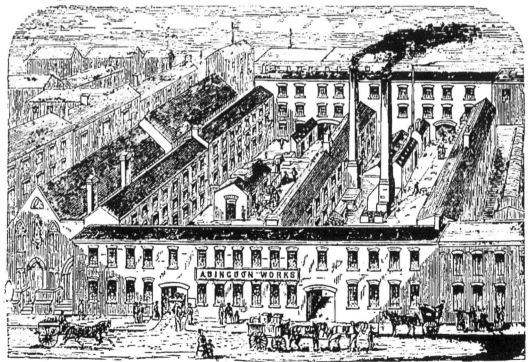

The Abingdon Works as seen from Shadwell Street.

In 1875 the company was incorporated with William Middleditch Scott (a gunmaker who later went on to form Webley and Scott), becoming the principal shareholder and Mabbutt the Managing Director. In 1896 the Abingdon Works Company was voluntarily wound up so that it could be restructured.

Along with all of the other engineering companies in

The Abingdon Light Car.

Birmingham at the time they were always interested in expanding their product range and, in 1903, started to manufacture motorcyles.

To start off they used engines bought in from other manufacturers, including Minerva imported from Belgium and Fafnir from Germany, but graduated to making their own 'Abingdon'engines. These engines, in their 350cc single-cylinder and 794cc v-twin variants,

would be used by other manufacturers including Ariel (see **Ariel**). After a brief experiment with forecar production the previous year, 1905 saw the introduction of the short-lived AKD tricar. This 5hp machine stayed in production for less than a year.

Thomas Mabbutt died in January 1906 and responsibility for running the company passed on to his son, George Prosser Mabbutt. Later that year the vehicle chain company, 'Albert Eadie Chain Company' (ECCO) in Redditch, run by Albert Eadie (see **Enfield** and **BSA**) was bought by the company and operations were merged under the name Abingdon-Ecco Ltd.

In 1908 new premises were acquired in Kings Road, Tyseley and production of AKD motorcycles moved there continuing, with a break for WWI, until 1932.

They had another excursion into car building in 1922 when they produced a light car called the Abingdon, not to be confused with that made by John Child Meredith (see **Abingdon/Meredith**). The car was powered by a Dorman four-cylinder 1490cc engine and had a three-speed gearbox, spiral bevel rear axle and steering gear all supplied by EG Wrigley (see Wrigley). At the prototype stage the car was fitted with a two-seater body but went into production as a four-seater. When Wrigley were taken over by Morris (see **Morris**

Commercial) they had only built twelve cars and, with the competition offered by the newly launched Austin Seven, they decided not to continue production.

George Prosser Mabbutt died in 1929 and was buried in Key Hill Cemetery. There are no known surviving motor cars though some of their motorcycles still exist.

Abingdon King Dick, as a company, does survive and now operates selling tools from premises on Roman Way, Coleshill.

The Abingdon Works in Bath Street.

Austin

The Austin Motor Company, Longbridge, Birmingham.
1905-1952

Technically, for the first six years, the Austin Motor Company wasn't in Birmingham but in the fields of Worcestershire. This changed in 1911 when Longbridge was absorbed into the City. The Company grew massively and by the outbreak of WWII had a site covering 100 acres and directly employed over 20,000 workers. This makes it the largest of the Birmingham marques by a large margin, and one of only three to survive the war.

Herbert Austin was born at Grange Farm in Little Missenden, Buckinghamshire in 1866. His father, Giles Steven Austin, was a farm steward and, along with his wife Clara Jane Austin (nee Simpson) tended to move from farm to farm following the work and, in 1870, had a position with Earl FitzWilliam on his estate at Wentworth in Yorkshire. Herbert went to the local school and Rotherham Grammar School before studying at Brampton Commercial College to become an Architect. Architecture never really suited the young Herbert and so when his mother's brother visited from Australia he accepted an invitation to return with him and take up an apprenticeship with Mephan Ferguson an engineering firm in Melbourne. He moved from company to company widening his experience and married a local girl, Ellen Dron, in 1887. A few days before his marriage he joined a small engi-

The Longbridge Works.

neering company, owned by Richard Pickup Parks, as manager and, through the contracts placed with them by Frederick Wolseley, he struck up a business relationship that was to give his career another direction.

Herbert Austin moved back to the UK and worked for Wolseley in Birmingham; at the same time he pursued other engineering interests and developed patents in partnership with Herbert Hall Mulliner the Birmingham coachbuilder for improvements to tyres.

He had been with Wolseley developing its car making arm for over 11 years before

Herbert Austin.

deciding to go it alone and start his own company. He had encountered difficulties dealing with a board of directors whose outlook were different to his own and, therefore, reckoned that he needed to have his own company.

He made estimates of the capital needed and organised financial backing from Frank Kayser (see Wolseley), Harvey du Cros Jnr. (see **Ariel**) and the Midland Bank but he needed a car factory and he needed it quickly.

In 1904 Archibald Millership had joined Wolseley from Lanchester (see **Lanchester**) and he joined Herbert Austin in setting up his new Company. Whilst searching for premises Millership suggested the premises at Longbridge that had been built by White and Pike, an established Birmingham printing company, to make cycle components and tin boxes.

The premises were ideal because, on top of everything else, they were sufficiently far from the 'dust and smoke from other manufacturers' in the city to avoid the finish of the cars being spoiled.

Austin needed to design his first car so he set to work at his home on the Chester Road in Erdington with two of his first employees Albert 'Joey' Hancock and A V Davidge, preparing drawings to be displayed at the Crystal Palace Motor

The original Austin Seven model 1909.

Exhibition in November 1905. On the basis of these drawings Austin received several orders for the car and work got underway. This first car had a 18-24hp, 5 litre, four-cylinder engine with a chain drive. The engine was mounted vertically despite his previous insistence at Wolseley that the horizontal arrangement was superior. The first car was unveiled at an inaugural lunch at Longbridge in April 1906 and the chassis of two limousines were displayed at the Olympia exhibition the same year. By the end of that first year 12 cars had been produced with a staff of only 50 workers.

The company was soon producing a range of cars with the original 18-24hp joined by a 40hp and 60hp models. All could be fitted with a range of bodies although Austin was keen to promote closed, limousine bodies rather than the open landaulette type, concerned that the English motor industry would lag behind the French if it didn't progress.

In 1909 the Swift Motor Company of Coventry, the firm set up by the Starley family and run by Harvey Du Cross, developed a 7hp car in collaboration with Austin. This car went into production at the Swift Works in Coventry after the prototypes had been built at Longbridge and effectively became the first Austin

An Austin Courtesy Car waits at New Street.

Seven. An example of this car can be seen at the Heritage Motor Centre in Gaydon.

Austin produced a range of cars over the years up until the First World War, eventually producing over a thousand a year. These were high-class coachbuilt cars with all of the operations necessary for car production from casting to upholstery being done in-house. Austin was proud that his cars were not only engineered well but also satisfied the exacting standards of his customers. In 1909 he introduced a 15hp Town Carriage and used one of these vehicles to act as a courtesy car ferrying visitors from the railway stations in Birmingham out to Longbridge so that they could inspect progress on their vehicles. The

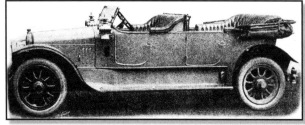

The 1914 Austin Twenty.

Austin Fifty was introduced in 1910 and stayed in production until 1913 whilst the Austin Ten first appeared in 1911 but only stayed in production for a year before being redesigned to effectively become a 12-14hp vehicle. A new 15-20hp car appeared in 1913 as did a 30hp vehicle with each cylinder in its 5700cc engine cast

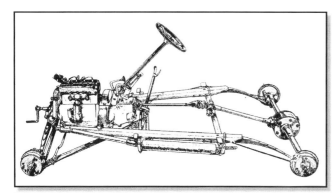

The 1922 Austin Seven Chassis.

The 1924/25 Austin Seven.

separately as was Austin's usual practice; but Austin was concentrating his efforts on a new 'Sports Twenty', the 20hp car that he wanted to put into mass production before war stopped play.

When the War started Austin found himself with a factory ideally suited to munitions production being away from the centres of population in case of explosion and having a wide range of founding, forging and engineering processes all available in one place. The workforce numbered about 2500 at the beginning of the war. This was to grow to over 20,000 on the back of Government contracts.

After the war Austin faced a dilemma. The factory had grown massively on the back of wartime contracts but he was now faced with the problem of how to use all that extra capacity in peacetime.

The first response was to concentrate on the production of a single model, the Austin Twenty. Inspired by Henry Ford's mass production methods in the US, and being impressed by the Hudson Super Six car he had owned during the war years, he used that as the basis for a single, mass produced model. Unfortunately, it was too big a car for the British market and the company got into severe financial difficulties. A new direction was needed.

In 1921 the government introduced a tax regime based upon the horsepower of a vehicle. This was disastrous for the manufacturers of bigger engined cars and promoted the development of the smaller car. Sir Herbert Austin, as he now was, realised that smaller engined cars were needed and tried to convince his fellow directors of the logic. The first manifestation of the change in direction were rumours in the press in April 1921 of the

1925 Sports Seven by Thomas Hughes, Sparkhill.

imminent announcement of a new 10hp model. This didn't appear but what did was the Austin Twelve, introduced in 1921 and a scaled-down version of the 'Twenty'. This car was to be an important part of the range for over fourteen years but, on its own, it wasn't going to cure the company's ills.

Austin wanted to introduce a small 6hp car that would appeal to the mass market and tried to convince his fellow directors of its wisdom.

With a lack of development capital available they resisted and, in April 1921, a receiver was appointed to oversee company affairs.

Sure that his small car would be the future, he decided to design and develop it himself at his Lickey Grange home and in August 1921 employed a talented, 18 year old draughtsman called Stanley Edge, who had been with the Austin company since 1917, to assist.

Stanley Howard Edge was born in Rowley Regis on 5 August 1903 the son of Elijah Edge from Brierley Hill, a coal miner who later became

Stanley Edge in 1921.

a cashier at a furniture company, and Emma Louisa Willetts, also from Brierley Hill.

He joined the drawing office at the Austin works as the assistant to the engine designer Jack Clarke and came to the attention of Sir Herbert.

He worked with Herbert Austin until the Easter of 1922 and, with the threat of taking the design to Wolseley hanging over them, the board approved the construction of three prototypes. The first two prototype cars were complete by Whitsun 1922 so that one could appear in the firms 'carnival' held on the company flying ground earlier used by Edwin Prosser when his biplane developed engine failure (see **Prosser**). This car, the Austin Seven, went on to save the company. Austin had intended for the car to be similar to the Rover 8hp car then in production at Tyseley (see **Rover**) with its two-cylinder air-cooled engine but Edge, inspired by the example of the small French cars of the day argued for a four-cylinder, water-cooled engine and got his way. The car was well received and went into full production, slowly at first with only just over 2400 produced in 1923 but output progressively increased to over 27000 per year by 1935. The Seven was a true car in miniature and the first to have stand-ardised all the main foot and hand controls in the positions that have now been accepted as the norm. It

Austin 16.

became a popular car to be produced under license by foreign manufacturers and was the car that launched BMW, Datsun, Jeep and Jaguar brands. Austin had been building race cars in the early years of the company but it was with the Seven built for sporting purposes rather than travel that Austin really took off. The company formed a race team in 1923, competing in fabric-bodied Sevens at Brooklands and in the Boulogne Motor Week held that year. One of the mechanics on that team, Leonard Brockas (see **Brockas**), worked for Austin from 1907 to 1958. The Seven spawned a large number of sports-bodied variants and, through clubs like the 750 Motor Club and the VSCC, is raced to this day.

The restructuring of the company in 1922 had brought two new faces to the company who, with Herbert Austin, were to shape the company between the wars: Ernest Payton, the Finance director and Carl Engelbach, the Production Director.

Ernest Leopold Payton was born in Handsworth in 1877 the son of Francis Payton, a manufacturing jeweller, and his wife Bertha Hopley. Charles Richard Fox (Carl) Engelbach was born in Kensington in 1877, the son of Lewis and Jessie Engelbach and had worked previously for Armstrong-Whitworth at their Newcastle-upon-Tyne car works.

In 1925 the company, inspired by developments on the other side of the Atlantic, installed its first, primitive, assembly line conveyor and, in 1927,

Austin 10.

launched the last two models of the twenties; the six-cylinder version of the Austin Twenty and the Austin Sixteen. The 'Sixteen' also had a six-cylinder engine and came in a number of saloon and tourer options.

By the end of the twenties, Herbert Austin believed that the market was improving and that there would be increasing demand for the larger vehicles then in production. However, the depression of late 1930 meant that it was the smaller cars that were more in demand and the 'light' Twelve that was launched in 1931 with a new all-steel body. This, it turned out, also wasn't what the market wanted.

What they did want were cars with engines of about 10hp, cars that didn't exist in the Austin range at that time. The response was to launch the four-cylinder Austin Ten in May 1932. By this time there had been a change in the body-design personnel. Herbert Austin had always had a great deal of input into the design of Austin bodies, but now had a new design assistant, Ricardo Burzi. Burzi was born in Italy and had been working for Lancia, but life became difficult for him when he accepted a commission to produce a lampoon of Mussolini in an Italian newspaper. Ridicule is something that budding dictators do not take kindly to and he was forced to leave the country. The Ten was very successful and, by 1933, was even outselling the Seven. With the launch of the four-cylinder light Twelve in 1932 the company now produced nine different chassis and 44 separate

Leonard Percy Lord.

models from a manufacturing site that had spread itself over 100 acres.

Herbert Austin was elected President of the Society of Motor Manufacturers and Traders in 1934 and was created a Baron in the 1936 Honours List, becoming Lord Austin of Longbridge.

1937 saw the re-emergence of bigger engined six-cylinder cars in the range with the launch of the Austin 14-6 in 1937 and the Austin 18-6 in 1938. Production now was in the order of 90,000 cars per year.

In early 1938 Leonard Lord took over as Works Manager and things changed. Leonard Percy Lord was born in Coventry in 1897 and raised at the city baths where his father was the superintendent and then the Hope and Anchor Inn in White Friars Lane where his father became the licensee. He started work in a munitions factory, moving on to a

Daimler engine plant during the First World War. By 1923 he was working for Morris rationalising their production methods before being seconded to Wolseley (see **Wolseley**), who had been taken over by Morris, in 1927 to do the same job. In 1932 he was promoted to General Manager at Morris but had a turbulent relationship with William Morris and in 1938 he resigned and headed for Morris's arch rival.

He hit Longbridge *'like a whirlwind'* and installed a new discipline amongst the workforce. Within eighteen months of joining the company he had launched a new range of cars including the Austin Eight in February 1939 using the same engine that had powered the 'Big Seven' launched in 1938 and a new Austin Twelve saloon. He also reintroduced commercial vehicles into the range and would have made further sweeping changes had the Second World War not intervened.

The company continued building cars into the war years though the Seven ceased production in 1939 with falling sales. The factory at Longbridge turned once again to wartime production of vehicles, aircraft and armaments and emerged at the other side of the War as a major car manufacturer once more.

The more recent history of the company is beyond the bounds of this book but Longbridge continues to be a car building works to this day, though now a mere shadow of its former glory. Little now remains of the original factory and demolition continues apace.

Herbert Austin died on 23 May 1941 and Ernest Payton took over as Chairman but, he too, died in 1946, at which point Leonard Lord took over. Carl Engelbach died in 1943.

Leonard Lord continued to steer the company through mergers and acquisitions until he eventually became the President of the British Motor Corporation. He became Baron Lambury of Northfield in 1962 and died in September 1967.

There are many thousands of Austin cars from the pre-war period surviving with the Austin Seven being a favoured car amongst touring and sporting enthusiasts.

Hitler inspects an Austin Sixteen in 1939.

Midland Red

In 1900 the Birmingham General Omnibus Company placed its first order for buses from Birch Brothers of London and asked that they should be painted red to stand out. At this stage they were still horse-drawn. By August 1905 when the Birmingham and Midland Motor Omnibus Company started operating, the cluster of existing companies that it absorbed into its new business were operating a mix of horse and motor buses. By 1913 the majority of buses were motorised and the livery adopted was that of the BGOC; red with black mudguards and a silver roof - the Midland Red was born.

The Birmingham Watch Comittee at this time restricted routes to those not already operated by trams which wasn't a problem until, in September 1913 the Birmingham Corporation extended its tram routes and decided to consolidate its tram and bus operations. Midland Red couldn't extend its services in the centre of the city so it concentrated on services that ran to and from the city boundaries. To gain the city's approval to operate these routes it had to sign an agreement to charge fares that would not compete with the city's.

Lorraine-Dietrich

Lorraine-Dietrich Ltd., Dale Rd, Bournbrook, Birmingham.
1907-1909

You could be forgiven for thinking that this doesn't sound much like a Birmingham Company but, for a couple of years, from 1907 Lorraine-Dietrich cars were made in Birmingham.

Lorraine-Dietrich was a French automobile and aircraft engineering company that was started in 1896 by a railway locomotive manufacturer called 'Société Lorraine des Anciens Etablissments de Dietrich and Cie' or, thankfully, 'De Dietrich' for short.

The Managing Director of their Luneville plant acquired the rights to build a car with a front mounted horizontal twin engine designed by Amedee Bollee. This car had a folding hood, three headlights and, unusually for the time, a plate glass windscreen. This they built until 1901 when they started building Belgian 'Vivinus' voiturettes or light cars under licence. De Dietrich competed with the likes of Crossley in Manchester and Itala in Turin as a prestige marque whilst trying to break into the 'super luxury' market with a series of six wheeled limousines.

In 1907 the company bought the Italian car manufacturer Isotta-Fraschini and the Birmingham company Ariel Motors (1906) Ltd. who occupied the Dale Road, Bournbrook factory vacated by Charles Sangster when Ariel moved car production to Coventry (see **Ariel**).

The 1909 Lorraine-Dietrich.

De Dietrich produced one model in Birmingham; a 20hp four cylinder engine with a drive shaft and live axle transmission which was exhibited at the 1908 Olympia Motor Show. It had a metal disc clutch and four speed gearbox. There were three options offered; a rolling chassis, an early Salmson bodied convertible and a Mulliner bodied cabriolet. The response could not have been too good as production shut down shortly after. The company continued to advertise in 1909 and remained in existence for a few years but was eventually wound up in 1912.

The Paris-Madrid Race 1903

De Dietrich cars participated in the infamous Paris-Madrid race held in May 1903, called by some the 'Race of Death'

A number of prominent figures in the early Birmingham motor industry also participated in this event, notably; Louis Antweiler of Mobile, Calthorpe and Mulliners, Herbert Austin driving a Wolseley and T.C Aveling of the Midland Automobile Club

The race was organised by the French and Spanish Automobile Clubs and was planned to cover a 1307 Km route. 224 racers were involved including Charles S Rolls and the Renault brothers. Eight people died during the course of the race and over half of the cars were involved in incidents, forcing the French Government to stop the race at Bordeaux and, eventually, ban open-road racing.

Newey

Gordon Newey Ltd., 77, 79 and 81 Bristol Street, Birmingham.
1907-1921

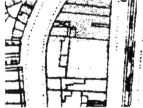

Gordon Newey's first venture into car manufacturing was in 1907 when he produced what is sometimes termed an 'assembled car' called the Newey-Aster.

Born Edwin Gordon Newey in Aston in 1884 he was the son of James Clement Newey, a Birmingham wire products manufacturer whose 'world famed' hooks and eyes have graced many a sewing box.

In 1905 James Newey died and passed the company on to his son Clement John Newey who, with his new found wealth formed Newey's Midland Garage Ltd in 1907 with himself as Managing Director, W J Kent and Edwin Gordon Newey as directors and premises in Station Street on a site that now lies between the Electric Cinema (opened in 1909) and the Old Repertory Theatre.

Edwin Newey not only built cars, he raced them as well, but chose the 8hp and 10hp De Dions when he took part in hill climbs and trials with Clement.

When this first car building venture folded in 1909 he formed a partnership with Harold

Haberdashery to Automobiles.

William Halstead as Newey and Halstead, carriage builders and motor agents, at 77 to 81 Bristol Street. This partnership didn't last long and in November 1913 they set up separate businesses, Halstead as a motor car agent in Kings Heath and Newey as a motor cycle manufacturer at 167 Barr Street and a motor car agent at the Bristol Street premises. In 1913, when the cyclecar craze was in full swing he turned once again to car making and produced a light car with a four cylinder 10hp Aster engine. When the First World War began it became difficult to obtain the French built Aster engines so, in 1916, he imported American built, four cylinder, 2.4 litre engines and put them into two and four seater models, badged as GNLs (standing for Gordon Newey Ltd).

The French engines became available again after the war and he resumed production of the Aster powered model and added a 12-15 model with a 1750cc Chapuis-Dornier engine built at

The Newey.

Puteaux, a western suburb of Paris. Ill health bought Gordon Neweys car making activities to a halt in 1921; winding the company up in 1922 he died at the seaside in Abergele, Wales in 1927 aged 41.

There was another Newey Engineering Company in Birmingham formed by Sidney Smith and Jonathan Frederick Newey at 36 Ashted Row, an automobile engineers dissolved in 1928, but it is not connected. None of the vehicles produced are known to have survived and neither have the premises, which were demolished when Bristol Street was widened.

BSA

Birmingham Small Arms, Armoury Road, Small Heath, Birmingham.
1907-1939

BSA is more famous today as a motorcycle manufacturer, being at one point the largest motorcycle manufacturer in the world, but it has a history of car production and an even longer history as a company.

The Birmingham Small Arms Trade Association was founded in 1861 in the Gun Quarter by 14 gunsmiths who aimed to redress the balance whilst competing against the Royal Small Arms factory at Enfield to produce guns following the outbreak of the Crimean War in 1854. The government-owned Enfield factory had introduced machinery and production techniques from America that outstripped the production of guns by the smaller and more hand-craft-orientated gun makers in Birmingham and a united front was needed. The Company acquired a 25 acre piece of land at Small Heath and built a complex of factory buildings there, lined along a new road called Armoury Road.

The move proved successful with the machine-production techniques attracting an order for 20,000 Turkish Infantry rifles in 1863. In the same year, the structure of the Company was revised with a Board of Directors chaired by John Dent Goodman in place of the original committee. In 1866 the company received an order from the Prussian Government, who were engaged in the Seven Weeks War with Austria at the time, for over 40 million cartridge cases and, though this was not their normal line of work they couldn't turn it down; so, for a time, the company became known as the Birmingham Small Arms and Metal Co Ltd. Over the next few years it grew to become the largest private arms manufacturer in Europe. However, armaments, like cycle making, was a precarious business and the Company had to be moth balled for a year waiting until 1868 before they got their first War Office contract. During another quiet period in 1880 a gentleman by the name of Edward C F Otto demonstrated his new invention to the Board (the 'Dicycle'), by riding it along the boardroom table and out into the street. They must have been impressed because this was to become BSA's entry into the world of vehicle production.

The company started to build the dicycle and then branched into the construction of more conventional cycles and tricycles alongside their armament work but orders from the British Government for Lee-Metford rifles to re-equip the British Army

The Otto Dicycle 1880.

Sir Hallewell Rogers.

halted cycle production for a time..

BSA bought the Eadie Manufacturing Company of Redditch (see **Enfield -Allday**) as they expanded production of bicycle components and at the same time looked to diversify further into car production. The appointment of Colonel EE Baguley as Manager and Albert Eadie as Managing Director of the Cycle and Motorcycle departments at BSA heralded the purchase of the Royal Small Arms factory in Montgomery Street, Sparkbrook in 1906 and the development of prototype cars. The premises were next door to the Lanchester factory (see **Lanchester**) who had purchased the Armoury Mills from the National Arms and Ammunition Company at the end of the 1890s. As the machinery for arms production was moved out of the building the new car came together with an 18-24hp four-cylinder, side valve engine but there was a bit of a problem with it; the chassis weighed in at over 26cwt and the test vehicle was seriously underpowered. Following modifications, the company had, by 1908, three models of car in production but they were not a commercial success, selling only about 150. Something had to be done to address the inefficiencies in the department.

Fording a South African river.

In an effort to expand the range of skills available to the company (Frank) Dudley Docker, 'Birmingham's Industrial Titan', who had joined the Board of BSA in 1906 and had a history of company mergers, negotiated with The Daimler Motor Company of Coventry to buy Daimler. Daimler were a highly profitable company producing Daimler and Rover cars (see **Rover**) but the merger was a difficult one putting both firms under a degree of financial stress. Technically, at this time, Daimler could be considered a Birmingham marque but that would be overstating the link with Birmingham.

The 1912 Tourer.

Docker's association with the company under the chairmanship of Sir Hallewell Rogers, an ex-Lord Mayor of Birmingham, wasn't without its controversy. The setting up of a

The 1915 Two-Three Seater with Dickey.

'secret reserve' of money that the directors could use without recourse to the shareholders meant that the Directors had a level of control over the company that made some feel uncomfortable. Following the merger Hallewell Rogers, along with Percy Martin and Edward Manville, who had joined the Board from Daimlers, was to exercise strong control over the company until his death in 1931.

By this time the company had produced their 14-18hp C1 type, a scaled down version of the prototype car with a four cylinder engine and cone-clutch, their 25-33hp B type otherwise known as the 'BSA-Itala', both in 1908 and their A1 type of 1909.

After the merger the company announced that their 'Daimler-BSA' cars would, from then on, be built in Coventry. Production of what were little more than badge-engineered

Daimlers continued there until the War halted production.

In 1914 a new multi-storey building was added on the Armoury Road site utilising a revolutionary construction technique - reinforced concrete. The American firm Truscon (The Trussed Concrete Steel Company) was responsible for design and construction via its British office and the estimating engineer at that time was Owen Williams who went on to design, amongst other things, Wembley Stadium and the reinforced concrete bridges that span the M1 motorway. The section of that building that still exists today may look as if it was constructed in the 60s but it is actually an important and, as yet, unlisted survivor.

In 1921, car production resumed and in 1922 the BSA air cooled twin, four-wheeler was launched with the cars leaving the factory tuned to do 50mph. In the same year the company opened a lavish new showroom in London to advertise its wares ranging from twist drills to the new cars.

Armoury Road Works in the 1960s. (Phyllis Nicklin)

Armoury Road Works in 2011.

The rear-wheel drive cars were eventually produced with four-cylinder and six-cylinder Knight sleeve valve engines and built in the Coventry Road works known as the Light Car Works up until 1924. It is estimated that about 1000 of these cars were made until competition from the Austin Seven helped to send it out of production.

The company took a break from car production until, in November 1929 the first of its front wheel drive cars appeared.

The BSA three-wheeler had a BSA modified version of the Hotchkiss 900 air-cooled, V-twin engine with a capacity of 1021cc adding, as standard, such refinements as electric starting, full weather protection and a reverse gear to the more usual specification of three-wheelers produced by the likes of Morgan.

In 1930 BSA purchased its neighbour in Montgomery Street, Lanchester, and merged Lanchester's activities with those of Daimler at their Coventry works but the light three wheelers continued in production in Birmingham.

The 1930, the three-wheeler came in sports and touring models with a four seater family version appearing in 1931. Also in 1931 BSA manufactured a three-wheeler delivery van based on the same chassis but these didn't look too stable; that probably put a lot of commercial buyers off.

The 1922 air-cooled twin.

They didn't stay in production for very long.

In the Autumn of 1931 the company went back into production of a light four-wheeled vehicle, the FW32 that came in two and four seater car and van versions. This was a short lived model however; and soon it too dropped out of production to be replaced by a car more similar to the small Lanchester which was introduced in 1932.

1933 saw the introduction of a more substantial three-wheeler with a water-

BSA at a 2011 Rally.

cooled, four-cylinder engine that was produced alongside the V-twin model until 1936. Returning again to four-wheeler production the T9 appeared in 1932, an altogether more substantial offering with a 9hp four-cylinder water-cooled engine. The TP had a weight problem, however, and the lack of power meant that it ceased production a year later in 1933. The next rear-wheel drive four-wheeled cars were 10hp tourer and saloon models of 1933 which were succeeded by an improved model that lasted until 1936. These were

manufactured at the Coventry plant. The company had had a chequered history of car production with a blur of short lived models but in 1935 they got it right and introduced the two-seater Scout. A sporty looking model, it had the same 9hp engine used in the three-wheeler and the T9, later upgraded to a 10hp 1204cc version, and came in a number of series. The Series 2 was a two-seater, the Series 3 came as a four-seater tourer or a two-seater coupe and, by the end of 1936 a plethora of different seating, engine and drive options were available.

BSA Scout at Birmingham rally.

The Scout was, by this time, the only model being produced but the variants were bewildering. It was time to rationalise and, when the Series 4 appeared, it only came in three seating options.

1938 saw the introduction of the Series 5 with improved styling and 12 volt electrics whilst the final model, the Series 6, appeared in 1939 just in time for BSA to cease production because of the war. These were the last cars produced by BSA as it concentrated on motorcycle production after the war.

The surviving BSA factory.

BSA still exists as a manufacturer of sporting rifles and they are still based in Armoury Road, Small Heath. However, the business now only occupies a small fragment of the original site.

There are a number of examples of the cars produced by BSA still surviving including three and four-wheeled types.

MP

Motor Plants Ltd., 102-104 Alcester Road, Moseley, Birmingham. 1908-1909

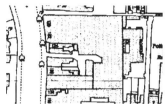

Hubert Berger Graham was born in Scotland in 1873 and trained as a mechanical engineer. By 1901 he was living in Birmingham with his wife and daughter, both named Mabel, and working as a consultant from offices in Winchester House, Victoria Square, which used to stand facing the Council House on the site where the 'Floozie in the Jacuzzi' now reclines.

Amongst his clients were the Forward Engine Company, the company that set Frederick Lanchester on the road to car production. (see **Lanchester**). In collaboration with Frank William Beeching and Forward's assistant manager, Alfred Pally Marks, he worked on patentable improvements to internal combustion engine design through 1902 and 1903; before Beeching moved on to employment at Kynoch's Lion Works. Hubert Graham was a keen early motorist and appeared in the Motoring Annual and Motorists Yearbook for 1904 but his aspiration was to actually make cars.

In 1908 Graham went into partnership with Archibald Meade Beatson from Bath in Somerset and Arthur Joel Smith; the licensee of the Red Lion in Park Lane, Walsall, to form Motor Plants Ltd. The company had a controlling interest in the Lawden Foundry in Bordesley Green and through that the Westwood Rim Company who made wheels under the original Westwood patents licensed from the then owners, Motor Components Ltd. (see **Ariel**) and a range of accessories. The company acquired premises at 102-104 Alcester Road Moseley next to the Prince of Wales public house and went into production of the 'MP' range of cars. The cars were a 16hp four-cylinder, 30hp four-cylinder and 45hp six-cylinder models which sold in 1908 for £365, £575 and £785 respectively. The 45hp model was only in production for a year and the other two models saw a drop of over 20% in their selling price in their second year before they too ceased production.

A Westwood accessories advert.

The company manufactured cars through 1908 and 1909 but went into liquidation and, like W A Lloyd (see **Walco**), made their way into case law when the actions of the liquidator were called into question. In 1911 Hubert Graham had moved to Charing Cross, London to work as a consulting engineer and was himself declared bankrupt. This bankruptcy was discharged the following year on the understanding that he would agree to pay the Receiver's fees.

Hubert Graham went on to become a designer and manufacturer of fire extinguishers in London.

Archibald Beatson went on to form the Car Clearing Bureau, Motor car agents and garage proprietors in London with Harold Gurney Walker Pike, an engineer from Birmingham, and his old school friend from Bradfield College in Reading, Charles Gilbert More, the father of the actor Kenneth More who, in 1953, starred in 'Genevieve' driving the sort of car that his father used to sell. This partnership broke up in December 1912.

Enfield

The Enfield Autocar Company Ltd., Fallows Road, Sparkbrook, Birmingham. 1908-1914

Mergers and acquisitions are nothing new in the motor industry. Enfield is a good example.

The company had its roots in Redditch where George Townsend opened a needle making mill, the Givry Works, in 1851. When his sons (see **Revolette**) took over the business, they started bicycle production and the business grew. It experienced financial difficulties which meant that, in 1891, the company was taken over by R W Smith and Albert Eadie.

Albert Eadie was born in 1862 in Birmingham, the son of Richard and Selina Eadie. His father had a Rose Engine engraving business in the jewellery quarter producing intricate, 'Spirograph' like designs on watches and other jewellery. He started as a clerk at his father's company and then moved on to become the manager of the cycle department at Perry's (see **Perry**). Whilst working there he met Smith who worked for Rudge and was responsible for supplying cycle parts to Perry.

Robert Walker Smith was born in 1855 in Stamford, Lincolnshire and moved to Wolverhampton to serve an engineering apprenticeship with the Great Western Railway. He then became the assistant works manager of Rudge Cycle where he stayed for nine years.

Smith and Eadie changed the name of the company to the Eadie Manufacturing Company, continued producing needles and cycle parts and won a large contract to supply rifle parts to the Royal Small Arms Factory in Enfield, Middlesex. They then started a company called the Enfield Manufacturing Co in 1892 to produce 'Enfield' bicycles, adding 'Royal' to their name in 1863 and adopting the motto; 'Made Like a Gun'.

In July 1896 a new company was registered to take over the manufacture of cycles called the 'New Enfield Cycle Company'. They dropped the 'New' the following year and, in 1898, they added De Dion engined motorized tricycles and quadricycles bearing the 'Royal Enfield' name to their range.

About the same time they formed a new company called the Albert Eadie Chain Company (ECCO for short) to manufacture chains for bicycles, a company which they sold to Abingdon King Dick in 1904 (see **Abingdon King Dick**).

In 1901 they produced their first 'Royal Enfield' motorcycle, a brand that survives to this day, though they are now built in India, and in 1904 started building cars. In March 1906 they formed the Enfield Autocar Company to take over the production of cars but in 1907 the motor

A 1909 Enfield.

The Enfield Autocar Model 183 Landau.

industry suffered a slump and the company got into financial difficulties. Alldays (see **Alldays and Onions**) bought the company, its machinery, premises and vehicles in production for £10,000 and, in 1908, moved operations to a new site in Fallows Road, Sparkbrook with Edward Tailby and William Allday in charge.

Albert Eadie continued in the business of motorcycle production and died at the 'Thatched House' in Sussex in April 1931.

Robert Smith stayed with the company until his death in 1933 at the age of 75.

The Enfield cars had been designed by Ernest Henry Lancaster, one-time staff engineer for the Automobile Club of Great Britain and Ireland and dealer in 'Clement' vehicles (see **Garrard**). These cars continued in production for a short while, presumably to use up the parts stock whilst new designs were developed. In November 1908 the company displayed three models at Olympia; a 10-12hp two-cyl-

The Enfield Autocar 18-22hp Engine.

The 1915 Enfield Light Car.

inder 'voiturette', an 18-24 and, the only Eadie model to survive, an updated 30-35hp. A fourth 18hp model was produced but not shown. In 1911 they introduced 12hp and 24hp models and, an early contender in the cyclecar market, the two-cylinder three-wheeled 'Autolette'. Later in the year this was replaced by a four-wheeled, 7-8hp model with a v-twin engine and, in 1913 another new model appeared.

This model came in two variants, a two-cylinder and a 9hp four cylinder engined option that became known as the 'Nimble Nine' in 1914. The car sold well, being particularly attractive to the growing numbers of women motorists, and went through a number of refinements up to its 1915 model, revealed in 1914.

The war halted production and the marque disappeared to be replaced by Enfield-Allday after the war (see **Enfield-Allday**).

A number of Enfields still exist but the Matchless Works in Fallows Road has gone, replaced by more an estate of more modern industrial units.

'Colonial road conditions' in Australia.

Enfields lined up outside the factory.

Veloce

**New Veloce Motors Ltd., Hampton Works, Peel Street, Spring Hill, Birmingham.
1908-1916**

Johannes Gutgemann arrived in Birmingham from Germany as a 19 year old in 1876 and married a local girl, Elizabeth Caroline Ore, in Kings Norton in 1884. He bought a pill making business called Isaac Taylor and Co of 36 Winson Green Road.

Gutgemann adopted the more English sounding name John Taylor and went into partnership with a cycle maker called William Gue to form Taylor Gue and manufactured cycles from the rear of the premises that backed onto Peel Street. The business expanded and diversified into forecars, rickshaws and, eventually, motorcycle making following the acquisition of Ormonde, a primitive motorcycle manufacturer and Kelekom, a Belgian engine manufacturer, both of whose businesses had failed in 1904.

The name Veloce was chosen to badge their new 2hp motorcycles and they moved to the Spring Hill premises in 1905 to start manufacture. The motorcycles didn't sell, however, and the company got into financial difficulties, being forced, into liquidation in June 1905 when one of their creditors, The Speedwell Gear Case Company of Broad Street, took action against them. Later in 1905 the business was revived under the name Veloce Ltd. to produce motorcycles and accessories.

John Taylor had two sons with Elizabeth; Percy John b. 1884 and Eugene Frederick b.1890. Percy apprenticed as a pattern maker and worked for some time in India selling Wolseley cars and sheep shearing tools. Eugene was apprenticed in the tool room at the New Hudson works on Summer Hill.

When Percy came back to Birmingham in 1907 he set up in business as New Veloce Motors with his brother and, by 1908, had produced a prototype 20hp car, the 'Veloce'.

In 1911 John Taylor became a naturalised British citizen and in 1917 the whole family anglicised their name from Gutgemann to Goodman.

The company was registered in January 1912 with John and his two sons as the directors until Eugene stepped down in favour of Harold John Lloyd in June 1913.

Meanwhile, in 1916 the New Veloce Company was wound-up to allow business interests to be amalgamated with those of the Veloce Co., and the combined company continued producing motorcycles under the 'Velocette' marque until February 1971.

The New Veloce Company was, itself, finally given notice of dissolution in 1921.

Percy John Goodman died in Stratford upon Avon in 1953 and his brother Eugene Frederick Goodman died in Shrewsbury in 1970. The Veloce car is not known to have survived and neither have the premises in Spring Hill where it was built.

Eugene and Percy Goodman.

Brockas

T Brockas Cycles, Chester Road, Sutton Coldfield. c1910

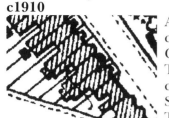

An example of a small cycle company turning its attention to car production was sited at the Beggar's Bush on the Sutton Coldfield border.

The company was run by Thomas Brockas, a mechanic specialising in sewing machine repair and cycle making born in Sutton Coldfield to Henry and Ann Brockas in 1857.

Thomas wasn't to be the only member of the family with a link to the automotive industry; his sister, Fanny Moreton Brockas, married William Hillman in 1873, the man who would go on to found the Hillman car company in Coventry at about the time that the photo below was taken. Thomas started out as a sewing machine mechanic in London living in Knowles Hill, Lewisham with his brother Henry (who had married Hillman's sister) and new wife Caroline Flora Ascough Lower from Coventry.

They settled in Lewisham with Thomas gaining the position of foreman in a cycle factory with Hillman and William Starley and raised a family that would eventually number nine children, moving back to live at No.3 Springfield, off Fentham Road, Erdington in about 1898.

Thomas opened a cycle business in the row of shops that faced the Princess Alice Orphanage at the Beggar's Bush and experimented with motorised vehicle building.

Based on the cycle technology with

The Chester Road cycle works.

which he was familiar the vehicle he produced was a late example of a forecar. By this time the forecar was being replaced by motorcycle/sidecar combinations and the day of the cyclecar was dawning so it would have had difficulty finding a market.

Thomas was probably prompted into this market by his sons, notably Leonard, born in 1889. Leonard Brockas went on to become the works mechanic for the Austin Racing Team, refining and maintaining the Austin Sevens that appeared through the twenties and thirties. He is pictured here with Lou Kings, Austin's chief tester in a 1923 Austin Seven racer. In 1931 he travelled with Malcolm Campbell to Daytona Beach where land speed records were set in a supercharged Austin Seven that he had built and, more famously, in 'Bluebird'.

Thomas Brockas died in 1935. The cycle shop is still there and is now a tyre garage. The car hasn't survived.

Len Brockas in a 1923 Austin Seven racer.

The Cyclecar

It is hard to imagine today, when cars are relatively cheap and available, how difficult it was for anyone less than comfortably off to acquire a car in the early years of the 20th century.

The fact that cars existed at all meant that the writing was on the wall for the motorcycle; the advantages of a vehicle that could give some protection from the elements and offer greater carrying capacity were obvious. The second hand market was limited. Cars hadn't been around long enough for any great numbers to trickle down and become an economical option; in fact the number of private cars licenced in Birmingham in 1912 was just over 1500 - half the number of car parking spaces in the Bullring shopping centre today.

The man on the street needed transport and the manufacturers had, up to that point, concentrated on satisfying the early adopters market, where the money was to be made. The response to this situation was the cyclecar. Cyclecars were a phenomenon of the period between 1910 and 1922. The manufacturer that set the trend was the French company of Bourbeau et Devaux Co. in Paris. They started producing 'Bedelia' cyclecars in 1910 with their most obviously motor cycle derived model; the tandem cyclecar.

What needs to be remembered about this time in the development of motor vehicles was that there was no 'right' way to do anything. Modern cars have superficial styling and performance differences but they nearly all conform to a few basic rules; a wheel in each corner, a driver in the front right or left hand seat with the main controls including steering wheel, gear stick, foot pedals and handbrake being in more or less standard positions.

These basic rules didn't exist before 1922. In fact it was the Austin Seven that finally put

A cyclecar picnic

Major F. Lindsay Lloyd.

to bed the argument about which order the foot pedals should follow - clutch/brake/accelerator - by becoming the first mass-market car to adopt this arrangement.

Bedelia, having no constraints, opted to put the driver and passenger in a straight line- one behind the other, as the name 'tandem' suggests but, and here is where it gets a little strange, the driver was at the back! And the oddness doesn't stop there. The driver had two gears at his command but to change from one to the other he had to take both hands off the steering wheel and manipulate the belt drive with the aid of two wooden poles, or develop a one-handed technique that would at least allow him to steer and change gear at the same time. This pattern was followed by a number of cyclecar manufacturers, notably the Birmingham company - Rollo.

A development of this was to put the driver and passenger side by side in an arrangement called the 'sociable'.

Not all of these primitive vehicles could carry two people so early examples tend to be called monocars or duocars. An all-encompassing term was needed.

Major F Lindsay Lloyd of the RAC is said to have coined the term 'cyclecar' in late 1910 but, by February 1914, he had come to the conclusion that, though the term cyclecar fitted the earlier vehicles, the later cars were just that - cars and, as such, should fall under the jurisdiction of the RAC rather than the Auto-Cycle Union.

The main characteristics of a cyclecar were that it would generally have a single or two-cylinder air-cooled engine with a lightweight body on a tubular steel frame and a belt or chain drive to the rear axle. There were many variants, of course with some having characteristics usually found on the more refined and substantial 'light cars'.

The main attraction of the cyclecar was that it was simple and cheap and, as such, buildable by enthusiasts at their own home. Magazines such as Light Car and Cyclecar promoted home-building and occasionally featured some of the better examples in their pages.

In 1913 'How to Build a Cyclecar' was published and, in its first chapter, described the best sort of shed in which to build one. Later chapters promoted companies who could supply the parts, axles, wheels, gearboxes, etc. many of whom were

A Bedelia Cyclecar from France.

Birmingham based. But the home-builders wouldn't have the cycle car to themselves and the new market attracted new car companies.

The cyclecar craze gathered pace rapidly with businesses that had previously concentrated on car component or cycle production being tempted into car building. The rise in the formation of Birmingham cyclecar companies was exponential; in 1911 there were four, in 1912, another nine appeared and in 1913 twenty-one more. This rate of expansion couldn't possibly be maintained. It wasn't. The bubble burst in 1914.

Britain entered the war in August 1914 and the world changed. There was a sudden dramatic halt in company formation whilst everyone's attention was focused on something else that hadn't happened before - a World War.

Alvechurch

The Alvechurch Light Car Co., Alvechurch Works, Bradford Street, Birmingham. 1911-1912

There was a massive expansion in light car and cyclecar manufacture in the years immediately before the First World War and in 1911 this boom was reflected in the gathering pace of creation of new car marques in the UK. There was a sudden upsurge in the number of manufacturers joining the fray and Dunkleys, typically, were early to responded to this.

The Alvechurch, later known as the A.L.C., was a light car manufactured by Dunkleys, the pram makers described earlier (see **Dunkley**) who made a number of forays into car production setting up separate Companies to keep the business affairs discreet from each other.

The company was set up by William Henry Dunkley's son, also called William Henry Dunkley, born in Kings Norton in 1888 and also a pram manufacturer, at his Arrow Ville Works in Alvechurch.

His partners in this venture were Minton Edwin Toddington, an engineer from Castle Bromwich and Alfred Thomas Blackwell of Northfield who operated from Grosvenor Chambers in Broad Street and acted as the Company Secretary.

The actual location of the works is open to speculation but may have been situated in the mill buildings (now, inventively, called 'The Mill' public house) in Alvechurch or, more possibly, in the Alvechurch Works in Bradford Street, Birmingham that sit alongside the site of William Henry Dunkley Snr's. English Motor Company works.

The car had an air-cooled V-twin 'Matchless' engine manufactured by Collier and Sons in Plumstead, London, pram wheels and belt drive. Unfortunately the belt drive suffered badly from slipping and this car-making episode ended disastrously when, with only two cars produced, the company went bankrupt.

In early 1913 the company was still in existence, though heavily mortgaged and with both Dunkley's still as shareholders, but Dunkley Jnr. had resigned his position as Director leaving Toddington and Blackwell to carry on with their solicitor joining as third Director. Minton Toddington, by 1911 was the landlord of the Four Oaks Hotel in Belwell Lane Sutton Coldfield presumably because his car manufacturing aspirations had ended by then. The long slow business of winding the company up was interrupted by the war and it was finally dissolved in February 1919.

Fortunately the foresight to separate the business activities protected the parent Company from the debacle but the experience taught Dunkley to steer clear of car production and focus on the pram business for the next dozen years.

There are no known surviving Alvechurch cars and William Henry Dunkley Jnr. died in 1970 in Weymouth, Dorset.

Minton Toddington died in Kingston Surrey in 1931.

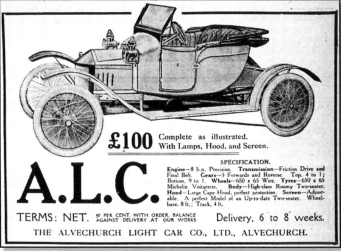

An advert for the Alvechurch.

Crowdy

The Crowdy Company, West Heath Works, Northfield, Birmingham.
1911-1912

Crowdy was a short lived, car company that operated for a time in Northfield, but the story of this car goes back all the way to 1902 in London with Danny Weigel.

Weigel was an early importer of Clement cars from France. His business associate was the wealthy Earl of Shrewsbury and Talbot and, between them, they had a desire to produce quality cars in Britain.

They formed a Company in 1902 and, while they undertook construction of a new car factory in Ladbrook Grove, London with Weigel as Managing Director, they imported Clement cars from France to satisfy the growing demand for cars, badging them as Clement-Talbots (see **Garrard**) and later, simply, Talbots. By 1905 Weigel had decided to set up in business in his own right as Weigel Motors Ltd. and started producing cars under the 'Weigel' marque.

Daniel Mitchel Weigel was an interesting character, by all accounts. Born in London in 1875, the son of an Austrian diamond merchant, he was described at the time as 'colourful' and 'bombastic', was prominent in motor tricycle racing before the turn of the century and a regular correspondent to the motoring journals.

He used his experiences driving in the Paris-Vienna race of 1902 and other events to design a series of race orientated cars, introducing the first British straight eight engined cars when he linked two 40hp engines in tandem for his 1907 French Grand Prix cars.

It was in this year that the Company moved premises to

Danny Weigel.

Olaf Street in Notting Hill. The Company continued producing cars until 1910 but got into financial difficulties and, in November of that year, its assets were bought by A E Crowdy, a former sales manager for Wolseley (see **Wolseley**) at their offices in Lancashire. Albert Edwin Crowdy was born in Blunsdon in Wiltshire in 1875. His father was a solicitor and 'Lord of the Manor' who bore the impressive name of Henry Crowdy Crowdy. Albert was a keen racing driver and mechanical engineer who had moved to Birmingham to

lodge with William Matthews on the Hagley Road at the turn of the century. His keenness for speed manifested itself in a £2 fine from the Birmingham Magistrates in 1904 for 'driving over 12 mph!'

In 1905, whilst living in Carlyle Road, Edgbaston, he patented improvements to car tyres and, in 1910, he patented a tyre-security wing nut, which he later marketed, whilst living in Manchester. This man moved around the country

Weigel and the straight eight.

and, when he bought the Weigel Company, he moved, temporarily at least, to London. Crowdy continued the production of the 25hp and 40 hp Weigel cars under the 'Crowdy' name from the Olaf Street works until the parts ran out. Crowdy then introduced further models including 19hp four cylinder and 29hp six-cylinder cars, with the dashboard

A E Crowdy.

mounted radiators, which had been a feature on the cars previously, moved to a more conventional position at the front.

In 1911 production was moved to the West Heath Works in Northfield, a former, purpose-built, roller skating rink, and he, allegedly, produced a further 4000 cars, though this is rather hard to believe.

Crowdy was not to survive for much longer, going out of business in February 1912. The company was bought by Arthur Wright, Ralph Ward, Lewis Radmore and William Miller as their way into the motor manufacturing business and renamed 'The Hampton Engineering Company' (see **Hampton**). A year later they started production of cars, including the Crowdy 12-6, using the Hampton name at Lifford Mills in Kings Norton, under three miles away.

Danny Weigel left the motor trade in 1914 and tried his hand at brewing Arrak, a distilled alcoholic drink made from the unopened flowers of the coconut palm, whilst in Sri Lanka (or Ceylon as it was then).

He later emigrated, with his wife Ruby and daughter Olive, to the United States of America and worked on the design of tyres and internal combustion engines. In 1946 he worked on improvements to the jet engine and died in Cuyahoga County, Ohio in 1948.

Albert Crowdy joined the army as a Lieutenant in 1914 and served in France. He stayed

The 'Weigel type' Crowdy.

with the Army after the war serving in Iraq and India, achieving the rank of Major. In 1922 he returned to England, where he spent some time working on his electronic inventions and died in Bath in 1965 at the ripe old age of 90.

There are no known surviving 'Weigel' or 'Crowdy' cars, but remnants of the West Heath works may still exist alongside the River Rea on the west side of the West Heath Road.

The definition of a Brummie.

It was almost a requirement of being a 'Brummie' that you were not born in the City. Of the 162 people featured in this book, who played a significant part in the development of the Birmingham motor industry 84 were actually born outside the City.

The reasons for this lie in the rapid rate of growth that the city experienced as it developed as a centre for manufacturing. At the time of Domesday Birmingham was a small village with a reputation for ironworking and a population of only a few hundred. The population grew slowly to 1300 by the early 1500s and by 1700 its population had grown to 15000. Over the next hundred years it grew rapidly to over 70000 people and by 1900 had reached half a million.

The birth rate cannot explain this growth rate but the magnetic attraction of an industrial centre to agricultural workers rendered unemployed by advances in farming technology can. The factories' demand for workers were safisfied by this influx. The current population is well over 1 million.

Dallison

**The Dallison Gearing & Motor Company, 37 Sutton Rd., Erdington, Birmingham.
1911-1913**

George Joseph William Dallison was born in Newington, London in 1892 to Joseph and Emma Dallison. He married Louisa Keevil in May 1894 in Camberwell and raised a family, moving to Lewisham in about 1900. (What is it about Lewisham and budding car manufacturers?). The family moved to Canada where he worked as an engineer before moving to Birmingham in 1910 to make his fortune.

He started life as a carpenter, following in the footsteps of his father, but changed his career path, setting up an engineering company in April 1911 to manufacture car parts and, eventually, cars. His company, 'The Dallison Engineering and Cycle Company', had three directors, himself, Joseph Ennever and Dr. Peter Campbell.

Joseph Aloysius Ennever was born in St Pancras in 1871 the son of William Joseph

Ennever, a pianoforte maker and brother of another William Joseph Ennever who was the inventor of 'Pelmanism', a memory training system popular in the first half of the last century that spawned a card game still played today. Peter Campbell was an MD and surgeon practising in Nechells.

In 1912 the company moved their production base to 37 Sutton Road opposite Erdington Abbey and close to Peter Campbell's house. George Dallison was, at this time, living at Oscott Villa on

The Dallison three wheeler.

Gravelly Lane, next door to Alfred Pilkington who managed the Premier Motor Company in Aston (see **Premier**). They must have had some interesting evenings in the Old Rose and Crown.

The Dallison cyclecar was considered a very racy design with its v-shaped radiator and streamlined body, however, the Company was dissolved in 1915 and George Dallison died in 1941. There are no known surviving cars and the site of the premises, now occupied by Colliers Car Showroom, is soon to be a Sainsburys store.

The Dallison four wheeler

Wall/Roc

**A W Wall, Roc Motor Works, Kings Road, Tyseley, Birmingham.
1911-1915**

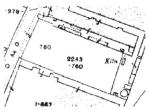

A W Wall were the manufacturers of one of the odder vehicles to emerge from Birmingham. A cross between a sidecar, bath chair and tricycle, it had a two seater body with tiller steering.

Arthur William Wall was born in 1873 in Balsall the son of William and Martha Wall. By the time he was 17 he was boarding with Charles Smith, a watchmaker, in Coventry, working as a cycle machinist but he wanted to experience life in London, so he cycled there - on a stolen bike! He hired a cycle whilst his own was in for repair but claimed in court that he ran out of money whilst in London and was unable to return it. It didn't help that he had given a false name, so he was fined £5.

In 1902 he married Alice Annie Newman who was born in India, the daughter of William Newman, whilst he was on military duty there. The marriage took place in Guildford where he started in business making cycles at 160 High Street.

With backing from Sir Arthur Conan Doyle, of Sherlock Holmes fame and with Henry Percival Rose and Charles James Whistler Hanson, the son of the painter of 'Whistler's Mother' as two of his co-directors, he set up his own company, A W Wall, to produce motorcycles in 1903. Also on the board were Conan Doyle's brother-in-law Patrick Stewart Leckie. By 1905 only Wall and Rose remained on the board with Conan Doyle's secretary and English cricketer, Alfred Herbert Wood overseeing.

The motorcycles, sold under the 'Roc' name, had 3hp engines and magneto ignition and, from 1905, a flywheel on each side.

The A W Wall factory entrance.

In 1905 a vertical twin-cylinder engine was tested in the Isle of Man Auto Cycle Cup by T H Tessier of the BAT motorcycle company but it didn't race. Over the next few years the range and sophistication of the motorcycles increased and the manufacturing base moved, in early 1907, to the premises in Aston Road and Dartmouth Street that were used at other times to produce the Alexandra (see **Alexandra**), Premier, PMC and Motorette (see **Premier** and **Motorette**).

In 1909 the 'Wall Auto Wheel' made its first appearance. Though devices that drove a vehicle along with a motorised wheel had been developed before, Wall's was the first to use a petrol engine. The Auto Wheel was a wheel driven by a motor that could be attached to a bicycle turning it into a motorcycle. It also provided the motive power of a number of vehicles produced by others. Some of these have survived, now proudly attached to vintage bicycles.

In 1911 the company moved to new premises on Kings Road, Tyseley and, in the same year, launched its idiosyncratic contender in the car market - the Wall Tricar. Unlike most three-wheelers on the market, Wall decided to put the single

Wall Tricar otherwise known as the Roc Egg.

Wall Tricar.

The Wall Auto Wheel.

A Wall tricar crashes in Elmdon while on a test run.

wheel at the front and steer it with a tiller. The front wheel was insulated from the frame with spring forks as on a motorcycle whilst the main body, with seating for two, was supported by long C springs. The Precision engine could be either a single or twin-cylinder air cooled type. The epicyclic gears to the main drive, reduction gear from the epicyclic gears, bevel gear to the magneto and gear for starting the engine were all contained in an aluminium housing bolted to the crankcase. There were two forward gears and no reverse as this was considered unnecessary bearing in mind the vehicle's tight turning circle.

The power was transmitted to the rear wheels through a drive shaft and bevel gears and a differential took up the slack when making tight turns. From March 1914 there was a steering wheel option but only on the passenger version and not on the commercial delivery version. Because of the form of the car the steering wheel, when adopted, was on a rather awkward horizontal steering column but it was practical enough for examples to still be on the road a dozen years later. The whole thing weighed in at 4 1/2 cwt and the twin cylinder option complete with body was sold for £101.17s. Despite its rather unusual design, the tricar did experience some popularity, being the vehicle of choice for, amongst others, the Dean of Trinity College, Oxford, and even acquired its own nickname; the 'Roc Egg'.

The company faded away in the mid twenties and was finally dissolved in 1927. The premises in Aston disappeared under the Expressway and the Tyseley factory has been remodelled to create offices. However, the main structure of the building and the entrance porch have been retained, even if the porch has been painted white.

There are two examples of the tricar known to have survived; a parcel delivery vehicle in New Zealand and a passenger tricar with tiller steering in Birmingham - unfortunately not the one in the UK, but the one in Alabama, USA, at the Barber Vintage Motorsports Museum. Arthur Wall died in Hampton in Arden in 1943.

The last surviving Wall Tricar.

Crescent

Crescent Motors Ltd., Britannia Works, Rolfe Street, Smethwick, Birmingham. 1911-1915

Another early entrant into the cyclecar market became one of only two car marques from Smethwick, the other being the even shorter-lived Rolfe (see **Rolfe**).

Crescent Motors was started by buckle manufacturer James Bailey, born in January 1858 in Tamworth and his son Bertram Morley Bailey, born in Walsall in 1889.

The first Crescents were of tubular steel construction and had an 8hp JAP v-twin, air-cooled, engine. They were built at the Pleck Motor Works in Walsall but there was a limited production run before the company changed owners and moved to new premises, Britannia Works, on the corner of Rolfe Street and Engine Street in Smethwick in 1913.

The new owners were retired barrister Edward Alexander Miller and his son, Henry Tavener Miller, an engineer, from Surrey who, along with Charles William von Roemer, another engineer from Herstmonceaux, developed a new version.

The version built at the Smethwick works was more substantial. It was fitted with a choice of either a Precision or a Blumfield v-twin, water-cooled engine transversely mounted with either a Cox Atmos or AMAC carburettor, (both Birmingham manufacturers), and a Bosch magneto.

The frame of the car was of solid-drawn tubes with brazed iron fittings and acetylene welded lugs for fitting the body. The Crescent was one of the first friction

The last surviving Crescent.

driven cars to arrive on the market and had a driven friction disc with a Ferodo lining from Derbyshire rather than compressed paper which had been previously more common. Crescent were so sure of this feature that they guaranteed it for 8000 miles. A countershaft connected to the friction drive drove the rear wheels via Brampton 'silent' chains made in Cookley, Worcestershire. Instead of a differential, the rear axle was fitted with a friction clutch.

The car, complete with hood, screen, lamps and tools cost £127 when launched in 1913 and Crescent anticipated production numbers would reach 500 for the 1914 season. They gained two more backers, in Ralph Carr-Ellison and Norman Holder who had already lent his support to Thomas Blumfield's business (see **Blumfield**) but the war was looming

The Britannia Works.

and the company went over to war production in 1915. Toward the end of the war the company ceased trading and was dissolved in December 1917. Only one Crescent is known to have survived but both the Walsall and Smethwick Works have survived, though in a poor state.

Rollo

Rollo Car Company Ltd., Watery Lane, Conybere St. & Bradford St., Birmingham. 1912-1913

In France, in 1910 Henri Bourbeau and Robert Devaux started to make what was to become one of the most popular of the first cyclecars.

They wanted to make scaled down cars so that they would be simpler and cheaper and so adapted motorcycle design principles. The first car they produced, the 'Bedelia', carried two people in a tandem arrangement with the driver in the rear seat. This was the format adopted by the first Rollo.

Rollo was a car company set up by Warne, Wright and Rowland Ltd. to capture some of the booming cyclecar market. Unlike most of their competitors who had come from a cycle making background, their usual line of business was screw, nut and bolt manufacture.

James Thomas Warne hailed from Bedminster near Bristol and had started the Company manufacturing machine-made screws in the late 1860s in partnership with William Henry Salisbury.

When he died in April 1880 the business was passed on to his wife, Harriet Mary Warne, who continued operating it under the name 'James Warne' until the turn of the century when Alfred Wright and John Rowland

The last surviving Rollo.

joined the business, thus changing its name to 'Warne, Wright and Rowland'.

Alfred Cecil Wright was born in Chipping Ongar in Essex in 1858 and moved to Birmingham with his parents John and Matilda in 1862, after attending boarding school at Melbourn near Cambridge.

His father had a company making gas cookers in Aston that later became 'Radiation' producing 'New World' gas cookers and developing the 'Regulo' thermostat that for many years lent its name to cooker temperature settings. Alfred's first business venture was making the fittings for umbrellas which he did for a number of years before joining forces with John Rowland.

John David Rowland was born in Moss Side Manchester in 1873 to Edward Rowland, a publican, and his wife Jane. His brothers William and Edward went into business building yachts in Bangor but John decided to serve an apprenticeship as a toolmaker before moving to Birmingham.

In April 1912 they were joined by Gerald Churchill Sambridge, the son of Henry Sambridge a brassfounder, born in Kings Norton in 1885, and the Rollo Car Company Ltd. was formed to develop cyclecars at premises in Watery Lane and Conybere Street.

Spurred on by an order for 100 cyclecars received in 1913, production moved to bigger premises at 314 Bradford Street, later used to manufacture the V.A.L. cyclecar (see **VAL**). The company developed a range that encompassed the three classic cyclecar types; a three-seater tandem with the driver at the back, a two-seater sociable with the driver and passenger side-by-side and a single seater monocar called the Pony.

All of the cars had a tubular steel frame with a two-cylinder, 8hp JAP, air-cooled engine on the tandem and sociable and a 4.5hp single cylinder Precision engine on the Pony. The drive on all three was by lapped belt between pulleys on a transaxle and drums on the rear wheels. The clutch was operated by use of a lever that moved the rear axle backwards relative to the car and putting the belts under tension. Moving this lever the other way pulled the rear axle forward so that the large-diameter brake drums were bought into contact with brake blocks mounted on the chassis. A second, foot operated brake acted on the transaxle.

The company only lasted for a short time and produced few cars, possibly curtailed by the impending war.

The 'Rollo Car Company Ltd'. went into voluntary liquidation in July 1913 but the parent company continued in business producing screws, nuts and bolts.

Lottie Berend at the wheel of the Rollo Tandem.

Alfred Wright had a number of business interests. He was also a director of William Bayliss Ltd. (Ironwork), The Sutherland Meter Company (gas meters) and, in partnership with William Dukes, set up the Warland Dual Rim Company (WARne, Wright and RowLAND) to market the removable wheel rims later fitted to a wide number of marques of car including Rolls Royce. He made a large amount of money from his business interests and was able to donate the Mostyn Collection of Welsh language manuscripts to the National Library in Aberystwyth before he died in Edgbaston in September 1920.

John Rowland continued with the company, registering patents for refinements to tools until shortly before his death at his Solihull home in 1937.

The Rollo Sociable.

Gerald Sambridge joined the Royal Warwickshire Regiment in 1915 and served in Nigeria, stopping on as a civil servant in Lagos until he relinquished his commission due to ill health in 1940 retiring to his house 'Karkara' on the Wirral. He died later that year.

After Alfred Wright's death the company was controlled by his sons and continued in business until the late fifties.

Only one Rollo has survived and has been carefully restored to it's original state.

The factories in Watery Lane and Conybere Street no longer exist but the later works in Bradford Street still stand.

The Rollo Pony monocar.

Kendall

The Kendall Cycle Car Company, 88 Shadwell Street, Birmingham. 1912-1913

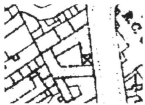

Fred Franks Kendall was born in Kings Norton in 1892, the son of Fred Kendall, a tailor and outfitter from Huddersfield, who had moved to Kings Norton and married a local girl, Sarah Ann Franks.

Fred Kendall was raised at the family home, 'The Homestead', in Birchwood Crescent, Sparkbrook, and set himself up in business in partnership with Allan Kell Bindloss, an aero engineer and the son of a GP from Lewisham.

They established themselves at 88 Shadwell Street, a site that is now landscaped open space (which used to be the site of the Kennedy Memorial mosaic) to the west of St Chad's RC Cathedral, and produced a cyclecar that they called the Kendall 'Carette'.

The Carette Chassis.

The 'Carette' had an 8hp V-twin JAP engine, positioned transversely and belt drive, with an alternative Peugeot engine and worm drive also available.

The epicyclic gearbox had two forward gears and a reverse gear operated by a foot pedal. This could be bought into action to give extra braking force in an emergency.

It was claimed to travel at up to 44 mph, have a chassis weight of 3.5cwt. and was priced at 92 Guineas on the road. The worm drive version complete with hood, lamps and screen could be bought for £130.

In 1912 the Carette made its debut at the Olympia Motor Show and the company manufactured cars through 1912 and 1913 but, before the First World War, operations came to a halt and the company failed. The dissolution of the company had already taken place by the time the war started suggesting that there may have been other issues that triggered its demise.

Fred Kendall joined the Royal Engineers and served in France. He survived the war and came home to marry Ethel D Hudson in Kings Norton in 1918 but his car building plans were behind him. He died in Solihull in 1955.

Allan Bindloss moved to Renfrewshire and turned his attention to experiments with gramophones, patenting improvements to the geometry of tone arms in 1917. He moved down to Surrey where he gained a glider pilot's licence and died in Worthing in 1962.

There are no known surviving Kendall Carettes and the works disappeared under the ring road redevelopment.

The Kendall Carette.

PDA

Pickering, Darby and Allday Ltd., Belgrave Garage, 233 Bristol St., Birmingham. 1912-1913

Pickering, Darby and Allday formed their Company in 1912 taking over the workshop premises of Pickering Brothers and Darby in Bristol Street to produce cyclecars.

Harold Cecil Pickering was born in Kings Norton in 1885 the son of John Pickering, a soap and candle maker and Sophie Allen. Sidney Darby was an engineer from Kings Norton and the two men traded from the premises in Bristol Street.

In 1912 the new business was registered and the Alldays joined the company. The Alldays of the title were John, born in 1857, a manufacturing jeweller and his son Gilbert who was an engineer and became the Company Secretary. They were not related to the owners of Alldays and Onions but this didn't stop Gilbert James (Jim) Allday from acquiring Alldays and Onions cars and, as time went by, he built a large collection of veteran cars.

In 1930 he joined the committee of the newly formed 'Veteran Car Club' and was their president for many years. He died in Cornwall in 1966 having given a large area of land around Pont Creek, Fowey, (the area said to have inspired Kenneth Graham to write 'The Wind in the Willows'), to the National Trust.

The PDA cyclecar was a four-wheel, two-seater with an air-cooled Blumfield twin engine and a water-cooled option.

Jim Allday and King Feisal.   Harold Pickering.

Both the engine and back axle were fixed to an underframe hinged off the front of the chassis so that a universal joint was unnecessary and the car featured transverse springing at the front. The steering column was adjustable and the vehicle was described as "*finely finished*" in the July edition of Motor Cycling magazine. The car was advertised as available in any colour and retailed for 105 Guineas. The PDA featured prominently in cyclecar runs and trials of the period, sometimes sporting a water-cooled Precision engine. By the end of October 1913 they had decided to wind up the company and it was dissolved the following year. No more than 15 cars were built and none have survived. The premises disappeared with the widening of Bristol Street.

PDA Light Car on a run.

Tyseley

The Tyseley Car Company, Tyseley, Birmingham.
1912-1913

Accessory companies, seeing the potential demand for mass-market motor vehicles and having the necessary manufacturing capability, joined the race. The Tyseley was a light car making venture of the Bowden Brake Company in Kings Road, Tyseley.

The founder of the company was Henry Arthur Lamplugh. He was born in Birmingham in 1872 the son of James Lamplugh who had a large saddle and leather goods making company in the city. His father's company made bicycle saddles, examples of which still survive and, for a time in the early 1900s, motor car tyres under the 'Pegasus' brand.

The Bowden Brake Company started manufacturing a tricar in 1912 with an 8hp water-cooled, twin engine.

In late 1912 the company launched a new light car that came in two body styles; an open two seater and a four seater doctor's coupe aimed squarely at the widely perceived market for inexpensive vehicles for medical men. In the 'Motor' magazine the reviewer said that it had '*an attractive appearance entirely free from faddishness or anything outré*'. Which must have been quite a relief.

The Tyseley open two-seater.

The car had a 1090cc, two-cylinder 8.4hp engine with the cylinders at an angle of 60 degrees to one another and magneto ignition. It had a two-speed and reverse gearbox but, because the car weighed less than 8cwt, the lower gear was only needed for starting and steep hills.

The engine, clutch and gearbox were combined into one unit supported by brackets from the side arms of the channel section steel chassis. The chassis had a pronounced dip in the middle to lower the step into

The Tyseley Doctor's Coupe.

the car to afford 'a low entrance', a feature not normally considered by their competitors. The wire-spoked wheels were detachable and were fitted with 650mm x 56mm Dunlop tyres. It had a wheelbase of 7ft and a track of 4ft and came complete with hood, side-screens, toolbox, spare wheel and lamps for 160 guineas.

Though predicted to create much attention the car didn't sell and the company turned back to brake production after a year. The company had some dealings a few years later with R Walker and Son (see **Bayliss-Thomas**) whose works were opposite, building saloon bodies with sliding doors for them.

No examples of the Tyseley are known to have survived.

Howett/Hail

Fowler and Cashmore, Hockley Brook Garage, Soho Hill, Birmingham.
1912-1914

An early entrant into the cycle car industry, William Henry Fowler was born in Birmingham in 1877. He formed a partnership with Walter Cashmore to open a garage next to Hockley Brook at the foot of Soho Hill.

Walter William Cashmore, born in Birmingham in 1855, was a manufacturer of gold and silver chains and, though the son of a tool maker, responsible for patents for cycle wheels, lead piping and small arms, his age indicates that he probably dealt with the business half of the partnership.

Their garage and workshop backed onto the former cable winding depot of the Birmingham Cable Tramway Company who ran cable cars, similar to those still surviving in San Francisco, from Colmore Row to Soho Road Handsworth. The cable tramway had opened in 1885 but by 1911 the cable system had been replaced by electric trams, possibly releasing workshop space in the depot in time for Fowler and Cashmore to set up business there.

The car that they produced under the Howett name had a 10hp V-twin, air-cooled Blumfield engine with a friction drive giving eight forward speeds and a countershaft with pulleys driving the rear wheels via belts. Steering was by an eccentric fixed to the end of the steering column which was a low-cost and simple option that made the steering 'irreversible' and resistant to wear.

It was a relatively wide car by cyclecar standards at 46 inches and cost £100. There was a water cooled option available for an extra £5 and a further option of detachable wheels.

The Howett.

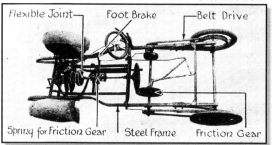

The chassis assembly.

The Howett wasn't the only car produced at Fowler's Garage. In early 1913 F N Hail collaborated with Fowler to produce a cyclecar aimed at commercial travellers, replacing the more traditional pony and trap.

It had four wheels and a two-seater body with a 2ft x 2ft 8in box on the back that was flush with the top of the seat back for carrying samples or small parcels. It was available with either a 6-8hp JAP or a 7-9hp Peugeot engine set transversely across the frame. The 20in diameter cast-iron friction-disk was fixed to the end of the prop-shaft and transmitted power to a countershaft and pulleys driving the rear axle via 1.5in wide v-profile belts. It had a Best and Lloyd lubrication system and a two-lever carburettor. The channel-steel frame had semi-elliptic springs at the front and quarter elliptic springs at the rear. The vehicle when complete cost about £75.

William Fowler emigrated to Canada in 1924, the same year that Walter Cashmore died in Handsworth. There are no known survivors of either marque and the premises in Hockley are no longer there, having disappeared when the Hockley Flyover was built in 1967.

Monarch (Haymills)

R Walker and Son, Kings Road, Tyseley, Birmingham.
1912-1914

The Monarch was an early product of another Birmingham manufacturing company aiming to diversify and capture some of the growing light car market.

The Walkers were a Birmingham family but they moved around the country. Reginald Walker Senior was a brassfounder, a maker of fire irons, born in Lincoln in 1860 but living and working in Birmingham by the time of the 1881 census.

His son Reginald Eric Walker, born in Eccleshall Bierlow, Sheffield in 1883, joined the business, managing the company, and later set up in business in his own right with his son Eric. The first appearance of the Monarch car was in late 1912 when production started at the Kings Road works in Tyseley.

The car was a light, two seater with the engine, and the two-forward plus reverse gearbox, built as one unit. The engine assembly was built into a tubular sub-frame and mounted on leather pads held tightly by a coiled spring to dampen the vibration of the engine.

The body was carried by a second frame with springing at front and back. The rear axle was also mounted on the subframe with power transmitted to the live back axle by a drive shaft in a torque tube. The first models had single-cylinder engines but this was later changed to an air-cooled 8hp Precision engine in a car priced at 110 Guineas with a water cooled option available for an extra 10 Guineas.

Both options had the same two-seater body shell with a dummy radiator on the air cooled version. In January 1913 the company announced its intent to *'turn out this machine in greater numbers that has hitherto been possible'* but mass production failed to materialise in the face of competition from the myriad of other cyclecar manufacturers that were

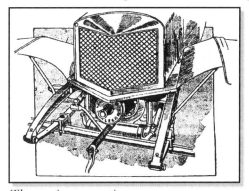

The engine mounting.

The assembled Monarch light car.

appearing in this period.

By 1914 the company was only using the car for promotion of its motor components and accessories business with no further intention of going back into full production, a promotional strategy also used by F E Baker (see **Precision**).

After the war the marque was revived for a range of motorcycles to be sold by Gamages, the London department store. None of the cars is known to have survived but the factory that produced them is still there in Kings Road, Tyseley.

R Walker and Sons aspirations to build cars didn't end with the Monarch. In 1922 they bought the Coventry firm of Bayliss-Thomas (see **Bayliss-Thomas**) and went into production again.

Reginald Walker died in Solihull in 1958

Hampton

The Hampton Engineering Company Ltd., Lifford Mills, Kings Norton, B'ham.
1912-1918

William Paddon had a business selling and repairing Standard, Arrol-Johnson and Benz cars but had an ambition to manufacture British Cars to his own designs.

In 1912 Albert Crowdy's car company (see **Crowdy**) failed and its assets were bought by a new company registered in December 1913 as the Hampton Engineering Company Ltd. The backers of the company were Arthur Wright, Ralph Ward, Lewis Radmore and William Miller.

Arthur Octavius Wright was born in Aston in 1868 and worked as a manager in a lamp manufacturing business before joining Ralph Ward in business as merchants dealing in trade with Australia. Lewis Radmore was born in Egg Buckland, Devon in 1883 the son of Lewis and Mary Radmore. He trained as a merchant's clerk trading in goods from West

William Paddon.

Central Africa and worked with William Percival Miller, his brother-in-law at WH Simpson and Sons, corn merchants and seedsmen in Broad Street.

These four entrepreneurs installed Arthur Wright, Lewis Radmore and Charles Apperley of Stroud as the company's directors. William Paddon managed the company, setting up operations at Lifford Mills in Kings Norton, a large old building that had previously been used for ebonite manufacture. Ebonite was a very hard rubber produced by vulcanizing rubber for a long period. Prior to plastics being invented it was used in many articles notably battery cases which, though usually plastic, are still traditionally black, an echo of their ebonite origins.

Initially he continued production of the Crowdy 12-14 car but replaced the engine with a larger one of 1726cc and rebadged it the Hampton 12-16. The 12-16 sold for £295 and was fitted with a four-cylinder Chapuis-Dornier engine, made in France to a monobloc design. The three-speed and reverse gearbox was built by E G Wrigley (see **Wrigley**) that drove through a leather-faced clutch to a bevel gear on the rear axle. The car had a 9ft wheelbase and a track of 51in. that could be supplied at 56in for use in the colonial market that the car was aimed at. The coachwork was, reportedly, of high quality with the door panels and trims being inlaid with mahogany.

Paddon added an 8hp cyclecar of his own design to the range in 1913 in response to the cyclecar boom. This car had a two-stroke, two-cylinder engine that probably never made it into the final production car. In 1914 he added the Hampton 10hp with its 1244cc water-cooled engine and shaft drive to the range. At this time Paddon, who was a keen motor sports

The 1914 two-seater Hampton.

enthusiast, made a number of ascents of the Nailsworth Ladder, a particularly steep public road near Stroud that is no longer open.

In November 1915 Arthur Wright and Ralph Ward who had a general merchant business together in London called Tulloch and Co went bankrupt, and circumstances at their car making venture were no better.

After the war the company made only one car, the Hampton 11.9hp with the choice of either a 1496cc or 1795cc Dorman four-cylinder engine, but the financial situation was becoming worse and the company was restructured in 1919 as a joint venture between Paddon and Charles Apperley of the Stroud Metal and Plating Company relocating to Dudbridge, Stroud.

Finances were still difficult and the company was bought out by John Daniel, one of the major shareholders, and re-christened the Hampton Engineering Company (1920) Ltd.

William Paddon left the company and joined the Autocrat company in Balsall Heath. (see **Autocrat**).

There are no known surviving examples of the Hampton cars that were built in Birmingham and the premises, Lifford Mills in Kings Norton, no longer exist.

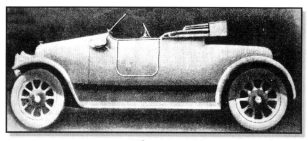

The 1914 Hampton Light car.

The Light car chassis.

Ascending the Nailsworth Ladder.

Car Accessories.

Henry Waterson had premises in Albert Street, Aston and regularly advertised his wares in journals and at trade shows. He dealt in car accessories, but with such a wide range that he could probably have progressed to car manufacture without too much effort.

At a show in 1899 he had two car bodies on show, one *'prettily finished in vermilion and black, lined white'* with nickel plated rails and covered spring cushions. The whole was carried on elliptical springs at the front and c-shaped springs at the back and, taken together with the accumulators, steering wheels, pinions, lubricators, horns, springs and petrol tanks, etc. that he had on display, all he needed was an engine and he could have completed the job.

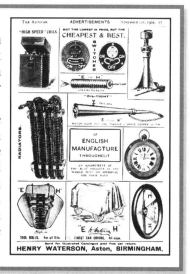

New Hudson

The New Hudson Cycle Co. Ltd., Parade Mills, Sandpits, Birmingham.
1912-1924

Edward Arthur Wilson started as a cycle manufacturer in the 1890s, trading as the New Hudson Cycle Extension Company in partnership with George Frederick Patterson from Birmingham.

Cycle production first started at the Priory Works of Joseph Harrison and Son in Alcester, near to Wilson's home at Bell Court in Bidford on Avon. The works had previously been used for needle production, a major industry in Alcester at the time, but were turned to cycle production in 1890. The partnership with George Patterson, who was involved in the sales side of the business, continued until 1896 when it was dissolved and Pattersons Company was merged with Wilson's to form the New Hudson Cycle Company Ltd. In 1899 Joseph Harrison and Sons, with Edward Wilson as the chairman, was wound up and cycle making transferred to Summer Hill in Birmingham.

The New Hudson.

Wilson had a network of business contacts that allowed him to sell his cycles through a number of dealerships in which he had an interest. Charles Dimmock and Co in Olney and Lloyd Cooper and Co of Watford were both part owned by Wilson but were sold off in 1901 and 1905 as New Hudson went from cycle to motorcycle manufacture. At about this time the company took over the New Revolution Cycle Company (see **Revolette**) in Liverpool Street whose site was then taken over by Lanchester for their Alpha Works. (see **Lanchester**).

New Hudson's first foray into car manufacturing was their four-wheeled cyclecar of 1912.

The Icknield Street Works.

An early entrant into the cyclecar market, it had two-seats, a shape reminiscent of a shoe and was sold for £85. Its 5hp engine was built by New Hudson and was fitted with a decompressor. The three speed gearbox was connected via a multi -plate clutch and had a chain drive transmitting drive to the live axle complete with differential. It had internal expanding brakes, 26 x 21/2 inch wheels and extra-heavy studded Dunlop tyres. Advertised as having the luxury of a motor car at motorcycle costs, to give an idea of performance, it was claimed to have driven up Sun Rising Hill with two passengers on board and power to spare! (see **Midland Auto Club**)

After WWI the company once more diversified from its core business of motorcycle manufacture into car building with a three-wheeled offering. Its return to the market was in December 1920 when the New Hudson Three Wheeler first appeared at the Cycle and Motor Show at Olympia. The vehicle cost £250 and had a 1200cc air-cooled v-twin engine with the cylinders set at 50 degrees to each other. The cam shaft engaged with the starting

handle at the front and a Lucas Magdyno at the back. The crankshaft had two cast aluminium arms to allow the engine to be fixed directly to the pressed steel frame. The cam shaft and pistons were lubricated by a drip-feed system from a one gallon oil tank fitted alongside the five gallon petrol tank behind the dash, under the bonnet. A single plate Ferodo-lined clutch drove a three-speed gearbox via an open shaft. The single rear wheel had full cantilever suspension and the front springs were quarter-elliptic. Both foot and hand brake operated on the rear wheel via Bowden brake cables. The rack and pinion steering was housed within the U-section cross-member at the front of the chassis giving it some protection from road dirt. A small locker containing tools was provided in the rear and a section of the rear hinged up to allow access to the rear wheel assembly.

Whereas the earlier car was built at the Parade Mills Works on Sand Pits at about the point where Summer Hill Street now joins it, the Three Wheeler was built at

1921 New Hudson chassis.

the company's Icknield Street Works.

Of the two works only the Icknield Street building still survives, having been used for many years for the production of Swan electric kettles. Of the cars produced, only one survives.

With trade becoming difficult, the business was acquired by H J Brueton in the twenties. Horace Joyner Brueton was born in 1882 in Birmingham and was brought up in the family's tobacconists shop in Broad Street by his parents Thomas, from Darlaston and Frances from West Bromwich. He was a successful bookmaker and developer who went on to be an Alderman of Solihull donating Brueton Park to the town in 1944. He was also another person to find his way into legal case law with 'Brueton v Woodward' defining the position on contracts as they relate to gambling.

Brueton had a workshop foreman called Alec Fraser who read an article in The Motor about a new braking system that was looking for a buyer. In 1929 the company acquired the patent for Girling Brakes from Albert Girling allowing Girling to pursue his business interests in the global market for postal franking machines.

The company supplied brake systems to Ford, Riley, Rover and Austin whilst still building

motorcycles but production of those stopped in 1933. In 1940 manufacture of motorcycles resumed with the autocycle which continued after a takeover by BSA but finally came to an end in 1958.

George Patterson died 10th September 1928. Horace Joyner Brueton died on the 5th July 1950.

The 1921 New Hudson.

Walcycar/Wall-Car/Wallycar

The Walcycar Company, Forest Road, Hay Mills, Yardley, Birmingham.

1913

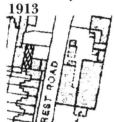

The Walcycar Company operated from premises in Forest Road, Yardley, near to the Coventry Road. The Company was owned by Arthur Wall who had also produced Roc cars and motorcycles and the Wall Tricar before parting company with the business that bore his name (see **Wall**).

Unlike the usual two and three-wheeled output of the A W Wall company the Walcycar had four wheels. The car had an 8hp twin cylinder air cooled JAP engine with a bore and stroke of 85mm, a two speed gearbox and a live rear axle. The frame was fabricated of pressed steel channel and it had both lever operated band and foot operated transmission brakes.

The advert for the car took the form of an allegorical cartoon describing the elopement of 'Wall' and 'Bessie' and the pacifying of her angry father by promising to build him a car. One can only wonder what was going on inside his head.

The works in Forest Road were only in use by Walcycar for just over a year before being taken over by Burgess and Garfield, motor engineers, in 1914. The building hasn't survived and neither have any examples of the Walcycar - or Wall-Car - or Wallycar.

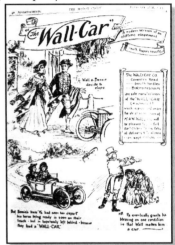

An allegorical advert.

Arthur Wall continued working on refinements to petrol engines, in collaboration with John White Jnr. (born in 1871, a city councillor and 'contractor' from Handsworth), until the mid-twenties. However, his car building days were behind him and the only thing he was producing were a string of patents.

The Walcycar.

Financial Backing

The degree of separation between the practical and financial parts of the motor companies varied widely.

In the smaller concerns, the aspiring motor car manufacturer was the engineer of the vehicle, which was fine whilst development work took place, usually side-by-side with the 'bread and butter' work, but when the time came to scale-up production financial backing was needed. These backers were sometimes intimately involved in the business but, more often, they were only there to provide the backing and had little interest beyond a return on their capital.

Even the largest manufacturers started from humble beginnings and, as 'Companies' turned into 'Limited Companies' tensions between the founders and the Board of Directors put in place to oversee the interests of the shareholders could grow. This could result in the original entrepreneur 'jumping ship' to start again as with Herbert Austin and Wolseley. In extreme cases they would leave their name behind, attached to a business in which they no longer had a direct interest.

Sherwood

Sherwood Brothers, Geraldine Road, Yardley, Birmingham.
1913

The Sherwood brothers made a brief excursion into car building just before the First World War.

Raymond Sherwood was a police officer who raised his family in a police force house in Frankfort Street, Hockley. He had two sons with his wife Sarah; Allen in 1877 and Albert Edward in 1879. Allen became a worker of German Silver, (a metal that was not actually silver but rather an alloy of copper and zinc that was popular for plates and bowls), and Albert became a cycle builder. In 1913 the two brothers went into business together as Sherwood Brothers. They acquired premises in Geraldine Road, Yardley from Arthur W Burgess who had also previously engaged in car building and aimed to produce their own cars.

As with all the other pre-war cyclecar manufacturers the business didn't survive the war years. The toll that the war took on the workforce was immense as was the financial pressure in an economy more geared to war production and thrift. The company, then with Albert and his wife Nellie as the directors, finally wound up in 1917. Remarkably their workshop still survives in the shadow of the Holiday Inn Express on the Coventry Road. Unfortunately there are no known, surviving cars and neither, apparently were any of their cars photographed.

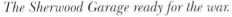

The Sherwood Garage ready for the war.

The workshop today.

Premises

A common feature of the early motor industry was the take-up of premises from previous motor building ventures that had proved their suitability. There are a number of examples of this in Birmingham.

The works on the corner of Dartmouth Street and Aston Road played host to five marques starting with Alexandra in 1905 then Premier/PMC/Motorette between 1906 and 1919. Whilst, in 1907, A W Wall produced some early vehicles there.

157 Clifton Road Aston played host to Maxfield from 1905 to 1914 and Barclay in 1933 and the pram works in Bath Passage were used by Leon L'Hollier till 1908 and then by Thomas McKenzie.

Brocklebank shared premises with Morris Commercial, Wolseley took over the Stellite Works in Drews Lane, Ward End from their stablemates at Vickers, the Electric and Ordnance Accessories Company. Lanchester's Alpha Works were where the Revolette was originally produced and the Roseberry Building in John Bright Street housed both 'Heron', 'Mobile' and P J Evans' showroom.

JAR

J A Ryley, Martineau Street, Birmingham.
1913

Riley is a well-known Coventry marque, but what we have here is the lesser-known 'Ryley' from Birmingham, spelt with a 'y', that had a short life manufacturing cars pre-WWI.

John Albert Ryley was born on a farm in Allesley near Coventry in January 1861. His father, a farmer of 57 acres near to where the Jaguar factory was later to stand, had descended from a family of watchmakers, a trade for which Coventry was well known. The family was wealthy and had investments in, amongst others, the Coventry Union Banking Co. In 1825 John Albert's grandfather had inherited £31000 (worth nearly £25million today) and so John, his brother and two sisters were worth a great deal of money.

In 1900 John Ryley formed Ryley, Ward and Bradford cars. They experimented with a light car called the 'Ryley Voiturette', that first appeared in 1901 with a 2.75hp, single-cylinder engine, later changed to a 5hp Aster engine, and disappeared by 1905 leaving Ryley with huge debts.

Ryley still had car making aspirations and set up a business in Birmingham to that end. He had one employee, his daughter Ethel, aged 16.

The car he produced was a two-seater called the

The 1913 Ryley.

JAR which had either a JAP or Precision air-cooled v-twin engine with chain drive to the two-speed gearbox and then a belt drive to pulleys on the rear axle. The car went the way of all cyclecars and was out of production within a year. The business, however, was highly successful and grew to become one of the major Midlands car parts suppliers until the 1960s, though the company itself was dissolved as late as 1996.

John Ryley died in Moseley on 30 December 1931 leaving the business to his son. His daughter Ethel married Thomas Gerald St Johnston and had a son, Eric, who went on to Cambridge University and, at the tender age of 29, became Chief Constable of the Oxford Constabulary. During his professional career he became technical advisor on Z-cars and introduced the 'Panda Car', which was coloured pale blue - his university's colour.

The Birmingham/Coventry Axis

There was an ongoing free flow of expertise and personnel between Birmingham and Coventry throughout the pre-war period at all levels.

Coventry was a centre of the car industry with many famous marques originating there. This was a natural progression from cycle and motorcycle manufacture much as it was in Birmingham. But many of the components, tubes and accessories came from Birmingham which, for centuries, had been an industrial centre on a scale that dwarfed Coventry.

It has been estimated that in 1929 as many as 27,000 workers were commuting into Coventry, most of them from Birmingham and it was not unusual for a car marque to be based in one city and then move to the other as ownership changed.

Coventry often took the lead attracting families like the Pughs and Pilkingtons who had started in business in Birmingham. Much of this was to do with timing; as one city would capitalise on a business, the other would gain the capacity to take over the next. What started in Coventry would often be passed on to Birmingham - and vice versa.

Wrigley

**E G Wrigley and Company Ltd., Foundry Lane, Soho, Birmingham.
1913**

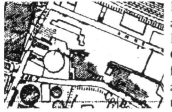

EG Wrigley were a major component manufacturer that made a brief excursion into car manufacturing.

Edward Greenwood Wrigley was born in Ashton-on-Mersey, Cheshire in 1868 the son of a wheelwright. He initially studied for the medical profession but, failing at this, he trained as a mechanical engineering draughtsman taking a position at the Tangye Cornwall Works in the early 1890s and, by 1896, had progressed to Chief Draughtsman.

He aspired to his own company and, in 1899, set himself up in business as a tool maker with a workshop at 232 Aston Road. The business was very successful and, in 1902, he moved into purpose built premises in Foundry Lane Soho, a short distance from the Tangye Works and over the road from the site of Matthew Boulton's Soho Manufactory, now occupied by Avery. His company made an extensive range of motor parts and specialised in axles and gearboxes. These found their way into a large number of cars, railway locomotives and tanks and financed an expansion of the works across Hockley Brook and along Anne Road. Though not badged as their products, a number of cars were designed and part manufactured, using the new flow production techniques developed there by Frank Woolard, under other marques but, in 1913, the lure of the cyclecar boom resulted in the production of cyclecars under their own name.

The E G Wrigley works in 2012.

The car had a 9.5hp V-twin engine available in either air or water cooled options. It had a two speed gearbox and an integral worm-drive rear transaxle. Steering was rack and pinion and the overall weight of the car was 5cwt. As was the usual case, the War curtailed their car building aspirations and the factory turned to war work, expanding massively in the process. In 1919 the company became involved with the ill-fated Angus-Sanderson car project in County Durham and over the next four years its losses mounted.

Despite announcing plans to produce two new motor car engines and starting to carry out development work, the company's financial problems became insurmountable and it went into receivership at the end of 1923. In 1924 the factory was acquired by Morris Commercial Cars Ltd for the production of commercial vehicles and specialist cars (see **Morris Commercial**).

What is now left of the factory stands derelict on Foundry Lane and is under constant threat of demolition.

The man that started the company, Edward Wrigley was forced to retire due to ill health in 1910 and moved to the Isle of Man to become a market gardener. He died at his home there in 1941.

The EG Wrigley Drawing Office.

Transmission Assembly.

Precision

F E Baker, 90 Moorsom Street, Birmingham.
1913

Companies formed to manufacture components were swept up by the cyclecar boom. Both Blumfield (see **Blumfield**) and Precision were engine makers first and foremost, but the temptation to compete with their own customer-base was too great.

Frank Edward Baker was born in Aston in 1883 the son of John and Emily Baker, a gun action filer and his wife. He worked for a time with Albert Eadie in Redditch (see **Enfield**) and, by 1904 had become the Works Manager at Premier Cycles in Coventry before setting up a company, in 1906, to manufacture cycle fittings under the 'Precision' name.

In 1910 he started building motorcycle engines at his 'Precision Works' in Moorsom Street, Aston and developed a strong demand for them after exhibiting at the trade shows. They were so popular amongst motorcycle manufacturers that he became a wholesaler

An advert from 1913.

and would often build engines to be sold under other brand names.

In an effort to expand his range he developed engines suitable for the cyclecar trade and, in 1913, built a car to demonstrate them.

A two-seater with a 'sociable' or side-by-side arrangement, the car was intended for test and demonstration purposes but the temptation to enter the marketplace could have won out but for the interruption of the War. Indeed, he had been building complete motorcycles since 1912 and, after the War, the company started to produce a new range of motorcycles following an injection of capital from the Scottish industrialist, William Beardmore who himself went on to produce cars from 1919. The level of involvement that Baker would have had is unknown but the engines at least could have been Precision.

During this period Baker was joined by Theodore James Biggs who had worked for Humber, Sunbeam and Raleigh previously and they collaborated on a number of motorcycle patents together.

The motorcycles that came from the new 'Precision Works' in Wychall Lane, Kings Norton were known as 'Beardmore-Precision' machines and the company had some success in races and trials but, during the early twenties, sales fell away and Beardmore pulled out of the partnership.

Following the separation Frank Baker went back into business in his own right, but in 1930 sold out to the James Cycle Company in Greet. He died in January 1941 in Birmingham.

There are examples of his engines and motorcycles still in use but the prototype cyclecar has not survived.

The Moorsom Street premises have been demolished and replaced by more recent industrial units.

The Precision Cyclecar.

Rolfe

Rolfe Manufacturing Company, Bridge Street, Smethwick, Birmingham. 1913

Many of the car manufacturers in Birmingham sprang from the cycle industry but few companies were bigger than the one that in 1913, briefly, produced a cyclecar called the 'Rolfe'.

The original 'Rolfe Manufacturing Company' was set up in 1911 by John Clarke, an engineer from Wolverhampton and Charles Edward Alcock, an accountant's clerk who lived on the Moseley Road. In 1913, the company was bought out by J A Phillips and Company who became one of the biggest cyclemakers in the country, second only to Raleigh, in the early part of the last century.

J A Phillips was formed by John Phillips, Ernest Bohle and Henry Church. The company was named for John Alfred Phillips who was born in Coventry in 1876 the son of a commission agent named Henry Phillips and his wife Sarah. He was joined by Ernest Wilhelm Bohle, who was born in Germany in 1872 and, as a consequence, was required to swear an Oath of Allegiance in September 1908 as the clouds of war gathered.

The third director was Henry Charles Church, the son of the Publican who ran the long-defunct Crown and Anchor in the equally long-defunct Jennens Row in Birmingham City Centre. Born in 1871 into an Anglo-French household he was the toolmaker of the trio and the longest-lasting member of the Company.

They had acquired premises at 77 Bath Street in 1896 a few doors away from The Abingdon Works (see **Abingdon King Dick**) and manufactured cycle accessories. The business expanded and, over the next 14 years they took over the cycle tyre company that shared their premises followed by the electroplaters next door at No. 75 and, finally, the gun makers at No. 74. In 1908 they looked to Smethwick for the much bigger premises that the tightly packed workshops in the Gun Quarter could not offer.

The Credenda Works were built as a plate glass manufacturing facility and were taken over by the Credenda Seamless Tube Company. J A Phillips and Co established themselves there and, by 1913, had vacated the Birmingham premises.

In December 1913, with the purchase of the Rolfe Manufacturing Company, they started producing motorcycles with both single-cylinder and V-twin engines, continuing production until 1914.

In 1913 they produced a cyclecar from the Credenda Works in Bridge Street but, as with so many other companies they had the facilities and capacity but the timing was bad and the war stopped production.

They built cycles and accessories from this base with a workforce numbering 2000 until 1919 when they were swallowed by Tube Investments as were Simplex, Accles and Pollock and Reynolds Tube.

The works lent their name to the 'Creda' washing machines, produced by one of Tube Investments' group of companies, but the buildings no longer exist. None of their cars is known to survive.

A contemporary advert.

Edwards

J L Edwards, 313 Franklin Road, Kings Norton, Birmingham.
1913

The Cyclecar craze prompted many enthusiastic amateurs to try their hand at car manufacture; one such amateur was Leslie Edwards.

James Leslie Edwards was born in 1881 in New End Lane, Kings Norton the son of Samuel Willets Edwards, a Farm Bailiff and his wife Harriet. He would have been expected to take a job in agriculture but instead he trained as a fitter and tool setter.

He was inventive and produced patents for such things as cycle stands and in-line skates in the early years of the last century.

In 1913, whilst living at 288 Franklin Road, Kings Norton, he turned his attention to building a cyclecar that could go into production. He actually produced two distinct versions of his car and called them the 'Brooklands' and the 'Traveller' models.

They were both powered by one of the new 8-10hp Precision engines and had a novel transmission designed to overcome the problem encountered in many cyclecars with friction drive, as was this, of the friction wheel flying to the edge of the disc. The drive comprised a leather faced cone clutch transmitting power by a shaft to a friction disc that made contact with a friction wheel fixed to the countershaft. The countershaft had pulleys to drive chains that drove the rear axle. The friction wheel was allowed to slip along the keyed shaft and was held against the friction disc using spring loaded thrust bearings. When changing gear a floor pedal would simultaneously disengage the clutch and relieve the pressure between the friction discs allowing them to part. The whole of the drive train was enclosed in a watertight space to protect it from the elements and road-dirt. A

The Edwards Cyclecar.   *A front view.*

distinctive feature of the car was the bonnet which incorporated two air scoops not unlike nostrils that drew air into the bonnet to air-cool the engine. The air was then passed underneath the car. The Touring model had a scuttle dash that was less deep than that of the Brooklands model and also had a side door to allow easier access. Both models sold for the same price - £95.

The car probably suffered the same fate as the many other cyclecars launched just before the war and Leslie Edwards continued to produce engineering patents related to the motor industry, joining forces with Alfred George Hackett, an engineer and draughtsman from Harborne, to register patents by the late thirties. He died in Birmingham in 1961 aged 80. There are no surviving vehicles and the location of the workshop is unknown, though probably in the back garden of his home in Franklin Road where the gardens are of an impressive length.

Hoskison

Hoskison Ltd., 95 Aston Road North, Birmingham.
1913

Hoskison was a marque that made a brief appearance in 1913 during the cyclecar craze and re-established itself after the war as a motorcycle company.

The company was based in Aston and was a collaborative venture between Harry Hoskinson, his brother Samuel, John Wathen and his brother William.

Harry, born in 1878 was a coachbuilder and Samuel, trained as a joiner, probably assisted his brother. They were born in Newhall, Burton on Trent to Henry Hoskison who was, at various times, a coal miner, grocer and publican of the Red Lion Inn in Newhall on the north-west side of Swadlincote.

They both lived as near neighbours in George Road, Erdington in 1913 and teamed up with the Wathen brothers to venture into cyclecar making.

William Henry Wathen, a toolmaker was born in 1872 and John Cornelius Wathen, a die-sinker, in 1876 to John and Annie Wathen in Birmingham. Their father was a die-sinker and ran a business with them, 'John Wathen and Sons' at 120 Barford Street Birmingham. The brothers patented a number of improvements to carriage lamps and other items of metalware in the late 1890s and early 1900s and, in 1912/13, the Wathens also turned their attention to motor vehicles.

1912 saw William registering a patent for gear cases and, in 1913, his father John patented a method of constructing a body 'suitable for Side-Cars, Cycle Cars, Motor Cars and the like'.

Unfortunately no photographs or artefacts from the Hoskisons and Wathens pre-war car building activities have survived but their motorcycle company which had appeared in 1919 as the Hoskison Manufacturing Company is better recorded.

This venture was based in Digbeth and produced lightweight motorcycles with a 292cc Union engine,

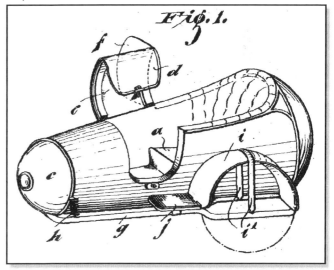

From Wathen's 1913 patent sidecar design.

two-speed Burman gearbox, chain and then belt drive to the rear wheel. They anticipated producing 2000 machines a year and were in production through 1920 and 1921. In 1921 they moved operations to Lozells Road and increased the size of the bikes. They produced two models with 348cc and 499cc engines again with Burman two-speed gearboxes and also offered a version fitted with a sidecar, echoing their pre-war cyclecar production. In 1921 Harry Hoskison died in Kings Norton and, by 1922 the company had disappeared and the remaining participants had moved onto other things.

In the case of Samuel Hoskison and John Cornelius Wathen this was tea. They set up the 'British Ceylon Tea Company' and traded as tea merchants from premises at 39 Carrs Lane. The partnership was dissolved when John retired in 1933 leaving Samuel to go it alone. John Wathen died three years later and Samuel Hoskison died in Solihull in 1942. Neither the premises or any of the cars have survived.

Carter

The Carter Car Company, 215 Bristol Road, Selly Oak, Birmingham.
1913-1914

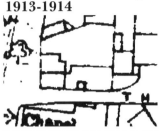

1913 was a very popular year to start light car and cycle car production with no fewer than nineteen new companies appearing, many of which only lasted the year as, with massively bad timing, Europe slid into the First World War.

Carter was one of these optimistic newcomers. Birmingham and Coventry had been major centres of cycle manufacture in the last decades of the 1800s, but they were not alone.

In 1883, in Stratford upon Avon, four men, David Carter, Edward and Thomas Birch and Stephen Barnard entered into a co-partnership deed to set up a bicycle manufacturing business. They took premises at 40 Guild Street in the town and David Carter oversaw manufacturing and training of local lads as apprentices. As the business expanded, they took on the neighbouring premises to house both the business and his wife Hannah and eight children.

The slump in the cycle industry took hold in the 1890s, the business collapsed and David Carter, a talented engineer, moved to Kings Norton to make a living building gas, oil and steam engines.

The draw of Birmingham as a major industrial centre proved irresistible and the business moved to premises at 215 Bristol Road on the corner of 'The Dingle' previously occupied by a

The Carter Cyclecar.

coal merchant and handy for the local fire station as it stood next door. It was here that he put his talents with cycle building and engine design together and worked on producing a cyclecar.

The cyclecar that he created was small and lightweight and, rather than the usual single or two cylinder engines found on typical vehicles of this type, it had a small four cylinder engine capable of producing 6.2hp, probably good enough for a cyclecar but not great.

The cyclecar was becoming very popular but the market was saturated with new companies and few would stay the course. Carter was not one of them and by the time WWI started David Carter had turned to car repair, though not before producing another, rather odd-looking car; this time a three-wheeler with a twin, air-cooled engine and belt drive. The premises have gone but if you venture down The Dingle you can still see the outline of the old fire station with its stables for the horses and the back wall of the workshop.

The Carter Four-Wheeler.

The Carter Three-Wheeler.

Armstrong

The Armstrong Motor Company, 8 and 14 Ryland Street, Birmingham. 1913-1914

Samuel Mills was a brassfounder with premises in Ryland Street and a staff of twenty. What he didn't have was any offspring to leave the business to, so when the time came, he handed the business over to his nephew Franklin Davies and his clerk Frederick Leggatt born in Chichester in 1844.

The company turned to manufacturing the ironwork for carriages and continued to operate from those same premises, with their foundry tucked into the middle of the block behind the buildings fronting onto Broad Street. In 1903, with Davies and Leggatt both approaching sixty years of age, the partnership was dissolved and Frederick William Leggatt continued to run the business 'S Mills and Co.' carriage brass founders.

In 1913 Frederick and his son, Franklin Warrenne Leggatt born in 1883, joined the fray in the race to build cyclecars forming the Armstrong Motor Company operating from Ryland Street in the original works and some adjacent works that had previously been occupied by J J Dobbs and Company, coach ironmongers.

The Armstrong.

Their first car appeared in 1913, a two-speed model that was soon replaced by an altogether more refined model in January 1914.

The car that they produced had an 8hp Precision engine with a choice of either air or water cooling and a friction drive composed of a driving disc attached to the drive shaft which also acted as a flywheel, and a driven disc mounted on a shaft which could be swung from one end. The clutch was effected by separating the discs by swinging the shaft around. Apparently this arrangement worked well, giving a greater clutch pressure on the lower gears and avoiding slipping.

Lubrication was by a Best and Lloyd drip system from a small oil tank in the scuttle. A countershaft with large pulleys drove the rear wheels via v-belts. Braking was by rim brakes on the rear belt pulleys augmented by a foot pedal operated external contracting brake acting on a drum on the countershaft. The car was marketed for 90 guineas complete with hood and screen and for an extra 10 guineas a chain drive and live axle could be substituted for the belt drive.

The car's production was halted by WWI, as were so many in this period and none of the cars have survived.

S. Mills and Co continued in existence after the war producing brass and aluminium motor sections and later in the thirties moved to new premises in Sycamore Road, Handsworth. The original premises in which the vehicles were produced no longer exist.

The engine and friction gearing.

Melen

F and H Melen, Express Works, Cheapside, Birmingham.
1913-1914

George Frederick Melen and Henry Corfield Melen were brothers, born in Redditch in 1868 and 1870. Their father, George, was a Maltster and an ale and porter agent for Allsop and Sons of Burton upon Trent. The elder brother, George, was an estate agent but, in a parallel career, he went into business with his brother Henry truck making in Cotteridge Road in Kings Norton in the early 1900s.

By 1912 George had moved his Estate Agency to Newton Chambers in Cannon Street and the brothers' business had moved to premises in Deritend to manufacture motorcycles.

They exhibited their first machine, a motorcycle and sidecar combination, at the Olympia Motor Show in 1912. This was fitted with a 6hp JAP V-twin engine, two speed gearbox and a belt drive and had a wicker sidecar. After a year they decided to branch into car building and experimented with an air cooled light car but eventually developed a car with a 9hp Aster two cylinder, water cooled engine.

They continued with production of their light cars from the Express Works on the corner of Cheapside and Sherlock Street (later demolished to make way for the Wholesale Markets), and by 1917 were producing about 145 cars per year.

Next door to the Express Works in Cheapside were the Arden Works of Thomson-Bennett, Magneto Manufacturers.

Peter Frederick Blaker Bennett, later Lord Bennett, who ran this company went on to become joint managing director of Joseph Lucas Ltd. When the First World War broke out Thomson-Bennett were the only manufacturers of magnetos in the country as they tended to be imported from the continent. The role they played in keeping vehicles on the road and aircraft in the air in the early months of the war was pivotal.

George Melen was the business man and Henry the technical expert so, when Henry died in March 1926, George had to restructure the company and renamed it Melen Ltd. In Henry's will he left £19,424 to his widow, Ethel and his brother, equivalent to over £3.5million today, and this enabled George to acquire a new factory in Sydenham Road, Small Heath next to the Alldays and Onions Works (see **Alldays and Onions**). It was at this time that George went into partnership with George Fisher, a fellow Estate Agent, to produce motorised three wheeled delivery cycles. In February 1939 George died leaving £35,711 to Enid Williams, described as a 'married woman' and George Fisher, his business partner. This is equivalent to over £6million today.

George Fisher carried on in business as an Estate Agent and the company he founded, Fishers, is still in existence today managing and letting property in the city.

An advert for the Melen.

The Melen.

Merlin

The New Merlin Cycle Co., Edgbaston and Balsall Heath, Birmingham.
1913-1914

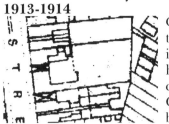

On Christmas Eve in 1801, a vehicle that lays claim to being the world's first successful, self-propelled, passenger-carrying vehicle made its way up Camborne Hill in Cornwall. It had been built by a local man, Richard Trevithick, who had christened it the 'Puffing Devil'.

Camborne had the character of a frontier mining town because rich seams of tin and copper were being worked and the town had expanded rapidly until it was a mass of drunken, brawling, lawless miners. The Rogers family lived in this town; all the men in the family were tin miners and the women either worked in Bickford's safety fuse factory or to support the men, so it was no surprise that, when the opportunity came, they made their escape.

Joseph Ivy Rogers headed for Utah in the States and the life of a Mormon but, in the process, he deserted his baby son, William, who was left behind in the care of his sister Elizabeth. Elizabeth married James Pope and they headed north to an area of the Black Country called 'French Walls'. The area was heavily industrialised with the Soho Foundry

nearby so work for James, a steam pump engineer, would be easy to find. James and Elizabeth didn't have any children of their own but they did have their nephew, William Ivy Rogers completing the family and so it remained until William met Ann and started his own family.

William moved around a great deal. He had a son, Telford Ivy Rogers, in Dudley Port in 1889, a daughter, Myrtle Ivy Rogers, in Smethwick in 1890 and his last child, Ivy Telford Rogers, in Wolverhampton in 1893.

He started off working as a turner on the lathes but soon turned his attention to the growing cycle business and started making cycles in a business partnership called the 'Merlin Cycle Company' with Mary Susannah Churchill from premises at 134 1/2 Great Charles Street.

The partnership was not to last, though, and it was dissolved

William Ivy Rogers.

Sam Cody.

in August 1891 leaving William to go it alone.

He formed a company called the 'New Merlin Cycle Company', the first of many cycle companies that he would control, and established himself in the growing business. He worked with George Hands at the Bard Cycle Company in Birmingham, (see **Calthorpe**), set up a manufacturing facility in Spon Street, Coventry and two more in Spencer Street and New Summer Street, Birmingham to manufacture the 'New Merlin' cycles and a sales outlet in Archway, London, with Philip Greville as manager. In 1897 he joined the Institute of Mechanical Engineers, moved his family to 'Calverley' in Boldmere Road, Sutton Coldfield and himself into offices in the newly built Coleridge Chambers next to the Victoria Law Courts. In 1898, the first of his businesses, the Collins Cycle Company, was wound up and the New Merlin Cycle Company found itself in danger of meeting the same fate.

In January 1898 the Cycle Engineers Institute was founded with William Ivy Rogers on the first committee alongside Charles

Garrard (see **Garrard-Blumfield**) and Charles Sangster (see **Ariel**). This organization was to grow into the Automobile and Cycle Engineers Institute with Herbert Austin (see **Austin**) heading later committees and still exists today in the form of the Motor Industry Research Association or MIRA.

William Rogers worked through his difficulties and continued to expand his business interests, moving his family to a house in Frederick Road, Stechford and forming new companies including the Coventry Frame Company in Union street, Coventry and the Balmoral Cycle Company Ltd in Bromsgrove Street, Birmingham.

Business was good so William was able to indulge in another of his interests - flying.

When the Midland Aero Club was founded in September 1909, William Ivy Rogers was the first Honorary Secretary and, in October 1909, he presented a paper to the Club entitled 'Impressions of a flight with Cody'. The Cody in question was Samuel Cody, a flamboyant American showman and pioneer aviator who had adopted Buffalo Bill Cody's name when he was younger. Samuel Cody developed large kites known as Cody War Kites that were deployed in WWI, worked on 'Nulli Secundus' the first British airship and made the first powered flight in Britain in the first British plane, the 'British Army Aeroplane Number 1', (also known as 'Cody's Cathedral') that he had built at Farnborough.

Merlin Components 1912.

Having twice crashed and modified this plane, the largest one in the world at the time, the third incarnation carried the country's first aircraft passenger, Colonel J E Capper, commander of the airship factory and on Monday 27th September 1909 William Ivy Rogers flew with Cody from Laffan's Plain.

In 1911 Ivy Rogers's companies were restructured with the Balmoral Cycle Company, which by this time had moved to Coventry, and the Coventry Frame Company being dissolved. The New Merlin Cycle Company, which had also by this time moved to Coventry, was moved again - to Edgbaston, where Ivy Rogers' first outing into car manufacture started. The New Merlin Cycle Company had premises at 3 Gough Road near to where the Woodview Primary School now stands, next to the Lee Bank Middleway. The Company started to manufacture components for cyclecars in 1912 at the beginning of the craze and made a name for themselves in the home-build market. This success extended to supplying other car makers and, in parallel, they started to develop cars to be marketed under the Autocrat name (see **Autocrat**).

The Merlin components business marketed parts, and by 1913 offered a complete rolling chassis with a 9hp two-cylinder water-cooled engine made by Thomas Blumfield, (see **Blumfield**), ready for bodywork to be fitted. There is one surviving known example of a Merlin car, in Australia, where many English built cars found their way.

Because of the cost of importing complete cars many vehicles were exported without bodies, a market that Merlin could readily access.

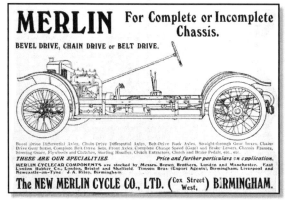

Merlin Rolling Chassis 1913.

Blumfield

Blumfield Ltd., 70 Lower Essex Street, Birmingham.
1913-1914

Blumfield Engine.

The Blumfield name was well known in Cyclecar circles as the manufacturer of engines aimed squarely at the cyclecar market which were fitted to the Crescent (see **Crescent**) and Merlin (see **Merlin**) cars. Thomas William Blumfield had a pedigree that meant that he was unlikely to resist joining-in when the craze for cyclecars took off.

He was born in Southampton in 1869 to Thomas Jonathan Blumfield and Dinah Blumfield (nee Double). Thomas senior was an iron and brass founder, who was born and lived in Ipswich and had, for a short time in the 1880s, been innkeeper of the Rose Inn there. Thomas was sent to Ipswich School, a boarding school founded in the fourteenth century, and when the time came for him to make his way in the world, he headed west to a job in the cycle industry in Coventry.

He teamed up with Charles Garrard and, when he married his wife Alice in 1894, became Garrard's brother-in-law. The two families lived near to each other in Acocks Green.

The two men went on to design and build the Garrard-Blumfield electric phaeton (see **Garrard-Blumfield**) using their contacts in the cycle industry to construct the car but by the end of the 1900s, had parted company to set up in business in their own right.

Thomas Blumfield established an engineering company in Clifton Road, Balsall Heath, Birmingham that produced its first motorcycle, powered by a Minerva engine, in 1903 and, by 1905, had also gone into production making cycles at premises on the Alcester Road.

In 1910 it was time to put his company on a firmer footing and get some serious financial backing. To this end he turned to an established family of Birmingham brewers.

The Blumfield works in Lower Essex Street today.

John Charles Holder founded his brewing company in 1872 in Nova Scotia Street on a site now occupied by the new Birmingham Ormiston Academy. The company was very successful and built up a large estate of public houses through which it sold its ales, including the Craven Arms in Upper Gough Street, the New Inns in Gravelly Lane, Erdington and the Selly Park Tavern all of which retain 'Holders' branding in their architectural features.

Sir John Holder, as he became, lived at 'Pitmaston' which used to stand between Highbury Park and Cannon

A Holders Advert.

Hill Park and had a keen interest in things mechanical being the proud owner of his own passenger-carrying, 10.25in. gauge miniature railway in the grounds of his house.

Three of Sir John's sons, Norman (see **Crescent**), Alfred and John, also had an interest in engineering and became Thomas Blumfield's co-directors and shareholders in 1910.

He started building motorcycles at his Lower Essex Street premises and this put him in a good position when the cyclecar craze started to supply an eager market with engines and other parts.

During this period many companies built prototype cyclecars and some went on to limited production before WWI brought things to a grinding halt.

There is record of at least one Blumfield cyclecar being registered in Dundee. It had an 8.9hp engine and weighed about 4cwt. Another five Blumfields were registered in Australia between 1914 to 1920 with the name of the last two anglicised to 'Bloomfield' because of anti-German sentiment in the country at the time, despite Thomas Blumfield's service during the First World War.

A number of his engines are still in use in surviving cyclecars and light cars but none of his own cyclecars have been positively identified, though there are 'unidentified' vehicles which could be candidates. In the early twenties Blumfield worked on patents for the Abingdon Works Limited (see **Abingdon King Dick**) in Tyseley and then, in collaboration with his son, issued a number of patents for improvements to engine design before leaving his son, Thomas Frederick Blumfield, to carry on the family business of engineering innovation alone.

'Pitmaston', or at least the Grade II listed building that replaced the original house, is now owned by the Church of Scientology. The premises at Lower Essex Street where much of his engine and motorcycle production took place are still there, now occupied by a firm of electrical engineers. Thomas Blumfield Snr. died in Birmingham in 1956 at the age of 87. Thomas Jnr. died in Solihull in 1987.

Beer and Cars

Thomas Blumfield was backed by the Holders Family, a family that had made its fortune brewing beer, but he was not the first. Charles Garrard (see **Garrard**), Blumfield's original partner and brother in law also gained backing for his manufacturing venture from a brewing family - the Showells.

At some time in their career a number of car makers found themselves serving behind a bar counter including Valentine Watkins (see **VAL**), Frank Taylor (see **Gerald**) and Minton Toddington (see **Alvechurch**). Still more were the offspring of licensed victuallers. Leonard Lord (see **Austin**) and Henry Charles Church (see **Rolfe**) were raised in public houses, as was Joseph Ashton Jarvis Evans (see **Ashton-Evans**).

The Melen brothers (see **Melen**) were the sons of a maltster and ale dealer.

VAL

The V.A.L. Motor Co. Ltd., 312-314 Bradford Street, Birmingham.
1913-1914

Some manufacturers tried to make their mark in one part of the car market, only to fail and try again in another. An example of this is V.A.L.

V.A.L were sidecar manufacturers, occupying premises next door to the Anchor public house in Bradford Street previously occupied by Rollo (see **Rollo**), that made a brief excursion into cyclecar production.

The company was founded out of the wreckage of the British Peerless company that had been wound up in the summer of 1913 (see **British Peerless**). The Chairman of British Peerless was Valentine Watkins, born in Aston in 1870, who also ran the St Martin's Hotel in Jamaica Row and it may be from his name that 'VAL' was derived.

The area had a number of significant early pioneers in the motor industry, notably Dunkleys (see **Dunkley**) whose premises were a few yards away in Bradford Street and Mill Lane and Anglo French (see **Anglo-French**), who were based just round the corner in Digbeth.

Production of the VAL started in 1913. It was powered by an 8.9hp water-cooled V-twin Precision engine with a separate friction drive and an asbestos lined cone clutch. A single pedal first operated the clutch and then separated the friction discs to avoid a flat spot being worn in the friction wheel.

The V.A.L. works today.

The engine was set transversely across the frame, in one unit with the clutch and gearbox, the whole being suspended at three points. The carburettor was initially operated by a Larkin hand control on the steering column, later replaced by a foot pedal and the ignition was provided by a Bosch magneto. The final drive from the transaxle to the rear axle was two enclosed roller chains and the brakes were of the expanding type within the hubs. The steering wheel's angle was adjustable and the suspension was by semi-elliptical springs.

The price of the vehicle, complete with hood, was £125. Unfortunately the engine was an outdated specification and the car did not sell well, so production ceased in 1914.

The building in which the VAL was built still stands in Bradford Street, next to the Anchor public house, a remarkable survivor in itself. There are no surviving examples of the cyclecar. Watkins died in 1955.

The V.A.L. engine.

Jennings

**The Jennings-Chalmers Light Car Co., Albert Works, Scholefield St., Birmingham.
1913-1915**

The Jennings-Chalmers Light Car Company was another short-lived car manufacturer that appeared in response to the cyclecar craze.

Their premises were the Albert Works in Scholefield Street in the Bloomsbury area of the city, between Aston and Nechells, a road that has now completely disappeared under green space and tower blocks. It is a very significant area because less than thirty feet away was the original works of the Forward Gas Engine Company that Frederick Lanchester joined and where he leased a workshop to start his experimentation with car design (see **Lanchester**). The Lanchester monument is sited in the green open space of Bloomsbury Village for this reason.

The company was formed by Arthur Jennings from Bromsgrove and Thomas Chalmers from Leith in Scotland. Thomas Edward Bain Chalmers was born in 1888 the son of Thomas Chalmers a grain merchant and Elizabeth Clark Bain. He studied at Edinburgh University and gained a B.Sc. in 1911 and in 1913 he became an associate of the Institute of Automobile Engineers.

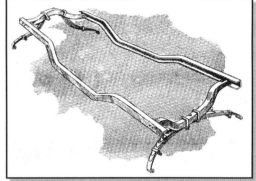

The Jennings chassis.

Arthur Jennings was a carpenter, born in 1885, the son of Herbert Jennings, who was also in the building trade. In 1910 he had teamed up with William Edwin Ward, another 'Bromsgrovian' to work on cycles and tricars but that was only the start of his ambitions.

The Jennings Light Car was designed to be dust and water tight from starting handle to back axle. This was achieved by bolting the gearbox directly to the crankcase and enclosing the universal joint within a spherical head on the torque tube. When first announced, the car was driven by a 90 degree twin-cylinder JAP engine which came through 'an extensive trial with pronounced success', but was replaced with a 1098cc two-cylinder 9hp Dorman unit when production started in earnest, connected to a three speed and reverse gearbox. It had a large diameter cone clutch and a bevel drive on the back axle. The car sold for 150 guineas complete with hood, screens, three lamps and toolkit. In 1915 an alternative four-cylinder 10hp engine became available at a total cost of 185 guineas.

The war started and the partnership was dissolved by mutual consent in July 1915.

Thomas Chalmers joined the Tank Corps in September 1915, attaining the rank of Captain. In 1918 he was decorated for conspicuous gallantry for saving tanks that had been ditched during an action and were under heavy hostile barrage. Arthur Jennings wasn't so lucky, he also served in the army but died, at home, in November 1918.

The Jennings.

Motorette

The Premier Motor Company, Aston Road, Birmingham.
1913-1915

The Motorette was another product of the Premier Motor Company in Aston (see **Premier**). The company had a chequered history of importing and badge-engineering cars from the continent but, occasionally, produced vehicles of their own manufacture.

Launched in 1913, the Motorette was built at the Company's works in Aston Road and bore more than a passing resemblance to its earlier PMC three-wheeler and to the A.C Sociable.

It was powered by a small, single cylinder, water-cooled engine with two, heavy, outside flywheels. The power was transmitted via a multi-disc clutch and two speed gearbox. Cooling radiators were positioned to either side of the engine. Steering was described by the Light Car and Cyclecar Magazine as 'interesting'.

Production of the Motorette continued up to the beginning of the First World War but it went the way of all Birmingham cyclecars and the company was wound up in the summer of 1915.

There are no known surviving examples.

The Motorette with hood up.   *The Motorette with hood down.*

Light Car and Cyclecar Magazine

With the interest in cyclecars, came publications to satisfy the public curiosity and keep them abreast of developments. The leading title was Light Car and Cyclecar Magazine, published weekly from December 1912 for a cover price of one penny, rising to 3d by 1934 when the 'cyclecar' was dropped from the title. The magazine continued as Light Car magazine until 1953 by which time it cost 1s 6d.

Published by Temple Press, who also published 'The Motor' from 1902 it championed the light car movement and is an invaluable source of information on early motoring. The editorial offices were in Burlington Chambers on New Street and, later, on the corner of New Street and Bennetts Hill.

Stellite

Electric and Ordnance Accessories Co. Ltd., Drews Lane, Birmingham.
1913-1919

Birmingham has had long association with the manufacture of arms and ammunition, and this is reflected in the history of some of the car marques, notably BSA (see **BSA**) and Accles-Turrell (see **Accles-Turrell**). Stellite is another marque that grew out of what was, and remains, an arms producer.

The story of the Stellite begins in Sheffield in 1776 when a firm called Naylor and Sanderson started producing steel. The daughter of the founder married a man by the name of Edward Vickers and he joined the business. The business grew and moved into steel casting, gaining a particular expertise in casting church bells.

Edward Vickers had made a great deal of money investing in the railways and was able to gain control of the company, bringing his sons into the business. The business continued to grow and diversify into many areas of heavy metal fabrication, moving into armaments manufacture in 1890 and purchasing the company that manufactured Maxim machine guns in 1896. The company now changed its name to Vickers Sons and Maxim. In 1901 Vickers bought the car making arm of the Wolseley Sheep Shearing Co and installed Herbert Austin as the manager of a new Company called the Wolseley Tool and Motor Car Company (see **Wolseley**). The

1914 Stellite.

Wolseley car brand was initiated and developed under Austin and, when he left to start his own company in 1905, it continued under the leadership of John Siddeley, producing cars that were aimed squarely at the top end of the market.

In the run-up to WWI the fashion for light cars was developing and Vickers wanted to take advantage of this market. They had made a brief excursion into car making in 1908 but their problem was much the same as Mercedes experienced with the Smart car; they

The Cheston Road, Aston Works.

didn't want their expensive brand tainted by association with a cheaper, mass market, vehicle, so they used a different marque for the 'lesser' cars. In this case the marque chosen was Stellite.

Their factory in Cheston Road, Aston was adapted in 1913 to produce this new range of light cars designed by Wolseley and they proved to be very popular. To cope with the demand a new factory was required. So Vickers, via its subsidiary The Electric and Ordnance Accessories Company Ltd, built one at Drews Lane in Ward End in 1914 that would allow the expansion of the Stellite brand and at the same time allow the production of armaments on a site away from the City centre in case of explosions!

The Ward End works covered an area of 65 acres by the time it was completed and included the distinctive administrative block fronting onto Drews Lane. During the war years the factory produced fuses and shell cases in workshops alongside its car production. The Stellite

Stellite Advertisement.

car had a wooden chassis, a four-cylinder engine built by Vickers with overhead inlet and side exhaust valves and a two speed gearbox powering the rear wheels via a cone clutch and worm final drive. The two speed gearbox was replaced with a three speed box later

The Works, shortly before demolition in 2011.

in 1914. The car had two seats with a third, rather precarious 'dickey' seat that folded out from the rear.

After WWI the company continued to produce Stellites but, in September 1919, the ownership of the factory was transferred by Vickers to the Wolseley Motor Company and production of the Stellite ceased. There were probably about 2500 Stellite cars produced of which five examples are still known to exist. One of these resides in the heritage Motor Centre at Gaydon. The factory in Ward End was, in more recent years, the base for Leyland DAF vans but, since that company failed in 2009, the buildings covering most of the site have been demolished. Only the offices fronting on to Drews Lane survived - until 2011.

The Drews Lane, Ward End Works.

Autocrat

The Autocrat Light Car Co., Edgbaston and Balsall Heath, Birmingham. 1913-1926

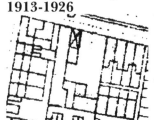

William Ivy Rogers had two companies producing cars; New Merlin (see **Merlin**), which catered to the cyclecar market producing components and rolling chassis, and Autocrat which produced complete cars.

The history of the two companies go hand in hand as they progressed from works in Gough Road, Edgbaston to Cox Street West in Balsall Heath and then to Edwards Road in Balsall Heath, the only one of their factory buildings to still survive. The last of their premises, which they held at the same time as Edwards Road, was in Spring Road, Hall Green.

William Ivy Rogers started producing cycles around 1890 and built up a large business around them. In 1911 the business hit trouble and the restructured New Merlin Cycle Company appeared in premises at the end of Gough Road alongside a new company, The

William Ivy Rogers (No 3).

Autocrat Light Car Company. His partners in both of these ventures were Joseph Theophilus Foster, born in 1863 in Birmingham and Ellen Elizabeth Anne Howell born in Aston in 1886.

The first Autocrat cars started to appear in 1913 and quickly prompted a move to new, more spacious, premises in Cox Street West which were reported to be '*very busy and being further extended*'.

There were two and four cylinder engine options available for 135 and 160 Guineas respectively and both versions featured a totally enclosed transmission.

They were designed to be a miniature car of Rolls Royce quality, being described as the 'Aristocrat of Light Cars'.

The two-cylinder model had a 9hp 1099cc engine and a multi-plate clutch connected via a tapered shaft with flexible couplings to a three-speed and

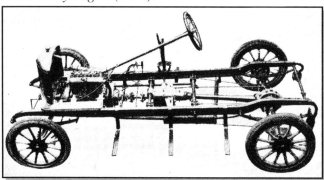

Chassis of the 1914 model Autocrat.

reverse gearbox. From the gearbox, drive was transmitted via a carden shaft enclosed in a torque tube to a bevel gear on the back axle.

The frame was of channel section steel with a sub-frame carrying the engine and gearbox. It had internal expanding and external contracting brakes operating on the back wheels and was suspended on four semi elliptical springs, the rear ones having shock absorbers. The bodywork was identical on both engine options having what was described as a 'sporting' design and finish with two seats.

Production of the car continued into the early part of WWI but, when the restrictions on leisure car production appeared in 1916, the company focused on producing a light van and a light lorry, both of which had been introduced in 1914 to help fill the gap left as delivery waggon horses were called up for war work.

After the war, production resumed and the company moved to new, larger premises in Edwards Road, Balsall Heath.

The post-war cars all had four cylinder engines, an 11.9hp 1526cc model offered for £440 and a larger model for £525. The prices were much higher and the cars more substantial.

The Works in Edwards Road in 2011.

In 1920 William Paddon, the builder of the Hampton car (see **Hampton**) joined the company following a restructuring of Hampton's finances and, in 1922, the company made its final move to Spring Road in Hall Green.

Production continued until March 1924 when the company was finally wound up, at the instigation of James Arthur Smith of the Acocks Green Motor Body Works, who had experienced trouble being paid. The company and its stock of cars was bought by Calthorpe (see **Calthorpe**) in 1926, but they were expe-

The late model Autocrat.

riencing problems as well and that company also collapsed later that year.

There is only one car known to have survived, having been restored by the apprentices at Dormans Diesels in Lincolnshire who had supplied the original engine for the car when they were based in Stafford. William Ivy Rogers died in Birmingham in 1935 at the age of 71. Ellen Marston (nee Howell) died in 1958 in Sutton Coldfield and Joseph Foster died in about 1931.

Miss Howell takes an autocrat into Cannon Hill Park in 1913.

McKenzie

**McKenzie Motors Ltd., Bath Passage and Charles Henry Street, Birmingham.
1913-1926**

A run in a McKenzie.

The 'McKenzie' was the product of another Birmingham perambulator manufacturer that turned into a car builder.

Thomas Clyde McKenzie was born in Scotland, the son of another Thomas Clyde McKenzie, who was established in the furniture business with a company that survived in Birmingham until the 1960s. Our Thomas was born in 1868 and married Ivy Gwenllian Bentley from Merthyr Tydfil in 1895.

In the early 1900s Thomas McKenzie acquired premises in Great Hampton Street and started manufacturing perambulators and invalid carriages.

In about 1908 the pram business and premises in Bath Passage of one the original Birmingham car makers Leon L'Hollier (see **Anglo-French**) became available and he moved production there.

He added side-car and car body building to his services and, in 1913, he diversified into car building just as L'Hollier had done.

His first car appeared at the Olympia show in 1913, an open two-seater with a four-cylinder 1162cc engine and three speed gearbox. In 1914 a modified version appeared but both had engines and carburettors apparently built by McKenzie. The 1915 model had a four-speed gearbox and, by now, a four-seater was available in the range with access to the rear seats through a small door in the front bench seat, but, in 1916, the Ministry of Munitions brought motor vehicle building to a halt and the company returned to its earlier core business.

For many of the companies that formed in the pre-war period that would have been the end of the story, but McKenzie managed to restart car production.

After the war Thomas's son, Thomas Alec McKenzie, who was born in Birmingham in 1896, joined the company. He had served in the army overseas, had a degree in Mechanical Engineering from Birmingham University and had gained experience at the Daimler works in Coventry.

Soon after car-building resumed in 1919 the company changed its name to 'McKenzie

The McKenzie engine.

Motors Ltd'. and set up a London dealership that sold into a market hungry for cars. The company also acquired further premises at 181 Charles Henry Street and moved car production there.

The post-war cars took up where the pre-war cars had left off, with similar body styles but a bigger, 1330cc, 11.9hp Alpha engine made by Johnson, Hurley and Martin of Coventry and, after 1920, a 10.5hp Coventry-Simplex engine. The engine was pressure-lubricated and fitted with a Cox Atmos or Zenith carburettor, a Thomson-Bennett magneto (of course) though this was replaced in later models with a BLIC magneto. Electrics were by the Birmingham company, Powell and Hanmer who were established in 1893.

The transmission comprised a Ferodo lined cone clutch connected to a three speed gearbox, a drive shaft with two 'unusually large' Hardy universal joints and a worm drive to the full floating back axle. The suspension was half-elliptic springs to front and rear.

The two seater version was put on the market for £395 and the four seater was priced at £425. As was common an unbodied chassis was also available for £340.

The McKenzie two seater.

In 1923 a new model with an 8.9hp, 1074cc Coventry Simplex engine and a gearbox and rear axle by E G Wrigley (see **Wrigley**) appeared.

Competition in the car market was fierce in the mid-twenties with the big manufacturers able to offer keen pricing. Small manufacturers, like McKenzie, couldn't compete on cost and so went to the wall unless they could upscale to mass-production. Thomas McKenzie Snr. didn't like mass production as it compromised the quality of the cars, so they ceased production in 1926, though he did move on to back Henry Denley who took over the Rhode Motor Company (see **Rhode**) in 1929.

No McKenzie cars are known to have survived and the only part of the premises in Bath Passage that remains is the back wall. Due to a quirk of ownership a fragment of brickwork is still lodged between two modern buildings in the service area.

Thomas Clyde McKenzie died in June 1933 in Solihull, Thomas Alec Mckenzie went on to work for Benfords Ltd. and patented a new concrete mixer in 1942. He died in Winchcomb, Gloucestershire in November 1971.

The last piece.

Pram Makers

Five of the Birmingham marques were the product of the firms who also manufactured perambulators, **Anglo-French, Dunkley, Alvechurch, McKenzie** and **Prosser**.

The prams of the time were substantial, upholstered, coachbuilt or wicker constructions with wire spoked wheels and sophisticated suspension so their builders had most of the manufacturing processes for vehicles already in place. All that was missing was the power train. A typical pram of the time is shown in the photograph on the right. This is the one pushed by Harry Bensley for 6 years across 12 countries whilst wearing an iron mask, for a bet between John Pierpont Morgan the American millionaire and Hugh Lowther the Earl of Lonsdale (see **Anglo-French**).

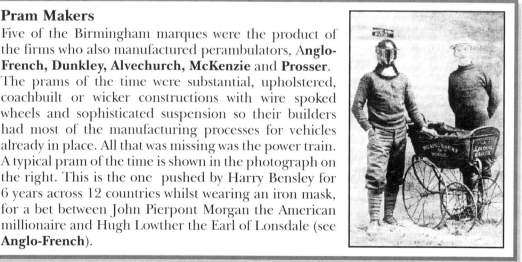

New Imperial

New Imperial Motors Ltd.. 41 Princip Street, Birmingham.
1914

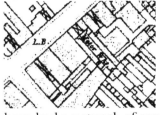

Norman Downs started in business making cycle fittings in 1887 under the name New Imperial but would later be swept up by the cyclecar craze.

Norman Tuckwood Downs was born in Nottingham in 1875 and, initially, set out to be a draper. He trained as a drapers assistant in Marylebone, London, a position probably found by his father Robert, who, as a commercial traveller, would have had a network of contacts all over the country.

After a move to Birmingham he set up in business making cycle fittings and, following the acquisition of Hearl and Tonks, a failed cycle business, went into production of complete bicycles in 1899. As with many other manufacturers operating in the highly competitive cycle market of the 1890s, he experimented with motorcycles as the next popular craze and produced his first machine in 1901. Unfortunately this failed to sell and, though he registered The Imperial Cycle Company with the intent of manufacturing motor cycles and cars in 1903, it was nearly ten years before he tried again.

In 1908 he formed a limited company called the New Imperial Cycle Company, worked on improving roller skates and, in 1910, launched

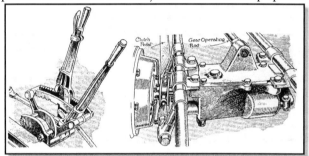

The New Imperial gear change and clutch.

another motorcycle. This machine fared better so, in 1912, the company changed its name to New Imperial Motor Company and a range of three motorcycles was produced. Building on this success, Downs turned to cyclecars and introduced a light car at the Olympia Motor Show in November 1913.

The New Imperial car had a four-cylinder, 1093cc water-cooled engine driving a three speed gearbox via a Ferodo lined plate clutch. Power was transmitted via a driveshaft to a bevel gear on the back axle, which was fitted with a differential. Suspension was by semi-elliptic springs at the front and three-quarter elliptics at the back. The car was under 6cwt and so qualified as a cyclecar and was offered at £145 but, as the war approached production ceased almost before it began.

New Imperial went on to produce successful motorcycles in the post war period with over 300 machines per month being built by the mid 20s. In 1929 the company moved to a 6 acre purpose built factory in Hall Green and, during the 30s, the company built many notable race bikes.

In August 1936 Norman Downs died at Barton-on-Sea, Hampshire and, in 1938, the company was liquidated. The company was bought by Solomon Joseph, Birmingham's only WWI flying ace, and his company Clifford Coverings. The name 'New Imperial' was later bought by Jack Sangster of Ariel (see **Ariel**).

The New Imperial.

Adcock

A J Adcock, Handsworth Garage, 47 Crompton Road, Handsworth, Birmingham. 1914

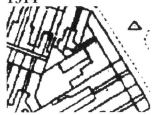

During the winter months of 1913 'Algy' Adcock experimented with a belt driven cyclecar at his garage on the corner of Crompton Road and Church Hill in Handsworth.

Algernon John Adcock was born in 1883 in West Bromwich the son of a milliner, also called John, and his wife Harriet. Algernon was brought up by his parents at their shop at 170 High Street, West Bromwich until the family moved to Thornhill Road in Handsworth at the end of the century.

He trained as a motor engineer and by the age of 18 was actually employing others to work with him. He married Edith Alice Williams in Coventry in 1909 and, by 1913 had established the business on Crompton Road, Handsworth.

He opted to use quite a large engine by cyclecar standards - a De Dion 10-12hp engine with a 100mm bore and 160mm stroke. A short drive shaft from the engine drove a bevel wheel on the countershaft that carried the belt pulleys on either side of the car in typical cyclecar fashion. The belt pulleys were tensioned, in typical cyclecar fashion, by moving the rear axle backwards and forwards to create a primitive clutch. There were quarter elliptic springs to front and rear supporting

The Handsworth Garage today.

a two seater body constructed with an ash frame. The steering was via cables linked to short lengths of chain that were tethered to a sprocket on the base of the steering column.

He demonstrated the car to Light Car and Cyclecar magazine in February 1914 but the car was yet another victim of the imminent war.

After the war he abandoned all thoughts of car making and instead teamed up with Leslie John Beard to form Adcock and Beard at premises at 236 Broad Street continuing as a motor repair and maintenance engineer, as did so many others. In 1922 this partnership was dissolved and he went it alone. He died in Birmingham in 1947 at the age of 64. The premises on the corner of Crompton Road still exist and are in use to this day as a motor garage. The prototype car that he built and in which he is pictured with his wife in the passenger seat, is not known to have survived.

Algy and his wife in the Adcock cyclecar.

The Adcock Cyclecar.

U.M.B.

Universal Motor Body Builders Ltd., 37 Sutton Rd., Erdington, Birmingham. 1914-1916

Universal Motor Body Builders produced cars from works facing the Abbey in Erdington a few doors along from another aspiring car maker, Dallison. (see **Dallison**).

Both companies wanted to take advantage of the cyclecar craze and UMB launched their car in the summer of 1914. The company was formed by Samuel Hamstead, (often misspelled 'Hamstaed', including by himself!), who was born in Romania in 1881, and Joseph Hamstead his brother.

They had a coachbuilding business in Sherbourne Road, Balsall Heath, and, in 1914, they bought another company in Erdington.

The Parry Motor Company, operated from 37 Sutton Road with two principals; George Mills Parry, a coachbuilder and Joseph Peter Trafford, a motor engineer who lived next door at No.35. The partnership between Parry and Trafford broke up in February 1912 and the businesses were amalgamated, with the Hamstead brothers and Robert Henry Williams as directors.

The car that they produced, from the Erdington premises, had a pressed steel frame with a sub-frame carrying the engine and gearbox. It had semi-elliptic springs to the front and three-quarter elliptic springs to the back, the whole supporting a three-seater body where the rear seat was fixed, rather than folding as with a Dickey seat.

The engine was four-cylinder with opposed side valves and a lubrication system that used needle valves to let oil into four troughs under the big-ends. The valves were operated via a linkage to the throttle lever.

It had a three speed gearbox and multi-plate clutch with power being transmitted to the rear wheels via a drive shaft with pin-type universal joints at each end and a worm drive to the rear axle.

The company produced cars into the early war years then ceased production, was liquidated in 1916, and dissolved in mid 1918.

UMB intended to produce six cars per week at a price in the region of £175 and it is not known how many were actually produced, however none are known to have survived.

The site of the premises is now a Colliers car showroom and will shortly be a Sainsbury store.

Army Recruitment

At the start of 1914 the British Army had a reported strength of 710,000 men including reserves, of which around 80,000 were regular troops ready for war. By the end of World War I almost 1 in 4 of the total male population of the United Kingdom of Great Britain and Ireland had joined; over five million men. Of these men 2.67 million joined as Volunteers and 2.77 million as conscripts (although some volunteered after conscription was introduced and would most likely have been conscripted anyway). There were no reserved occupations as there were in the Second World War so the impact upon manufacturing would have been dramatic. The car dealerships also struggled, with 18 of George Heath's staff of 52 signing up by November 1914.

West

E J West, Villa Road, Handsworth, Birmingham.
1914-1920

Enoch John West was born in Exhall near Coventry in 1864, and had a long, illustrious history of car production in Coventry but, it is fair to say, he was not good at managing the finances of his Companies.

He was a pioneer of car manufacturing and designed his first car, a 2.5hp air cooled 'voiturette' in 1899. This was followed by 3.5hp and 4.5hp models produced under the 'West' and 'Progress' marques between 1900 and 1903, but the company failed. In 1904 he started another company producing cars under the 'West-Aster' marque which also ceased trading in 1906.

In 1911 he joined forces with Franklin Dennison and tried again producing cars under the 'West' and 'Ranger' marques between 1912 and 1913. He produced cars with his

A 1906 West.

own badges on the radiators, but also supplied cars for other companies and had previous contact with the Birmingham car industry, building a large part of the cars produced under the 'Heron' name described earlier (see **Heron**). It was in Birmingham that the business, now under the control of Franklin Dennison, had one last try at car making at the beginning of WWI.

The company reappeared in Villa Road, Handsworth in 1915 in premises on the corner of Terrace Road shared with the Dennison Watch Case Company. The owner of that company, Gilbert Dennison, was born in Boston the son of Franklin Dennison and grandson of Aaron Luft Dennison, a dynasty of influential watch makers that continued manufacturing in Birmingham until 1967. Dennison was another aeronautic pioneer, holding the post of secretary in the Midland Aero Club at the time that Ernest Thompson Willows, the Welsh airship pioneer and

The Willows airship after flying over Birmingham in 1911.

Willows Airship Advert.

holder of the first airship pilot's licence issued by the Royal Aero Club, made his demonstration flights over Birmingham. With a little help from George Heath, (see **Car Garages**) Willows moved into premises in Villa Road Handsworth in 1911 to build his fourth airship but all was not going to go smoothly. The finances of the E T Willows Company, aeronautical engineers, were unstable and the company was forced to wind up in 1913.

The workshops that he used were now vacant and so in 1914

E J West and Company Ltd. moved in to set up another car making business. The cars that would have been produced in Birmingham are most likely to be either the 'Pilot' or 'Ranger' cyclecars. The Pilot had a four-cylinder 1244cc engine, friction drive and four

speeds. It had a final chain drive and sold for £150 complete. The Ranger, introduced in 1912, had a two-cylinder 964cc engine with a leather cone clutch a final chain drive and sold for £121.

The Ranger also came as a light delivery van which could carry loads up to 5cwt with its v-twin Precision engine. After the Ministry of Munitions order of November 1915 spelled the end of the cyclecar, delivery van production could still continue and so was seen as a lifeline to the car manufacturers.

The Ranger Cyclecar.

The Ranger light van is the most likely vehicle to have been produced up until the end of the War but, as vans of the period tend not to have survived, it is hard to be certain.

EJ West on the right.

They stayed in business right though until 1920 with the possible involvement of Enoch West who was, during the war years, the manager of the White and Poppe engine works in Coventry.

On 23rd August 1920 the final attempt at car making came to an end when a resolution was passed to voluntarily wind up the company.

None of the vehicles produced in this phase of his career are known to have survived but the Birmingham venture was one of the longest periods that the company had managed to hold together so it is always possible that there are cars existing today wrongly attributed to his manufacturing ventures in Coventry or badged by other motor companies. He died in Kenilworth in 1937 at the age of 73. The premises in Villa Road no longer exist having been replaced by Osborne House - an NHS facility.

Motorists in Birmingham

In early 1914 the Birmingham city treasurer reported that the number of horse-drawn carriage licences had fallen from 1792 in 1912 to 1597 in 1914 and that the number of Hackney Carriage licenses had fallen from 727 to 654 year-on-year. In contrast the number of private motor cars licensed had risen from 1554 to 2020, motor taxicabs had risen by 167 to 808 and motorcycles by 769 to 3341.

Horses were being supplanted by motorized vehicles and that was before the effect of the loss of horses to the war effort was felt. The days of the horse and cart were numbered.

The First World War

Britain entered the first World War on 4th August 1914 and it had a dramatic effect on the car industry in Birmingham. Some manufacturers, like Austin, won large government contracts and grew strongly; others lost their way or their workforce.

Lanchester, Austin, Wolseley and Alldays and Onions, all geared up for war production expanding their workforces and diversifying into heavy vehicles and aircraft, but the choice for the myriad of smaller car makers was more stark. Both the production base and the target market for light cars was populated by men of just the right age to find themselves in the trenches of France. As war became imminent the country was rife with rumours. Airships were sited over a number of British cities and brought the horrific possibility of fighting on the home front. Cyclecar enthusiasts put a brave face on it, predicting that the

demand for cars would remain strong despite the war and even musing on the ways that their cars could further the war effort.

They were wrong. The cyclecar craze had seen its best years already and most of the cyclecar makers that had set up with such optimism simply disappeared within the first year of the war.

A few manufacturers kept going with much reduced production levels, but the market had gone and, in November 1916, the government forbade the manufacture, assembling or erection of any new or used motor

An armoured cyclecar!

vehicle unless a specific order had been placed by the military. The cyclecar was doomed. The 'Light Car and Cyclecar' magazine became much leaner during the war years and relied upon the second hand market to bolster its advertising income. It did have one more idea to promote however, and that was parcel vans.

The restrictions on 'pleasure' vehicles meant that other avenues needed to be tried and parcel delivery vehicles were seen to fit the bill. In the early months of the war large numbers of horses were commandeered and delivery rounds had to be serviced somehow. A number of manufacturers took up this suggestion and developed small vans. Amongst these were Alldays and Onions, West, Calthorpe and Autocrat who all produced proposals for light delivery vans in 1914. The war wasn't the only obstacle for the car builders. Spanish Flu also hit their target market, and then there was the depression...

The Calthorpe 10hp Light Van.

The Autocrat 10-12hp Light Van.

The Great Depression

After the First World War there was a new flowering of car companies as the country recovered from its effects and people started to look to the future again with a little more optimism and certainty. As the twenties dawned the rate of increase in the number of car companies increased steadily, but the writing was on the wall for many of the simpler cyclecars and primitive light cars when Herbert Austin introduced the Austin Seven in late 1922.

The keen pricing of the Seven meant that many of the other car producers were forced to reduce their prices to compete, but they couldn't reduce their costs at the same rate. Inevitably the number of marques fell so that by the beginning of the depression in 1929/1930, there were only nine surviving marques in Birmingham. By this time over 80 marques of car had come and gone.

The Great Depression started in the US when, on 4th September 1929, stock prices started to fall and, on 29th October, the stock market crashed, a day forever after known as 'Black Tuesday'. The US economy was in a spiral dive and the government responded by introducing the Smoot-Hawley Tariff Act in an attempt to protect US industry from foreign imports. The result of all this was a global downturn in trade with cities like Birmingham that were dependant upon industry and manufacturing being hit. There was a growing feeling of unrest amongst the work force as unemployment rates doubled and the economy slowed to a crawl. By 1932 there were clashes between police and protesters in Birmingham and other industrialised cities and a series of hunger marches took place to demonstrate the inequalities highlighted by the downturn.

Birmingham had it easier than many of the more northern cities because it had its secret weapon - the car industry. Car sales grew during the thirties as, at long last, the demand for more affordable cars was being catered for. Birmingham was well positioned to take advantage of this with its car production capacity boosted by factories that had grown on the back of war work. But it wasn't good news for all of the car makers.

The depression took its toll and further thinned down the number of car companies to just four by the start of the Second World War: Austin, BSA, Singer and Morris Commercial.

He'd had better days.

Vintage Cars 1919 - 1930

The First World War had seen many car manufacturers disappear, a reflection of the huge losses suffered in both manpower and resources during the conflict. To compound this an epidemic of Spanish Flu at the end of the war depleted the light car building and buying generation.

As the country got back onto its feet, car making got off to a slow start. The surviving companies from before the war were searching for new peacetime markets and the smaller companies were not appearing at anywhere near the rate that the period immediately before the war promised. The cyclecar craze was a particular casualty, with only a few new cyclecars being launched from Birmingham.

When the new car makers did appear there was particular growth around 1922. Austin launched its Seven and light cars rapidly took over from the cyclecars that had previously held sway amongst the less affluent motorists.

The opening years of the twenties had a stylistic effect on the cars of the time, the most noticeable feature being the adoption of solid wheels. This fashion lasted only three or four years and went hand-in-hand with the flapper era. The beginnings of streamlining that would be adopted with gusto in the thirties, were just starting to appear in the twenties and the closed saloon car became the norm with hooded open tourers being reserved for more sporting uses. In 1918 over 90% of cars were open. By 1930 over 90% were closed.

A traffic jam in the Twenties.

Standardised controls replaced the idiosyncratic choice and location of pedals and levers that characterised earlier cars. The moving of gear and brake levers to the centre of the car rather than to the driver's right, a subject of much debate at the time, meant that the driver's door became a more practical option.

There were many technical advances that became established during this period, including detachable wheels, brakes that operated on all four wheels (something else that was the subject of great debate), chrome plating rather than nickel or paint and electric lighting and starting. In 1921 motor taxation was introduced which used the horsepower rating of the car to define the tax bands. This tended to dissuade the otherwise cheap American cars from flooding the market but it also had an impact upon the ranges being offered by domestic manufacturers.

In the early mid Twenties the motor industry became depressed and companies started to cut their prices, gradually at first but at an increasing rate as competitive price took over from other considerations when selling cars. There were casualties and a further thinning out of the industry just in time for the depression.

The only manufacturers that stood any real chance of surviving these conditions were larger ones with enough resources to ride the storm until their competitors had been knocked out of the marketplace. Austin was a good example but even they sailed very close to disaster with their one model strategy immediately after the war. It was only the widening of their car range, and particularly the introduction of the Austin Seven in 1922 that turned their fortunes around.

Enfield Allday

Enfield Allday Motors Ltd., Great Western Works, Sparkbrook, Birmingham.
1919-1924

The Enfield name had appeared as a Birmingham marque in 1908 and lasted until the outbreak of the First World War when production was halted (see **Enfield**).

In 1918 the Alldays Company (see **Allday and Onions**) returned to car production with a new company called Enfield-Allday, again controlled by William Allday and Edmund Tailby from the main company. They had their hopes pinned on a single 10hp car called the 'Bullet' designed by the Works Manager, Arthur William Reeves.

Reeves had worked for Crossley before the war as a designer and may have been spotted by Alldays when he presented a paper on 'Works Organisation' at the Institute of Automotive Engineers with Cecil Kimber, who later went on to found MG motors. The 'Bullet' had a five-cylinder, radial, air cooled engine and tubular steel frame and sported an oval shaped radiator.

Augustus Bertelli (see **Reaba**), who had taken over as works manager, was not at all impressed and said that it would be uneconomic to produce, but the car was launched at Olympia in 1919... and flopped. The company was in danger of missing the post-war car boom, having invested heavily and ending up without anything to sell.

The task fell to Gus Bertelli to rescue the situation and, newly promoted to General

1920 two-seater Enfield Allday.

Manager, he designed a four-cylinder 10-20hp car of more conventional appearance. The car was launched in 1921 but by this time the car boom had turned into slump and the car, priced at £575, was far too expensive to compete. The car was, however, winning races and, to build on this and, bearing in mind his sporting background, Bertelli opted to increase the power of the car with a 12-30hp model complete with four-speed gearbox launched in 1923. Despite lowering the price by over a third the car didn't sell and so, in April 1923, the company went into liquidation.

The 1921 sports model Enfield Allday.

Alldays revived the marque a few months later at their Waverley Works in Small Heath and produced a wide range of different body styles aimed at the end of the market that could afford them. They were popular, but the parent company collapsed in 1924 and, as part of the restructuring, the car building company turned into Alldays Motor Repairs Ltd. ceasing car production. Alldays and Onions still exist (see **Alldays and Onions**).

Gus Bertelli continued as a freelance consultant before starting Reaba. Arthur Reeves went on to attempt to market his design as the 'Reeves Radial' but failed. He then joined forces with Frederick Mountford at the 'Fremo' works. At least one example of the Enfield Allday has survived.

Ashton Evans

Ashton Evans Motors Ltd., Floodgate Street, Birmingham.
1919-1925

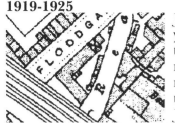

Joseph Evans and Company were established in the closing years of the nineteenth century producing brass tubes from their Liverpool Street Works. The Company branched into manufacturing parts for aircraft and locomotives from their mills on the banks of the River Rea and, just after the war, they turned their attention to car making.

Joseph Evans was the son of a labourer born in West Bromwich in 1863. By 1891 he was living in Castle Bromwich with his wife Mary who had been born in the village, and running the Coach and Horses pub on the Green, but he had manufacturing ambitions. By the turn of the century he had set himself up in business as a brassfounder and had moved to live on the Chester Road in Boldmere which is where his son Joseph Ashton Jarvis Evans was born in 1896.

During WWI the company produced parts for aircraft and airships and the workforce was expanded to cope, but when the war ended the company faced a common problem - what to do with the workforce in peacetime?

It was with his son, generally known by his third name Jarvis, that a new Company was formed in May 1919 called Ashton-Evans Motors Ltd.

The company was set up to use some of their excess manufacturing capacity to build cars and later that year they

The 1921 chassis with triangulated suspension.

A 1925 four-seater, Ashton Evans car.

produced their first model. This first car was designed by E Bailey, who had previously worked previously as a designer for Sunbeam and was badged as an 'Ashton'. The car was notable for having the two rear wheels only eight inches apart and separated by the crown wheel to avoid the need for a differential - a feature that wasn't repeated in their later cars. There were few, if any of this car sold and so they turned to another designer for their next attempt.

The next car to be produced was the Ashton-Evans badged Model 20 designed by T Bedford which went in to production in 1920 and was a more conventional design.

The 1921 model had a Coventry Simplex engine and an inverted cone clutch to the exclusive design of Ashton Motors and a three speed

The Liverpool Street Works.

gearbox. The power was transmitted by an open prop shaft through a Hardy joint to a full-floating rear axle with a bevel gear. The suspension system was distinctive in that it had long transverse springs at front and back and two triangles formed by the torque rods and axles connected to the front and back of the gearbox.

The company continued producing cars until May 1923 when a boardroom reshuffle took place. Joseph Evans was, by then, in his sixties and he stepped down to be replaced on the board by Jarvis's wife. Two months later she was replaced by Henry Belfield who

The Ashton Evans.

was, himself, replaced in September 1923 by Henry Caleb Curry of Hall Green (son of Henry Caleb Curry and father of, yet another, Henry Caleb Curry) who had previously been employed as the Works Manager.

In 1925 a new company was formed, Ashton Engineering Ltd. who operate from the same premises to this day. Of the 250 cars estimated to have been made very few of them appeared after 1924, but they were available until at least 1928 when their manufacture was 'temporarily' ceased. As with many temporary actions, this became permanent and no further cars were produced. The company was finally dissolved in May 1929.

The Works still stand in Floodgate Street on the edge of the River Rea and in the shadow of the railway viaduct.

The Joseph Evans factory has mostly gone but parts of it still survive abutting that same viaduct, a little further along, and next door to one of Birmingham's few surviving cast iron gentlemans' 'Temples of Relief'.

Joseph Ashton Jarvis Evans died in Bromsgrove in 1970.

No cars are known to have survived.

The Floodgate Street Works.

The British Industries Fair

In 1923 Ashton Evans were appointed the official car for the British Industries Fair at Castle Bromwich. The cars were used to ferry visitors from the centre of Birmingham out to the exhibition hall that used to stand on the corner of Castle Vale.

The Fair was built in 1920 and for two weeks every year it was the most visited attraction in the country and often visited by the great and good.

The building was demolished in the 60s to make way for the housing estate which also occupies the old Castle Bromwich Aerodrome, and the NEC assumed its role.

The station that served the fair has also gone but may yet be reinstated.

Gerald

The Gerald Cyclecar Company, 452 Moseley Road, Birmingham.
1920

The Gerald cyclecar was first announced in March 1920 whilst still in its prototype form and, by August, was at a stage where it was considered ready for production.

It was designed and built by Frederick Dudley Gerald Taylor from Tottenham who was born in 1891 the son of James and Elvera Taylor.

In 1919 he was living in Salisbury Road, Moseley and, whilst there, patented a variable speed power transmission gear. The 'Gerald' Cyclecar appeared in 1920 with a modified 8hp water cooled JAP engine. The engine was mounted longitudinally so that the crankshaft was parallel with the axles, fixed to the front axle and a tubular crossmember on the chassis. Transmission was via a Ferodo lined cone clutch to a roller chain from the engine to a countershaft, then via a single rubber belt running over variable pulleys to the solid rear axle.

The front wheels were 3ft 6in apart, whilst the rear were 2ft apart reducing the drag on the outer wheel when cornering on an axle without a differential.

The large diameter pulleys were enclosed by a metal cowling and were both operated by a single lever, so that when one was opened the other was closed, keeping the belt under even tension. The drive ratios that this arrangement produced were infinitely variable between 3 to 1 and 12 to 1. The front axle, being solidly fixed to the chassis, wasn't sprung, so the front wheels had springs built into the hub assemblies. The rear axle had leaf springs and 'dash-pot' shock absorbers. The body was a two-seater with the rear wheels enclosed by the skirt of the body, dispensing with the need for rear wings.

A Gerald cyclecar without bodywork.

Gerald Taylor could only handle small scale production so entered discussions with bigger manufacturers with a view to going into mass production.

The discussions came to nothing and the car disappeared shortly afterward. By 1924 he had moved to Brighton but was still working on vehicle related patents.

The premises where the car was built still exist on the Moseley Road and, when seen, explain why production numbers would have been limited. Few of the cars will have been built and there are no known examples of the car surviving.

Taylor became a pub landlord, running the Fox and Hounds Inn at Potsgrove, Bedfordshire for a year up until his death in Aylesbury in September 1939.

The expanding pulley.

Topham

Arthur Topham, 17 Poplar Avenue, Kings Heath, Birmingham.
1920

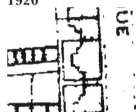

Arthur Topham was one of many who had home-built their cyclecar. The difference was that Topham wanted to see his go into production.

In June 1920 Arthur Topham revealed his home-built vehicle in the pages of 'Light Car and Cyclecar' magazine and declared his interest in finding a manufacturer who would take up production.

His was no basic DIY project; the car was well finished and would not have looked out of place alongside the offerings of the established manufacturers.

The three-wheeler car had an aluminium body with seating for two and a curved metal hood over the rear wheel that could be hinged to give access to the two brake systems, an internal expanding brake and an external contracting band type.

The car was driven by an 8hp JAP engine fitted parallel in the frame with a chain drive to a Sturmey Archer three speed motorcycle gearbox. From the gearbox a second chain transmitted the power to the rear wheel. The body was suspended by helical front springs and long leaf springs at the back. The engine was fired-up by a kick-starter on the off side and apparently fired easily.

The car could reach speeds of 35-40mph over undulating roads, was rigid, strong and, most

The Topham from the side...

important, stable. To aid wheel changes the car incorporated jacks to the front wheels and a double jack to the back wheel that folded away when not in use.

The reviewer from the Light Car magazine had a few issues with legroom but otherwise found it a '*praiseworthy effort*' and the photographic evidence supports this view.

Arthur Ireland Topham was born in Bethnall Green in 1887 the son of Joseph Topham and Patience Ireland. His father was an ironworker as was his father before him, also a Joseph.

Arthur's brother, William Guest Topham had an on/off association with the Lanchesters (see **Lanchester**) working for them, intermittently until they were taken over by BSA.

He too had built three-wheeler cars at home and had managed to sell one to BSA (see **BSA**).

Unfortunately Alfred didn't find a manufacturer so the car never went into production. Arthur Topham died in 1956. The prototype hasn't survived.

...and front.

Rover

The Rover Co. Ltd., Hay Hall Road, Birmingham.
1920-1925

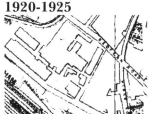

With the building of the post-war Land Rover car plant at Lode Lane and the unification of British marques under the Rover name in the seventies at Longbridge, 'Rover' became associated with Birmingham in more recent years, but the Company didn't start in the City.

Rover is a Coventry company that started as Starley and Sutton, a cycle company, in 1878 and, after experimenting with an electric car in 1888 and tricars in 1903, started conventional car production in 1904.

But Rover did produce cars in Birmingham before the war, and a large number of them at that. John Young Sangster, more commonly known as Jack Sangster, had a long as-

sociation with the Birmingham Motor industry. Born in Kings Norton in July 1896 he was the son of Charles Sangster who had founded the Cycle Components Company (see **Ariel**) and was educated at Hurstpierpoint College in Sussex before engaging in an engineering apprenticeship.

The apprenticeship was interrupted by the First World War when he joined the Birmingham Battalion of the Royal Warwickshire Regiment and served in France. His brother Frederick was killed in action in 1916.

Returning from the war he joined his

The Rover 8.

father's firm, the Cycle Components Manufacturing Company in 1918, and proceeded to design a small, low cost car.

After a short period of manufacture, the design for the car was sold to the Rover Company and Jack joined them as manager of a new factory acquired to facilitate production of the 8hp car. The car was built at the Tyseley plant in Hay Hall Road and had its body fitted at Rover's Coventry plant.

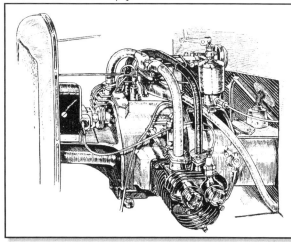

The Rover 8 engine.

The car was a sales success, filling the gap for a mass produced light car that had opened up following the war as manufacturers were re-gearing themselves for peacetime production.

The Rover 8 had an air-cooled side valve horizontal twin engine with 998cc capacity, though this was increased to 1135cc in 1923. Being air cooled, the engine didn't need a radiator so, as was common practice at the time, a dummy radiator was fitted. The engine, being a horizontal twin, was somewhat wider than the bonnet making it necessary to project the cylinder heads out to either side under protective metal cowls which acted as air scoops. A current owner of one of the surviving cars confirms that *'indeed you can see the cylinder heads glowing cherry red at night after a run'*. Power was transmitted to the rear wheels via a drive shaft with worm gear to the rear axle. A starter motor was an optional extra until 1923.

One possible reason for the improvements that came in 1923, and the accompanying massive drops in price, was the appearance of the car's Nemesis in 1922 - the Austin Seven (see **Austin**). The car was sold for £230 when it was introduced but by 1925 the price had dropped to £139. This was in an effort to compete with the Seven which was brought to the market for £165 and was also a more substantial and refined vehicle. The efforts to compete came to nothing and the car was taken out of production in 1925.

There were around 17000 Rover 8s produced but there are only about a dozen survivors. This may be attributed to the rather primitive cars becoming somewhat of an embarrassment to their owners. Whatever the reason, few remain and even fewer are on the road.

Part of the remaining Rover works.

In 1923 another event occurred affecting the future of the company - Jack Sangster resigned.

He rejoined his father's company and, by 1932, was joint managing director alongside him. In 1932 Cycle Components went bust and Jack bought most of the companies assets to form Ariel (see **Ariel**). He expanded the Ariel company over the next decade and alongside it acquired the bankrupt Triumph Motorcycle Company from the receivers which he also nursed back to health. He sold both companies, Ariel in 1944 and Triumph in 1951 to BSA for a handsome profit. Following the sale he joined the Board of BSA (see **BSA**) and, in 1956, became chairman.

He died in March 1977 in London aged 80.

The premises in Hay Hall Road still exist, though they are now almost unrecognisable being covered with profiled metal cladding. There are still some glimpses to be had, if you look around the back.

Lady Drivers
They don't caption photographs like they used to...

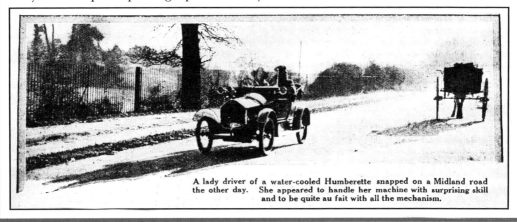

A lady driver of a water-cooled Humberette snapped on a Midland road the other day. She appeared to handle her machine with surprising skill and to be quite au fait with all the mechanism.

Hands

GW Hands Motor Co. Ltd., Lion Works, Barn Street, Birmingham.
1921-1924

George Hands had been building cars since 1904 under the Calthorpe name, as described earlier (see **Calthorpe**) but, by 1921, disagreements between the directors of the Calthorpe Company had reached such a pitch that he took a 12 month break from the business before deciding to produce cars under his own name.

His first business premises in 1895 were in Adderley Street with a shop and offices in Digbeth, and it was in Digbeth, in Barn Street, that he set up the 'Bard' and then the 'Minstrel and Rea' cycle companies.

When production of Calthorpe cars started in Cherrywood Road, Bordesley the premises had been turned over to motorcycle production so it was in these works that he worked on his 'Hands' cyclecar.

By December 1921 the first Hands car was on test. It was a light four-seater with a 1088cc four-cylinder water-cooled engine and separate three-speed gearbox with a central gate change. The chassis had four quarter elliptic springs and the car was fitted with disc wheels as were very much the fashion

George Hands.

in the early twenties. This was joined by 10.5hp 1498cc and 11-22hp 1296cc models in 1922 and 1923 that came in two-seater, four-seater, deluxe two-seater and coupe body styles.

The biggest car in the range, the 15-45hp, 1860cc, six cylinder model was launched in 1924. It had a fabric-lined cone clutch, a three-speed and reverse gearbox and spiral bevel gears for the final drive. It had four-wheel braking with the front axle 'specially designed to take the strain'. It could attain speeds up to 65mph and fuel consumption of 40mpg.

Unlike the other models which had Dorman engines this car had an engine produced in-house.

During his period in the wilderness George Hands worked on designs for other manufacturers, notably a firm little known outside Russia called 'Dux'.

The Russian firm had been in existence since 1901 but stopped car production in 1906 to concentrate on aircraft building. The last gasp of the company post war was obviously intended to be another car but whether it made it to the market is unknown.

His differences with the other directors put to one side, George Hands rejoined Calthorpe in 1924 and continued production of the six-cylinder 'Hands' car under the Calthorpe name.

About 150 Hands cars are thought to have been built and a few still survive.

The 1922 Hands.

The engine in the Hands.

Rhode

The Rhode Motor Co., Rhode Works, Rushey Lane, Tyseley, Birmingham.
1921-1934

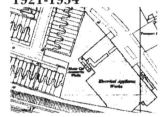

Rhode is not a marque that is widely known today and only three cars are known to have survived, but in the years between the end of WWI and the beginning of the Great Depression, the Rhode was a well known and popular car.

Mead and Deakin at Tyseley had already had experience in car making with the Medea light car (see **Medea**) but after the War they turned to a more substantial model.

Their first car was a 9.5hp model with a 1087cc OHC engine. The gearbox was supplied by EG Wrigley (see **Wrigley**) and the rear axle was basic, having no differential. The car also lacked a starter motor, though this could be an option for an extra £15 on the £250 selling price.

The Rhode engine.

It was known as the 'Occasional Four' as it was generally expected to be used as a two-seater but could accommodate another two passengers, under the hood and protected from the weather rather than on a 'dickey seat'. The car was produced until 1924 and proudly advertised as '*made in a British factory from British brains by British labour and with British capital*'.

In 1923 a sports model was introduced with a more streamlined, two-seater body and a 'livelier' engine.

Late in 1923 a new 10.8hp Rhode appeared with an OHC 1232cc engine. This was a full, four-seater selling for £275 and was fitted with a differential on the back axle introduced '*purely as a sop to the public and not because it is anymore necessary on this chassis than it was on its predecessor*'. The front seat in this car was a full-width, bench seat with fore and aft, sliding and tilting adjustment. The car came

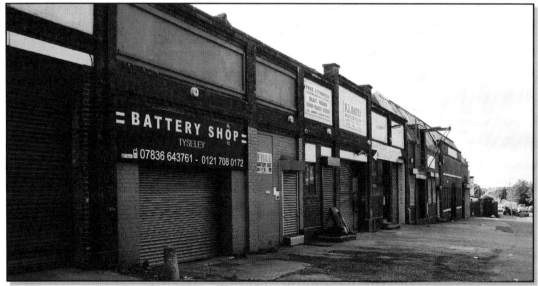

Rushey Lane Works.

172

in at just under 15cwt and could achieve petrol consumption of 35-45miles per gallon. A trade van option of this car was made available in 1923.

A feature of all of the Rhode cars was the bonnet height. Though essentially a light car it gave a feeling of enclosure and protection from the weather but meant that the eyeline of the driver and passengers was only just above the top of the bonnet.

In late 1925 the 11-30hp car was introduced with a four-door saloon and a four-seater sportsman's coupe among the variants. The engine had been tweaked to improve power output and smoothness of running and the car was generally made more 'substantial'.

The sporting model featured a rather unusual windscreen that was formed of four facets that parted the air vertically and horizontally.

The 1921 9.5hp Rhode.

With the sale of EG Wrigley to Morris, Wrigley components were no longer available and so the gearbox was now made in-house.

Production by 1926 was averaging 50 cars per week and an estimated 2500 cars had been produced up to 1928.

In the early twenties Henry Denley joined the company and appeared at trials meetings driving Rhode cars along with Fred Mead.

Henry Bernard Denley was born in 1885 in Birmingham, the son of William Henry Denley, a toolmaker of Deritend who had worked with his son refining file and hack-saw design during the early years of the century.

The 1923 9.5hp Rhode.

In 1929 Henry Denley joined forces with Thomas Clyde McKenzie (see **McKenzie**) to form Macbee Ltd. at McKenzie's invalid carriage works in Webb Lane, Hall Green.

They bought the Rhode Motor Company from Mead and Deakin and production was moved to the Webb Lane works. In 1930 the 1496cc Rhode 'Hawk' appeared. This had a Meadows engine, as engine building facilities were not available in the new factory, and a four speed gearbox.

The 1925 sports model roadster.

The car sold for £365 but only 50 cars were produced before Macbee Ltd. was wound up in 1934 following the death of Thomas McKenzie. In 1932 McKenzie and Denley had bought the remnants of 'Star' of Wolverhampton from Guy Motors (see **Universal**) and Denley continued in business selling their spares until the sixties. Mead and Deakin was dissolved as a company in February 1932.

In the early thirties Mead joined forces with the twins Fred and Stan Smith in a coach-building firm called 'Meredith Coachcraft' to produce the 'Trinity' body which could be an open two or four seater or a closed four seater. They built this body on about 30 cars, mainly the Riley and Wolseley Hornets but the company closed down in 1934.

Excelsior/Bayliss Thomas

The Excelsior Motor Co. Ltd., Kings Road, Tyseley, Birmingham.
1921-1929

As was the case with Birmingham, Coventry attracted a large number of immigrant workers and expanded as an industrial centre through the 19th century.

Three men who were attracted to Coventry were John Thomas born in Banbury in 1933, Thomas Bayliss born in Birmingham in 1844 and John Slaughter, born in Marylebone, London in 1860. They all worked at the Coventry Machinists Company, which started as a sewing machine manufacturer before becoming the first cycle maker in Coventry on the back of an order for 400 velocipedes from France in 1868. In 1874 the three men formed Bayliss, Thomas and Slaughter in Coventry to build 'Excelsior' cycles in their own right with Slaughter as the Works Manager until he left in the early 1880s and the Company became, simply, Bayliss-Thomas and Company.

In this form the company grew over the next thirty years, producing a wide range of cycles and motorcycles reacting to the twists and turns of the vehicle markets. In 1909 the company experimented with car production with a three-wheeled prototype, with an air cooled engine replaced by a 9-13hp engined four-wheeler that achieved limited production numbers. The venture wasn't a success and the company concentrated on motorcycle and sidecar production. Because the Excelsior name was already in use by a Belgian car maker the Bayliss-Thomas marque had been adopted for their vehicles but when the company was taken over by R Walker and Sons from Birmingham in 1920 the Excelsior name came back into use.

The 1921 Excelsior.

R Walker and Sons was run by Reginald Eric Walker, originally from Sheffield, and his son Eric. They had ventured into car manufacture immediately prior to the First World War but their efforts foundered at the outbreak of war and they returned to general manufacturing (see **Monarch, Hay Mills**).

When they bought the Company it was re-registered as the Excelsior Motor Company and production was moved to the Kings Road premises in Tyseley that had previously been used to build their Monarch marque cars. The Coventry works in Lower Ford Street was sold to Francis-Barnett who made their motorcycles there

Kings Road Works.

until the 1960s.

In July 1921 the Excelsior car appeared with a 10hp water-cooled engine with a separate three-speed and reverse gearbox, all mounted on a separate frame with four points of suspension. The engine was fitted with a fan and a Cox carburettor manufactured in Lower Essex Street.

Power was transmitted to the rear wheels via a die-pressed, steel plate clutch with Ferodo linings, a drive shaft fitted with Hardy joints and a spiral-bevel drive on the rear axle. It had quarter elliptic springs all round with provision to prevent the car settling down at the front in the event of a spring breaking. Being 1922, the car had the almost obligatory solid disc wheels and, due to the design of the front end, was reckoned to hold the road well and handle very lightly. To increase driver comfort both the foot pedals and steering column were adjustable and the car had a total weight of 12cwt.

Before the car went into full production the name was, once again, changed to Bayliss-Thomas and a number of refinements were made.

It had a Coventry-Simplex engine, Moss Gearbox from Aston, Wrigley back axle from Smethwick (see **Wrigley**) and Michelin tyres. It was sold, with full equipment, for 300 guineas

The Bayliss-Thomas light car.

and for an extra 5 guineas the car could be fitted with an optional dickey-seat.

The price reductions that many car manufacturers had to make in the tight market conditions of 1923 meant that soon after launch the price was dropped to £295, including dickey, a total drop of over £47 on the original intended price, delivery to anywhere in the UK was free. Two and four-seater models were available and, in 1923, a Bayliss-Thomas Junior model was introduced for £295 (and an extra £15 for a starter). This had an 8.9hp four-cylinder, water-cooled engine and an occasional four-seater body with slightly staggered front seats. The arrangement of the front seats allowed access to the rear by hinging the passenger seat sideways with the passenger seatback passing behind that of the driving seat. The company also collaborated with the Bowden Brake Company, (see

A Bayliss Thomas with a Birmingham tram.

Tyseley), whose works stood on the opposite side of the road to produce a saloon with sliding doors.

The company acquired a new works in Coventry and production of the car was split between the two sites. It continued in production until 1927 though the 'Excelsior' motorcycle continued to be built up until 1965. Britax, the car accessory maker, bought the 'Excelsior' name and produced a number of Britax-Excelsior motorcycles in the 70s.

About 1000 cars were produced by the company and a handful still exist. The works in Kings Road still exists and is used by a storage company.

CWS

The Cooperative Wholesale Society, Kings Road, Tyseley, Birmingham. 1922

The Co-op as a business model, with the company being owned by the customers and the profits being redistributed as dividends first appeared in Fenwick in Scotland in 1761 when a group of weavers grouped together so that they could buy oatmeal cakes at a discounted rate. This simple idea spread rapidly as the attraction of people grouping together to get bulk discounts became apparent.

The Cooperative Wholesale Society was set up as a Co-op of Co-ops allowing the individual local Co-ops to group together in a federation that further increased their buying power. The English Cooperative Society extended into production of goods that would be sold through the network including cycles, motorcycles and, eventually, cars.

The Society had previous experience in car production with a model called the 'Bell' produced at its factory in Manchester from 1905 to 1915, and a further attempt after the war to build a slightly more substantial model that sold in limited numbers. Not to be beaten the CWS gave it another try in the early 20s. The Tyseley factory in Birmingham had been producing motorcycles under the 'Federal' and 'Federation' names since 1919 but, in 1922, they decided to produce a three wheeled car. The car only enjoyed limited success so the venture was abandoned after a year and they re-focused on motorcycle production which continued until 1927.

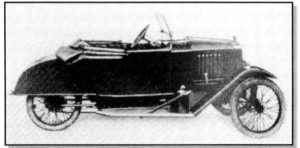

The CWS three-wheeler.

Kings Road Works.

Road Signs

In 1921 the Ministry of Transport unveiled a new, standardised design of road warning and direction sign.

Though signs that used symbols instead of words had been in use on the continent for a number of years the British had maintained an ad hoc system with wide regional differences in appearance.

The signs introduced in 1921 remained in use until the Anderson Committee of 1957 introduced new signs designed for the first motorway and the Worboys Committee of 1963 bought in the system of signage that is still in place today.

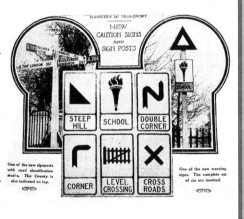

Prosser

Prosser Automobile Co., 57 Water Street, Snow Hill, Birmingham.
1922

Continuing the great Birmingham tradition of combining car building with pram manufacture. Edwin Thomas Prosser, who ran a perambulator making business called Bentley and Co in Water Street, launched a light car called the Prosser in 1922.

Edwin Prosser was born in Wolverhampton in 1895 the son of Alfred Prosser who had moved from Birmingham with his family and worked as a stonemason before setting up a brick and tile manufacturing company.

His business was obviously successful as his son, Edwin, had the wherewithal to learn to fly only a few years after the Wright brothers had made the first powered flight. Having piloted a Bleriot plane at the age of sixteen he was presented with flying certificate number 526 from the Royal Aero Club in 1913.

He was involved with the Birmingham Aero Club building model gliders and held the gliding distance record for a time before moving on to full sized powered aircraft, acquiring a French built, Coudron biplane, in 1913.

He flew this on a number of navigation and demonstration flights and, later in 1913, travelled to Australia where he also gave demonstrations and partnered garage proprietor and Australian aviation pioneer Robert Graham Carey in

Edwin Prosser in 1913. purchasing a 1914 Bleriot biplane that had been abandoned on the dockside in Sydney. The plane had been left by the French stunt pilot Maurice Guillaux when he returned to Europe to play his part in the war. Having been taught to fly by Prosser, Carey gained the first Australian issued pilot's licence and the first Australian commercial flying permit. The plane was used at Ballarat Flying School with Carey as manager and Prosser as pilot and mechanic. The Bleriot still exists and is on display in the Powerhouse Museum in Sydney.

In 1916 Prosser enlisted in the Australian Flying Corps, rather wisely as a mechanic rather than as a flyer considering the life expectancy of pilots at that time. He sailed on the HMAT Aeneas from Melbourne and joined the conflict. He survived the war and was discharged in April 1919.

Prosser continued to fly but, on one occasion, his Coudron experienced engine trouble. He flew the plane to the Austin Works at Longbridge (see **Austin**) to repair the engine and had his photo taken on the airfield there. He had links with a number of Birmingham motor manufacturers, like Herbert Austin, through their shared interest in aviation and so, when the time came to set up his own car making business, he would have known the right people and had some useful connections.

The vehicle that he produced from his works in Water Street was the eponymously named

Edwin Prosser in his Coudron biplane.

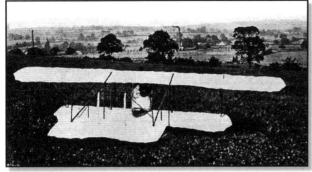

Prosser landing at Longbridge.

'Prosser' a light car powered by a 10.5hp four cylinder Coventry-Simplex engine with a three-speed and reverse gearbox from E G Wrigley (see **Wrigley**) and a shaft drive with Hardy flexible universal joints.

There were two variants available; a two seater and a four seater, both with Leatherite upholstery and sporting the disc wheels that were in vogue at the time.

The cars were put on the market for £295 (and an extra £20 if you wanted a starter motor) and came in one standard colour - dark blue, with nickel plated fittings and a mahogany dashboard.

The suspension on the car was considered particularly effective with its long and prominent semi-elliptic springs at both front and back. The car also had combined head and side lights avoiding the need to have lights mounted at the front of the car in an area considered vulnerable to damage.

The general opinion of Light Car and Cyclecar magazine was that it was 'nippy' and stood up well in hill-climbing ability when compared with the other light cars on the market. The premises in Water Street were owned by J F Ratcliff rolled metal manufacturers. The owner of the business, John Francis Ratcliff, was the first person in Solihull to own a motor car (an American Hupmobile) and the family lived at Hillcroft, the immediate neighbour of Herbert Austin at Lickey Grange. Alas, Edwin's foray into car manufacture lasted for only one year with the introduction of the Austin Seven probably too strong a competitor for a fledgling business. The twenties were a period of consolidation in the car industry with fewer new marques appearing and many joining forces to form companies of sufficient scale to survive in an increasingly competitive market. Edwin Prosser died in Northampton in 1966.

The works in Water Street were demolished and the site is now occupied by the offices of the teachers' union NASUWT.

The only known surviving piece of the factory's output is a radiator badge. No complete cars now exist. As the soldiers returning from the First World War would have said; 'ça ne fait rien'.

The Two Seater Prosser.

The Four Seater Prosser.

R and B/Reaba

Bertelli Ltd., Kings Road, Tyseley, Birmingham.
1923-1925

> *Location of works unknown.*

William Renwick and Augustus Bertelli were keen to break into the sports car market and took their first faltering steps in designing and building their concept car in Tyseley, but they went on to greater things under a completely different name.

Dominico Augustus Cesare Bertelli was born in 1890 in Genova, Italy and immigrated to Cardiff with his parents when he was a young child. His brothers, Alfredo and Enrico were both coachbuilders and he had an enthusiasm for motoring and motor sport from an early age. In the early years of the century he travelled back to Italy and worked as a designer for Fiat but eventually moved to Kings Norton, married and had children. He worked for Enfield Allday (see **Enfield Allday**) at the same time as A W Reeves, who had designed cars for Crossley in Manchester, and William Somerville Renwick from Stirling in Scotland who had worked for Armstrong-Siddeley in Coventry.

'Bert' Bertelli was a talented designer and teamed up with Renwick, who had come into a sizeable inheritance, to form the engineering company Bertelli Ltd developing a 1.5 litre four cylinder engine that could be sold on to other car manufacturers. In the process they patented a number of developments in engine and vehicle technology and built a car known as the 'Buzzbox' at their workshop in Tyseley based upon a car that had been built for Bertelli while he was still at Alldays.

Augustus Bertelli.

Other backers for the project included Woolf Barnato who became a director of the company. He was another of the 'Bentley Boys' who had inherited a massive amount of money from his family's diamond mining activities and went on to control the Bentley company as a result of his investments. The Buzzbox has had a chequered history but it still exists and currently resides in Surrey.

In 1925 the opportunity came to take their ambitions on another step and, with the backing of Lady Charnwood and her son John Benson who were already major share-holders, they bought an ailing company run by Lionel Martin and Robert Bamford and called it Aston-Martin.

The Buzzbox.

Over the next few years they developed the Aston-Martin with the help of Augustus's brother Enrico who coachbuilt many of the cars of that era and, by 1932 when the reins were handed over to David Brown, had established a reputation for high quality sports cars.

Augustus Bertelli made his last appearance with a patent for a grass drying machine in 1946 and died in 1979 at Henley in Oxfordshire at the age of 89. William Renwick went on to work for MG and producing patents for engines and died in 1962.

Morris Commercial

Morris Commercial Cars Ltd., Foundry Lane, Soho, Birmingham.
1923-1968

With a name like 'Morris Commercial Cars' you would expect this company to be focused on car production, but nothing of the sort; this company specialised in building commercial vehicles with a side-line producing cars.

William Richard Morris was born in Worcester in 1877 the son of Frederick Morris, a draper's clerk from Witney and Emily Morris from Cowley, both in Oxfordshire. In 1880 his father took a position as a farm bailiff at Headington (also in Oxfordshire) and the family moved into a house in James Street Oxford. When he left school he was apprenticed to a local cycle repairer and dealer but within a few months had set himself up repairing cycles in his own right in a shed at home and later from a shop in the High Street.

In 1901 he started designing motorcycles and by the following year had moved into garage premises from which he sold and repaired cars. In 1912 he designed and started production of the 'Bullnose' Morris at a disused military training camp near Cowley and his car building activity took off. Pausing to carry out munitions work during the first world war he resumed car production in 1919 and by 1925 had introduced Henry Ford's production-line techniques and was building 56,000 cars a year. In 1923 he decided to build a lorry capable of carrying a one ton load to bridge the gap between the car derived light vans and heavy lorries that were the usual products of British manufacturers. He aimed to compete with the ten foreign companies, mainly American, who were then offering one ton machines in Britain and for that he needed a new production base. The existing car factories simply didn't have the space to accommodate commercial vehicle production, whilst car production was expanding, and so the production facility developed by E.G.Wrigley, (see **Wrigley**) newly vacated in Foundry Lane Soho, provided a great opportunity to acquire a ready built factory.

By March 1924 the factory was producing components for the Morris Cowley motor car, and production of the T-type one-tonner and a factory expansion plan was underway. New

William Morris (2nd right) with his family.

TD Touring Car 1926.

commercial vehicles were developed through 1925, notably the 'Roadless Lorry' which had wheels at the front and crawler type tracks at the rear and, in May 1926, the 'D' type appeared. The 'D' type was a six-wheeler built to meet the specifications of a War Department Subsidy type lorry with the new 15.9hp four-cylinder, 'Z' type engine built at the Soho Works. Shortly after the introduction of the lorry a six-wheeled touring car variant, the 'TD' appeared possibly developed as a military staff car. The car had the 'Z' type engine but the bonnet, scuttle and radiator shell was remodelled to give it a more car-like appearance. The touring car seated five people and incorporated a folding map table, folding hood and retractable side screens.

In 1926 Morris Commercial was tasked with producing a version of the Morris Oxford intended for the export market. To cope with the demands of the roads found in the colonies the car had to be more 'heavy-duty' than the normal Morris cars and so the Empire Oxford was born. The car used the same 'Z' type engine as the 'TD' produced at the Soho Works and the gearbox, front and rear axles were all also produced there, though the final assembly was at Cowley. The car didn't sell as well as expected, only about 1740 were produced, but it continued in production until 1929. Four examples are known to exist today.

In January 1929 the 'G' type international taxi was announced based on the same mechanical components as the Empire Oxford. This too did not achieve its anticipated sales targets but continued in production until 1932 by which time about 840 had been built.

In 1927 Morris personally bought the bankrupt Wolseley Motor Company (see **Wolseley**) against competition from Herbert Austin, amongst others. The company was developing a car with an 8hp overhead cam engine and Morris used this to develop the Morris Minor. Though the Morris Minor was assembled at Cowley the chassis and running gear were produced at the Foundry Lane site and the engine was to the Wolseley design. In 1929 the original MG midget , the M-type, was also based on the Wolseley original.

In 1931 the '6D' saloon cars appeared. Evolved from the

'G' Type Taxi Chassis 1929.

6D Saloon Cars lined up outside works 1931.

earlier six-wheeled 'TD' type but bearing little resemblance to it, the '6D' had a stiff, semi-box section steel chassis and six-wheel braking. The 4,256cc six-cylinder engine was built at the Adderley Park works, originally for the 'Viceroy' bus chassis and developed 74 bhp. The saloon body had a rear passenger compartment with seating for four separated from the driver by a glass screen. The bonnet, front and rear bumpers were made by Fisher and Ludlow at their Rea Street factory in Digbeth. Fisher and Ludlow are familiar from their operations at Castle Bromwich after the war but the company has been operating in Birmingham since it was founded in 1851. The company still exists, though now owned by an American holding company. Despite the size and weight of the '6D' it had striking performance and had a recorded top speed of 75mph as demonstrated by the company's senior road tester on the Chester Road, heading toward Sutton Coldfield.

In 1938, the combined car building enterprises became the Nuffield Organisation, in the year that Morris became Viscount Nuffield of Nuffield in Oxfordshire. He died in 1963 at the age of 85. His home of 30 years, Nuffield Place, has been offered to the National Trust.

Monarch (Castle Bromwich)

The Monarch Motor Car Company, Castle Bromwich, Birmingham.
1925-1928

Location of works unknown.

The market for mid-sized family cars in the mid-20s was saturated, with cars from Austin, Standard, Humber and Singer all competing in the marketplace. Monarch was launched into this market in 1925 from an unusual direction.

Sir Richard Butler was born near Oxford in 1850 and, at the age of four, was taken to Australia by his parents. He was educated in Adelaide and became a farmer but he had political ambitions. In 1898, after winning a by-election, he became Minister of Agriculture. He resigned this post soon after and held a number of ministerial positions over the next two decades. In 1919, he left government 'in unfortunate circumstances' having been implicated in irregularities discovered in the 'Wheat Scheme'.

At about this time the long-established Australian agricultural engineering firm of May Brothers and Co in the town of Gawler, north of Adelaide, were experiencing difficulties with their businesses so looked to diversify into automobile manufacturing. To this end they formed a public company with J H Jones of Adelaide and Sir Richard was appointed chairman. In October 1924 he announced that, because of supply problems elsewhere, the Monarch Motor Company of Castle Bromwich would make most of the parts.

Sir Richard Butler.

A prototype car was built with a 13.9 hp OHV Meadows engine, a four speed gearbox and a Salisbury spiral bevel rear axle but the company announced their intention to produce their own 2121cc engine. The bodywork was a saloon produced by Mulliners and the whole package was priced at £525.

In 1925, disaster struck with the death of Sir Richard and May Brothers engaging in a legal wrangle with JH Jones that would finish the parent company off.

A Monarch chassis was pictured by Autocar at the British Industries Fair (BIF) in Castle Bromwich, the only Birmingham-built car on display.

The Monarch chassis at the BIF.

The Monarch.

The only thing that remains of May Brothers, a company that employed over 300 Australians, is the name of the street that their works once stood on - Foundry St. in Gawler. In Castle Bromwich there isn't even that. There is some evidence that the Monarch company built a car marketed in Australia as the Chic but it is possible that the prototype built for the company headed by Butler was the only car built by the company and it may still exist - a car was found in 1986 that has been identified as a Bean from Wolverhampton and restored. The car had features that didn't quite fit with that identification, could this be the missing Monarch?

The location of the factory used by the Monarch Motor Company isn't known which is why the map at the top of the page is missing. Perhaps someone knows?

Brocklebank

Brocklebank and Richards Ltd., Oozells Street and Adderley Park, Birmingham. 1925-1929

The story of the Brocklebank car starts in Liverpool and in a completely different sphere of business.

Captain John Brocklebank was a shipmaster and shipbuilder who emigrated to New England in 1770 to establish a ship-building works in Maine. When the War of Independence broke out he decided to return to his hometown of Whitehaven in Cumbria to continue his business and managed to build up a fleet of eleven ships.

When he died, in 1801, his sons Thomas and John took over and despite the trials of the Napoleonic wars continued to send ships all over the world. In 1819 Thomas Brocklebank expanded the company from a base in Liverpool and by 1844 had built the fleet up to fifty vessels. At this time he took on his cousin Ralph and nephew Thomas Fisher to continue the family firm. The younger Thomas adopted the family name and was made a Baronet in 1885. The Whitehaven shipyard was closed in 1865 and the headquarters moved to Liverpool. The company passed through two further generations of Brocklebanks, becoming a limited company in 1898 and ceasing to be family owned in 1911, when shares were sold to the trading firm of Edward Bates and sons and, shortly after, was absorbed into Cunard.

The chassis production line.

Major John Jasper Brocklebank was born in 1875 the son of Thomas, the second Baronet. He fought in the Boer War and WW1 gaining the rank of Brigade Major in 1916. Due to the restrictions on car manufacturing during the war the American car industry had managed to gain a foothold in the British and European markets and Sir John decided by 1921 that it was time to build the English answer to the American car. He teamed up with the engineer R W Richards to form Brocklebank and Richards Ltd. and in 1925 established the company in premises on the corner of Oozells Street and Broad Street, with further works at Adderley Park in the corrugated metal sheds that had been erected to house aero engine production during WWI. Brocklebank provided the finance and business acumen and Richards provided the engineering expertise, designing the cars, laying out the works and designing the tools. The cars first appeared in 1927 and had a number of advanced features, including a hydraulic brake system and a hinged instrument panel on the dash that allowed easy access for repair and maintenance. They had a six-cylinder 15hp engine and a choice of body styles including a Gordon England fabric saloon, 'Weymann' fabric saloon and a four/five seater tourer.

There are a few Brocklebanks remaining but the only confirmed one in the UK is owned by Sir Aubrey Brocklebank, having been repatriated from South Africa where it had been restored by his cousin after use as a courtesy car in a nudist colony.

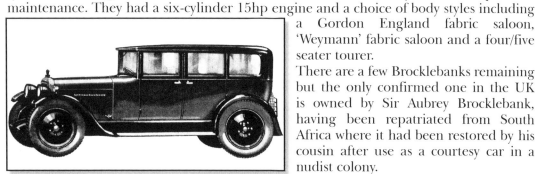

The Brocklebank.

Hinks

James Hinks and Son Ltd., 102/104 Ledsam Street, Birmingham.
1927-1932

The Hinks was a short-lived marque of car produced from works in Ledsam Street.

James Hinks and Son was an old Birmingham firm of lamp and chandelier makers. The company had started in the 1840s when James Hinks (born 1817 in Atherstone) had joined up with his son Joseph to form a company to carry out wood turning and japanning. In 1843 they dissolved their partnership and James teamed up with James Syson Nibbs (b1819 Clapham) and formed Nibbs and Hinks and manufactured an 'Oxidate Condensing Lamp' that had been invented by Nibbs. The lamp was exhibited at the Crystal Palace Exhibition in 1851 and used in the Crimean War; it was, in fact, the one used by Florence Nightingale 'The Lady With the Lamp'.

In 1858 Nibbs and Hinks was dissolved, James Hinks and Son was reformed and James Hinks and his son started to patent improvements to lamps, percussion caps, button and metal box manufacture amongst many others. The company was incorporated in 1873 and re-incorporated in 1888. As James aged, capital was extracted from the company to pass on to his son. In 1905 James died but, by then, Joseph had retired and was living in Milverton near Leamington so the company carried on under his son Harry Dain Hinks. Harry had a son Walter James Hinks and it was he that would carry the company forward.

The company's first foray into car related manufacture was as Christensen and Hinks in 1927, formed by Henry Ebbe Christensen and Walter Hinks to manufacture a device called the Frikke Brake. This was designed to apply a braking force on the steering column of cars to reduce 'stagger and wobble' whilst driving, particularly in cars that were 'old and worn'. The invention was patented in 1927 by Christian Frikke from Esbjerg in Denmark and introduced to Walter Hinks by Christensen, who was himself Danish.

The company only existed for two years before Christensen and Hinks parted company, leaving Walter Hinks to continue at the Ledsam Street premises as Hinks and Co. In this form Walter built cars under the Hinks name. Little is known about the cars and none are known to have survived.

Florence Nightingale.

The Slowing Pace

Of the 114 Birmingham Marques 80% had appeared by the start of the First World War and most had disappeared by its end. In the post war years the rate of company formation was steady but markedly slower.

The business was maturing and had entered a phase when size mattered. Small manufacturing companies could no longer compete with the economies of scale that the larger companies could employ. The competitive edge offered by innovation in the early years was less, diminishing as the major design elements of motor vehicles were settled and protected by patents.

The rate of formation of new marques slowed still further as the world headed toward the Great Depression and the financial backing necessary to allow a new venture to compete against the established players became more difficult to find.

The world was a different place in the interwar period. The Great War had a lasting effect on the country's manufacturing base concentrating the means of production in fewer, larger companies. A trend that would continue...

Singer

Singer and Company, Coventry Road, Small Heath, Birmingham.
1927-1939

Singer is well known as a Coventry car marque, and most references to the Company reflect this, but Singer and Company had a large car production plant on the Coventry Road, Small Heath (on a site now occupied by an Asda store) that, before the war, was responsible for a major part of the Singer car company's output.

George Singer was born in Kingston, Dorset in 1847, the son of George Singer, a farm bailiff and Hellen, his wife, who managed the dairy and, on leaving school, he worked for a firm of marine engineers in Greenwich. Moving to Coventry he joined the Coventry Machinists who had started as a sewing machine manufacturer but, by 1867, had moved into cycle production and in 1869 had incorporated as Coventry Machinists Ltd.

Coventry Machinists had an important role in the early car industries of both Coventry and Birmingham as a number of car makers worked there early in their careers, including the founders of Bayliss-Thomas (see **Bayliss-Thomas)**, Thomas Brockas and William Hillman (see **Brockas**) and James Starley (see **Ariel** and **Rover**).

In 1875 he set up Singer and Co. with his brother-in-law, James Charles Stringer, to make 'Challenge' cycles and tricycles and the business continued as cycle manufacturers with over 300 workers at its factory in Alma Street, Coventry until 1896, when it was incorporated as the Singer Cycle Company Ltd.

The premises in Alma street were sold to the Pneumatic Tyre Company, control of which had been transferred by John Boyd Dunlop to William Harvey Du Cross. William, and his sons Harvey and Arthur, would go on to play an important part in the formation of Austin (see **Austin**), Ariel, (see **Ariel**) and Dunlop in Birmingham.

George Singer.

Singer moved to Canterbury Street in Coventry and, in 1900, the company's first motorised vehicle was unveiled - a motorcycle with the engine in its wheel. The company became registered as Singer and Co. Ltd. in August 1905 with George Singer and James Stringer as directors, though Singer himself by this time described himself as 'a retired cycle manufacturer'. It had its first taste of car production making four-wheeled cars with 8hp and 12hp engines made under licence from Lea-Francis.

The following year they branched into production of cars to their own design with a four-cylinder, 12-14hp Aster engine and, over the next few years added 8-10hp, 12-14hp and 24-25hp cars to the range, all with four-cylinder engines but only the biggest having a shaft drive. The Lea-Francis designed car dropped out of the range and, by 1909, all of the cars were powered by White and Poppe engines.

In 1909, it became a private company following the death of George Singer in the January of that year. Singer was dead but the company that bore his name continued producing cycles, motorcycles and cars and, in 1911, launched the light car that was to become their first big seller - the Singer Ten.

Powered by a 1100cc engine built in their own works, the other cars in the range would nearly all have Singer engines by the outbreak of the First World War.

The Singer Factory in Small Heath

The war put a stop to car and motorcycle production with only car production restarting after the war.

After the war Singer bought Coventry Premier Ltd., a car manufacturer which had started producing a three-wheeler in 1913 during the cyclecar boom and had a minor legal wrangle about use of the 'Premier' name with the similarly titled Birmingham car maker (see **Premier**).

Following its acquisition for £97,000, Singer replaced the three-wheeler with a more substantial four-wheeler and added it to their range.

Singer went through a period of expansion in the early twenties, taking over the Coventry Repetition Company, Sparkbrook Manufacturing Company and Calcott Brothers before making their debut in Birmingham with the purchase of a large, multi-storey manufacturing plant on the Coventry Road in Small Heath previously owned by BSA (see **BSA**). In September 1926 Singer introduced the Singer Junior with its 848cc OHC engine and produced these from the Small Heath works. The Singer Ten, which by now had been in the range for fifteen years, was renamed the Senior and had a bigger 1308cc, 10-26hp engine. This car too would now be produced at the Small Heath Plant.

In 1928 the Singer Senior was redesigned and given a bigger, 1571cc engine, wider track and improved steering and brakes.

By 1929 Singer were the third biggest car producer in the country with only Austin in Birmingham (see **Austin**) and Morris in Cowley, Oxford (see **Morris-Commercial**) making more cars. The majority of the 100+ cars per day that they built were Juniors or Seniors and they were substantially built in Birmingham.

In 1931 the Singer Ten appeared with a 1261cc four cylinder engine.

The Singer Junior.

The Singer Senior.

It followed the trend of having an overhead camshaft engine but it was a short-lived model being swept away by a side-valved Singer Twelve in 1932.

The last two models produced before the war in Birmingham were the Singer Bantam and its open tourer version, the Roadster.

The Bantam was launched at the Motor Show in 1935 and was the first car produced by the company with a pressed-steel body. There were two and four-door 'Popular' and two and four-door 'De-luxe' versions and these were joined in 1939 by the open tourer, Singer 9 'Roadster' but production of all of their cars suffered from falling sales due to lack of competitive pricing and was brought to a halt by the outbreak of the Second World War. Production of Singer cars continued in Birmingham after the War but that is another story...

Reg Baker (centre) and Singer Tens on the production line at Small Heath in 1931.

The Veteran Car Club

By 1930 the car had been around for over thirty five years but it was only in 1927 that any thoughts of celebrating motoring heritage manifested itself in a London to Brighton Run to mark the anniversary of the Emancipation Run in 1896. After holding the event for three years the organising body formed itself into the Veteran Car Club of Great Britain at the end of 1930.

The Club was formed for Veteran and Edwardian cars built before 1918 and heralded a new-found appreciation of, and keenness to preserve, early cars.

Early Classic Cars 1931 -1939

By 1930 most of the pre-war car manufacturers in Birmingham had come into existence and the majority had disappeared again.

The industry was dominated by big companies who had grown, merged and swallowed other companies whole. The number of marques had shrunk and the days of the small workshop trying its hand at car making were long gone, or nearly...

There were still to be a few hardy entrepreneurs who would challenge the big players, but their efforts were short-lived and generally only made any money if they captured a niche market.

Of the companies that started in this period, only one, Patrick Motors, lasted for longer than a year; the others had failed or moved on in a matter of months.

The Thirties opened with a new piece of motoring legislation, the Road Traffic Act 1930 which made testing for some driving licences compulsory, introduced a minimum driving age, swept away the 20mph speed limit and made third party insurance a legal requirement. The Act introduced measures to combat dangerous and careless driving and paved the way for a Highway Code.

In 1931 the first edition of the Highway Code was published with a cover price of one penny with guidance for motorists, pedestrians and the drivers of horse-drawn vehicles.

The concept of 'looking both ways before crossing' was codified for pedestrians as were the system of hand signals for motorists. Motorists were also instructed to look out for white lines which were beginning to proliferate.

The Minister of Transport, Lord Hore-Belisha, introduced The Road Traffic Act 1934 which included a number of now familiar measures including pedestrian crossings with 'Belisha beacons', a compulsory driving test for all new drivers, L-plates and re-introduced a speed limit for vehicles carrying fewer than seven people, by this time generally set at 30mph.

Reflective 'cats-eye' studs appeared in roads for the first time in the mid-thirties, the invention of Percy Shaw from Halifax, who patented the idea in 1934. They have been manufactured by his company Reflecting Roadstuds Ltd. since 1935 having become popular during the black-outs in World War Two.

Leslie Hore-Belisha.

Toward the end of the decade the Motor Vehicles (Construction and Use) Regulations made it a requirement that windscreens should be made of safety glass and that windscreen wipers should be fitted. The steering, brakes and wipers were all to be in good condition; speedometers became compulsory and dipped headlights were introduced.

Horse-drawn vehicles had nearly disappeared by this time, no longer competing with the well over 2,000,000 cars on the road by the start of the Thirties.

Most of these cars were built in Britain which, by 1932, had overtaken France as Europe's leading car producer, a position maintained until the mid Fifties.

Despite the reduced number of car manufacturers in Birmingham the city's share of the market was substantial, with Austin alone having nearly a quarter of the market by the end of the decade.

An endangered species?

Patrick Jensen Motors

Patrick Jensen Motors Ltd., 479-581 Bristol Road, Bournbrook, Birmingham.
1931

Jensen is well known as a producer of cars such as the Interceptor from their works in West Bromwich and, if this was their only production base then they would fall outside the scope of this book. But the Jensen Brothers originally hailed from Birmingham and their first foray into car building was in partnership with Patrick Motors in 1931.

Joseph Albert Patrick was born in Leeds in 1847 and moved to Birmingham in 1889. He worked for the Britannic Assurance and was later to become its Chairman. Joseph's son Albert Morton Patrick, born in Leeds in 1874, bought Edgbaston Garages Ltd on the Bristol Road in order that a more secure job could be found for his son Joseph. Joseph was aiming to become a stockbroker but the collapse of the stock markets at the end of the twenties made it clear that a career in the stock market was rather less than secure.

Seeing that the motor industry was growing he decided to combine his son's interest in motoring with a sound engineering business and entered into a partnership with the Jensen Brothers to sell and service small cars and coachbuild custom cars onto light car chassis.

Frank Alan Jensen was born in Moseley in 1906 and his brother, Richard Arthur Jensen was born in 1909. Their father, Frank was a provisions merchant who bought his sons a 1923 Austin Seven. The brothers first experience of coachbuilding was the 'Jensen Special Number One' based on the car that their father had bought for them. The car caught the attention of Standard Motors so they built a

Alan Jensen.   *Richard Jensen.*

second car based on a Standard Nine chassis, 'Jensen Special Number Two'. Following the partnership with Joe Patrick they were given free rein to develop the Edgbaston Garage as they wished and promptly changed the name to Patrick Jensen Motors. This didn't sit well with Joe and before the year was out the partnership had been dissolved. The Jensen's next door neighbour George Mason introduced the brothers to the long established but failing coachbuilding firm of W J Smith and Son and Jensen Motors Ltd. was born.

Black Country Manufacturers

Coventry was not the only close competitor to Birmingham's car makers. In the Black Country were some serious players.

Sunbeam were the first in Wolverhampton in 1899. In 1905 Star, also from Wolverhampton, produced their 'Starling' cars which were later renamed the 'Stuart' and in 1909 started the 'Briton Motor Company'.

Crescent (see **Crescent**) started production in Walsall in 1912 and Beans, initially based on the Perry (see **Perry**) were built in large numbers from 1919 but never achieved the market dominance they wanted.

Guy Motors in Wolverhampton (see **Universal**) specialised in commercial vehicles but built a few cars in 1919. 'New British' built cars in Cradley Heath for two years from 1921 and Clyno became the third biggest car producer in the country for a time after launching its car in Wolverhampton in 1922. Following the closure of Clyno, A.J.S. started building cars in Wolverhampton in 1930.

Patrick Motors

Patrick Motors, 479-581 Bristol Road, Bournbrook, Birmingham.
1931-1933

Following their disagreement with the Jensen Brothers whilst building the 'Bournbrook Special', Patrick Motors persisted with their intent to produce their own marque of car.

Joe Patrick was a motor sports enthusiasts and enjoyed a great deal of success driving his Patrick Specials. The Company had a growing reputation as a manufacturer of coachbuilt special cars based on Austins, Triumphs and Wolseleys amongst others and business developed through the early thirties despite the prevailing economic climate. By the mid thirties the predominance of the larger manufacturers made it difficult to compete and so the company concentrated on sales and servicing in the years up to

the Second World War. After the war the company diversified, forming 'Patrick Aviation' to use the skills of ex-RAF pilots to fly cargo planes between Elmdon airport and a range of European destinations but again they were squeezed out of the market by bigger companies who took over their routes. The company re-focused on car sales and servicing and changed its name to the Patrick Motors Group - PMG in 1953.

In the years since the War the company has absorbed a number of other Birmingham firms including Premier

Albert and Joseph Patrick.

in Aston (see **Premier**). The building that housed the company existed intact until very recently but the coachbuilding department has now been swept away by the same by-pass that finally destroyed the Ariel factory in nearby Dale Road (see **Ariel**). The remainder of the building still stands behind the shops on the Bristol Road.

Patrick Motors Group has, in more recent years, distanced itself from the motor trade, selling its last dealership in 1999 and restructuring itself as a property development firm, but the Patrick Motor Collection still exists (though now only viewable by appointment).

Joseph Patrick died in 1982 but there are a number of the cars he produced still in existence - including the one that started the Patrick Motor Collection.

Car Assembly Workshop.

A 1934 Patrick Special.

Barclay

Barclay Motors Ltd., 173-177 Clifton Road, Aston, Birmingham.
1933

By the thirties the British motor industry was mainly in the hands of a few major car manufacturers. The mergers, consolidations and take-overs had knocked most of the small car builders out of business so it was a brave entrepreneur who set up business in this climate.

Those that made the attempt usually targeted a niche market overlooked by the big players but not so Barclay. They decided to go for the family saloon market.

The company was started in modest premises at 173 - 177 Clifton Road, Aston, the same premises that had played host to the car building ambitions of Alfred Pericles Maxfield a quarter of a century earlier (see **Maxfield**).

The Barclay was a four door, family saloon with a 10hp 1122cc Coventry Climax engine, a gearbox from the Moss Gear Company, run by the Dukitt family in Aston who went on to supply Jensen, Jaguar and Morgan and universal joints by Hardy Spicer in Birch Road, Witton. The spiral bevel gears to the rear axle were supplied by ENV of Willesden and the bodywork was made by the Jensen brothers. As is fairly obvious this is what is known as an 'assembled' car with few, if any, of the components being manufactured in house - an arrangement not unusual in modern car production.

The frame of the body was manufactured by Rubery Owen, based in Darlaston. The Owen family owned the Newhall Estate in Sutton Coldfield and, as a result, Newhall Mill is now owned by Rubery Owen Holdings Ltd.

The interior was fitted out with 'Dunlopillo' upholstery and leather seat coverings with a fold-down arm in the middle of the rear seat. Each of the doors had a winding window with a glass louvre fitted at the head to reduce draughts and the whole thing was topped off by a Pytchley sliding roof.

The car impressed the reviewer from 'Autocar' magazine who, in the issue of 24 February 1933 considered it a 'promising newcomer'. Unfortunately that was how it was to remain; the car never did go into full production and the company had disappeared as quickly as it came.

The Barclay.

The Barclay engine.

HPS

Smallbone and Son, 116 Raddlebarn Road, Selly Oak, Birmingham.
1939

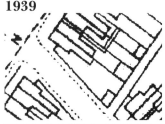

Smallbone and Son are the longest established, family owned car dealership in the City. Started in 1927 by Percy Smallbone they are still in business today on the same site.

Percy Andrew J Smallbone was born in 1891 in Aston but the family had links with Walsall where Percy's father Harry and his grandfather Samuel had both been in the electroplating trade.

He married Eva Freeman before the First World War and had a son, Harold Percy Smallbone, in 1915 and about this time started working at the Austin Works at Longbridge (see **Austin**).

In 1927 Percy started his own business, taking the premises in Raddlebarn Road that had, since 1912, been in use as William Bedford's cycle garage.

By 1931 Harold was old enough to join his father working in his garage and to complete a two year stint at the Austin works to widen his experience.

The HPS.

They repaired and maintained cars, but also bought and sold them, keeping meticulous notes of all their transactions. From these we know that a 10hp Jowett was bought in early 1939 and formed the basis for a car building project by young Harold.

The car that he built used the chassis and four-cylinder engine from the Jowett and used the radiator and parts of the body of a Rover 10-25hp Sports that was rebuilt to Harold's design. The car was badged as an HPS and sold in 1941 to a buyer in Kings Heath.

By this time the Second World War had intervened so any thoughts of building further cars would have had to be abandoned and, post-war, the company carried on with its main business as it does to this day under the control of Harold's sons who are prominent figures in the 'early car' movement and Austin enthusiasts.

This was not to be the end of Harold's automotive creativity as, in 1969, he toured the US and Canada demonstrating a pneumatic tyre bead expander he had invented and patented a number of ingenious ideas; self-cleaning rear-view mirrors, improvements to tyres, funnels and even a rotary engine during the 50s, 60s and 70s.

Percy died in 1950 and Harold in 1987. The car is not known to have survived but the premises have, fulfilling their original function.

Harold Smallbone and the HPS.

Atco

Charles H Pugh Ltd., Whitworth Works, Rea Street South, Birmingham.
1939

This is where the story of Birmingham's pre-war car industry comes full circle.

When the first Birmingham Company to manufacture in the City, Lanchester, was registered as 'The Lanchester Engine Company' in 1899 (see **Lanchester**) one of the Directors was Charles Vernon Pugh who was also Managing Director of his family's firm Charles H Pugh Ltd.

When he stepped aside his son, John Geoffrey Pugh, took over the reins and produced the last pre-war Birmingham car and badged it with the company's long established marque; Atco.

The last car to appear in Birmingham before the Second World War was rather smaller than average as it was intended for children rather than adults. The Atco Junior Safety-First Trainer was produced in response to a government Select Committee on Road Accidents report that urged an improvement in road safety training for children.

Charles H Pugh Ltd. had been making lawnmowers for many years under the 'Atco' name but had its roots in cycle and motorcycle making having established the Rudge Whitworth Company in 1894 by merging their own Whitworth Company with the ailing Rudge Cycles of Coventry. The cycle and motorcycles were all produced at their Coventry works but control of the Company came from Birmingham. At the head was Charles Vernon Pugh born in Rotherham in 1869.

The Atco Safety Trainer.

Following his death, control passed to his son John who also played cricket for Warwick-shire in the twenties.

The Safety Trainer was very much a real car in miniature aimed at the 7 - 17 age range. It was powered by a Wolverhampton-built Villiers 98cc, two-stroke engine with a cone clutch and chain drive. All the normal controls were provided; accelerator, brake, clutch etc. so that the child could become familiarised with the workings and control of a car. The car could achieve a top speed of 10mph. It wasn't intended to go on the roads but rather into schools and parks. This didn't stop one enterprising Oxford resident from registering his for the road in 1939 to eke out his restricted supply of petrol. The Atco trainer came in only one colour - lawnmower green with red upholstery and sported disk wheels with

An Atco publicity photograph.

Dunlop tyres. Though only 250 are thought to have been made there are a number of survivors including one each in the Beaulieu and Gaydon Motor Museum collections.

Charles Vernon Pugh died in Bognor on 23 August 1921. John Geoffrey Pugh died on 14 February 1964 in Hastings, Barbados.

Judging by the number of car manu-facturers who died at holiday resorts it really does seem that people liked to retire to the seaside.

Epilogue

Of the 100 or so car marques that sprang up in Birmingham, from the efforts of Garrard, Blumfield and the Lanchester brothers at the dawn of motoring onwards, only three survived the Second World War and carried on producing cars in the city.

Austin, Wolseley, BSA and Singer turned their factories over to war production and all but BSA restarted car building when the hostilities ceased. They were joined, or rejoined, by Rover, Jaguar and Land Rover. The City had demonstrated it's long established pre-eminence in metal product manufacturing and, in the process, had produced a large number of the cars on Britain's roads.

The small manufacturer finds it difficult to compete against the economies of scale that the bigger players have, but they can always dream that they will find that niche in the market that will allow them to endure. The evidence from the 100+ companies that have featured in this book is that there is little hope of finding such a niche as they all, ultimately, failed.

The reasons for their failure, however, are many and varied. Many bowed to financial pressure, some failed to find the backing necessary to go into mass production, some simply lost interest and pursued other goals. But the important thing is that it is "*Not that you won or lost—but how you played the game*" (see **Alexandra**).

The entrepreneurs whose vision led to the formation of so many Birmingham car companies 'played the game' and continued a great tradition of manufacturing in the city. The metal bashers, brassfounders, casters, steel toy makers, jewellers and gunsmiths all played their part in building the city's reputation. Their willingness to adopt new processes and techniques, to create things that probably didn't exist while they were growing up, and refine them in the process, are part of the city's industrial heritage.

The skills still exist, but for how much longer? In a culture that values retailing above manufacturing, financial services above actually making things, Birmingham has suffered... but, you never know.

The future of car design as seen from 1913.

Not Quite...

There are a number of companies that had an association with Birmingham but which couldn't, hand on heart, be considered Birmingham marques. These are the car companies that didn't quite make it:

Darracq 1903
Darracq and Co (1905) Ltd.
In 1903 a financial consortium headed by WB Avery of the Birmingham based Avery Scales Company bought the Alexandre Darracq's Company. In 1913 the company had premises at 280 Broad Street but, alas, production had been moved from France to a manufacturing facility in Fulham, London rather than Birmingham.

Mail 1903
The Mail is listed in some references as a Birmingham Marque but this is probably a case of mistaken identity and refers to a model rather than a make. Lanchester produced a car called the 'Mail' in 1897.

Tulip 1903-1906
Alex J Flewitt and Co.
The Tulip is also listed in some references but probably refers to the 'Tulip' style of phaeton bodywork sometimes supplied by Flewitts, also known as the 'Roi-des-Belges'.

Castle Three Motor Co 1919- 1922
Castle Motor Co.
The Castle Three was an attempt at making a slightly more substantial cyclecar. They appear in the Kellys Directory in Broad Street but the works was in Kidderminster.

Owen/Orleans
Orleans Motor Co.
The Owen has been a puzzle amongst automotive historians for many years as no examples of the cars they purported to produce have ever been seen. For a time there was a theory that they may have been manufactured in Birmingham but no factory has ever been identified.

New British 1921-1923
Charles Willetts Junior.
The New British was sold through its offices in Warwick Chambers in Corporation Street but the cars, and the business, was actually based in Cradley Heath.

Traffic in New Street in the early thirties.

Coachbuilders

So you are a reasonably well-off, aspiring motorist in the early part of the 20th century and nothing on offer from any of the new motor manufacturers suits your taste or purpose, what do you do?

Unlike today when opportunities for bespoke cars are limited, the early motorist had a number of coachbuilders who could design and build a body onto the running gear of another manufacturer.

These coachbuilders would originally have done just that - build coaches, but as their traditional market slowly dried up new opportunities appeared. The craft heritage was clearly apparent in many early cars with the 'horseless carriage' appearing as late as 1909 with the horses replaced by an engine in what was otherwise an unaltered vehicle.

Strange contraptions appeared in this crossover period but as the First World War approached cars settled into the form that we would broadly recognise as being a car.

The ability to produce a well crafted piece of coachwork didn't necessarily extend to any mechanical ability. There is a world of difference between woodwork and metalwork , between creating joints and manipulating sheets of material and cutting and grinding machine parts.

So, for a while, the disciplines existed alongside each other. Some companies, like Austin, wanted to build the whole thing and so employed their own, in-house coachbuilders to build the ash frames and panel them with sheets of aluminium, but others were either too small or wanted to leave the opportunity of a made-to-measure solution where the client would have his own coachbuilder just as he would have his own tailor.

Birmingham was home to a fine coachbuilding tradition with companies like Mulliners, Flewitts and Startin building bodies for cars from the Austin Seven to the Rolls Royce Phantom. There were dozens of coachbuilders offering their services in the city during the period up to 1939 with workshops in Aston, Bordesley Green and the city centre.

Little evidence remains of their businesses as all had gone by the mid-sixties. The factories are gone, the company papers have been archived at Gaydon and Kew but the companies still live on through the bodies they produced and their tell-tale badges.

There are too many to describe in any details so here are a few representative companies:

H.H Mulliners (Birmingham) Ltd.
Gas Street and Bordesley Green Road
Herbert Hall Mulliner was born in 1861 into a family with a long history of coachbuilding. His father Henry, his grandfather Francis and his great grandfather Francis were all coachbuilders as were his uncles and cousins. The HH Mulliner coachbuilding workshops were in Gas Street on a site now occupied, ironically, by a multi-storey car park. The company had showrooms in Broad Street just behind where the gilded statue of Murdoch, Boulton and Watt now stands. They built bodies for Calthorpe (see **Calthorpe**), Clyno and Sizaire-Naudin but are best known for their Austin bodies. Herbert Mulliner himself was chairman of the London Electric Cab Co. between 1896 and 1899. He also had interests in firms producing ordnance and scientific instruments and assembled a collection of English decorative furniture of national importance.

Flewitt and Co. Ltd.
Alma Street, Aston
John Alexander Flewitt, a Birmingham doctor's son , started the company in 1905 when his business partnership with George Ashley Martin came to an end. From 1912 they were initially known for building Rolls Royce bodies but after 1930 they predominantly bodied Austins. The company survived until 1965 working mainly on commercial vehicles.

Thomas Startin Junior Ltd.

Thomas Startin is a name recognised in more recent years as an Austin (see **Austin**) and Rover dealership, but started as a coachbuilding company in 1840. They coachbuilt cars but much of their work was of a more commercial nature. The company was started by Thomas Startin Junior but his father, Thomas Senior, was a coachbuilder, as were his two uncles and established a sizeable business by the mid 1800s. The company still exists, though these days they are based in Redditch and sell only foreign marques.

Meredith Coachcraft Ltd.

Meredith was started in the early thirties by F W Mead (see **Medea** and **Rhode**) and brothers, Stan and Fred Smith. The only body they produced was known as the 'Trinity' as it could be adapted to become an open two or four seater or a closed four seater. The company ceased trading in 1934.

John Marston's Carriage Works Ltd.
Cheapside

A long established carriage and coachbuilder that had works in Bradford Street in the city centre. Though mainly a commercial coachbuilder they did build landaulettes, limousines, cabriolets, saloons, torpedoes, and sporting bodies, notably on Rolls Royce and Daimler chassis. John Marston was born in Nuneaton in 1834 and, before starting the coachbuilding business, had sold patent medicines. He died in 1913 leaving the company in the hands of his son Charles.

W C Atcherley Ltd.
82-84 Sherlock Street.

The company was started by William Clive Atcherley, born 1885 in Shropshire, the son of a pub landlord. In the early thirties they worked with Brough on prototype/early production cars for a Brough Superior car on a Hudson straight 8 chassis.

A typical coachbuilding workshop in the twenties.

Component Manufacturers

In the early part of the last century the city lived up to its reputation of being the workshop of the world and just about any component needed to build or maintain a car could be sourced in Birmingham.

Rather than attempt to construct every part of their car, most manufacturers called upon suppliers and sub-contractors for components. There would not be room to include all of the Birmingham companies but here is a small selection:

ENGINES

Accles

James Accles (see **Accles-Turrell**) produced engines at his Holford Works in Perry Barr in the very early days of car manufacture. The engines were built to power vehicles produced by Harry Lawson's syndicate. Over 1000, similar to the De Dion engine were claimed to have been produced.

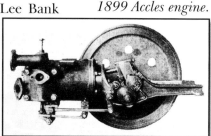

1899 Accles engine.

Linford and Willson

Harry Copeman Willson was born in Edmonton, Essex and moved to Birmingham to set himself up in the cycle business with William Almond Linford. Around 1900 Linford and Wilson branched into building 4hp Benz-type engines at their 'Astral Works' in Bell Barn Road near to what is now the Lee Bank Middleway. It ran at between 600 and 800 rpm, had a 4.5in diameter cylinder and a 5in stroke. It was designed so that water from the cooling jacket couldn't enter the combustion chamber in case of leakage and the valve seats were also cooled.

1900 Linford and Willson engine.

Precision

Frank Edward Baker, born in 1875 from Poole in Dorset, started his company in 1906 and by 1910 was building engines aimed at the motorcycle market. As the cyclecar craze took hold, 'Precision' engines appeared in many different marques of car including PDA, Rollo, Wall and briefly, in 1913, their own cyclecar (see **Precision**). After the First World War the company was taken over by William Beardmore and Company from Scotland and the 'Beardmore Precision' motorcycle went into production.

CHAINS

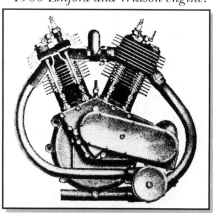

1920 Precision V twin engine.

Brampton Brothers

The Brampton brothers, Arthur, Charles and Frederick, inherited a brassfoundry in 1874 and established a business specialising in cycle chains in Oliver Street, Bloomsbury and Rocky Lane, Aston. Later they capitalised on their experience producing the heavy duty chains that were required to transmit the drive in early cars. The company was taken over in 1925 by the Coventry Chain Company.

TYRES

Clipper

Established in 1897 by John Davenport Siddeley (see **Wolseley**) The Clipper Pneumatic Tyre Company manufactured and sold pneumatic tyres and Westwood rims under licence from Dunlop.

They operated from their 'Clipper Works' at Aston Cross before moving to Alma Street, importing their tyres from the 'Continental Caoutchouc and Gut-

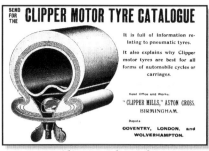

Clipper Advert from 1900.

tapercha Co.' in Germany (now, thankfully, known simply as 'Continental'). In 1901 Siddeley decided to turn to car manufacture and sold the company to Dunlop.

Dunlop

The Dunlop Pneumatic Tyre Company Limited was set up in 1896 with Harvey and Arthur Du Cross (see **Ariel**) as the joint Managing Directors. The registered offices were at Holloway Head and the works were at 'Para Mills', Aston Cross. They took over from John Boyd Dunlop's company acquiring patents and machinery for tyre production from the Cycle Components Manufacturing Company. At first, tyre manufacture was sub-contracted but, in 1902, production facilities were set up in Birmingham. In 1912 they restructured themselves and were renamed the Dunlop Rubber Company. In 1917 they built Fort Dunlop in Erdington which became the world's largest factory employing 3200 people

at its peak. The only tyre production now carried on in the UK is specialist, racing and vintage car tyre production on a small corner of the Fort Dunlop site.

ELECTRICS

Powell and Hanmer

Established a factory in Chester Street, Aston in 1893 producing fittings for carriages and, along with H Miller and & Co. and Joseph Lucas Ltd., also of Birmingham they dominated the cycle lamp market. When cars first appeared they responded to the new market by producing headlights. In 1914 they acquired new premises in Rocky Lane, Aston to produce dynamos. They were taken over in 1929 by Lucas.

Dunlop Advert from 1902.

Joseph Lucas

Joseph Lucas and his son Harry started in business

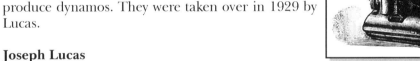

Lucas Headlamp 1906.

in 1872 producing pressed metal goods including lamps for carriages. In the late 1870s they made inroads into the growing cycle accessories market. In 1897 they formed Joseph Lucas Ltd. to buy Joseph Lucas and Son and, by 1902, they were supplying the car industry using their 'King of the Road' brand.

They took over magneto manufacturer, Thomson-Bennett in 1914 and, from then, concentrated on the supply of electrical equipment for cars. The company grew through a series of acquisitions till, by the seventies, they had over 100,000 employees. In 1996 they merged with the Varity Corporation in the USA and three years later were bought-out by TRW, and sections of the business have been spun-off ever since. In 2004 a UK based company acquired the rights to use the Lucas name on after-market auto-electric products and set up a new company with headquarters a little closer to Birmingham. 'Lucas Electrical' is now based in Coleshill.

The Thomson-Bennett magneto testing room.

MAGNETOS

Thomson-Bennett
In 1904 Peter Bennett of the Electric Ignition Company in Birmingham joined forces with James Thomson and Sons, an Edinburgh motor parts and accessories company to form Thomson-Bennett Ltd. They produced magnetos from their Arden Works in Cheapside (see **Melen**) and at the outbreak of WWI were the only manufacturers of magnetos in the country. The company merged with Lucas in 1914, with Sir Peter Bennett becoming chairman and managing director.

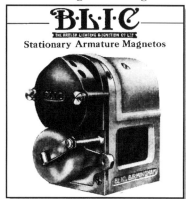

1923 BLIC magneto.

B.L.I.C
The British Lighting and Ignition Company Ltd. had their works in Cheston Road, Aston where the Stellite car was first built (see **Stellite**). They were part of the Vickers group and produced magnetos that were used on early Austin Sevens, amongst others.

TRANSMISSION

Moss Gear Co.
Founded by the Dukitt family from Moss Side in Manchester, Moss (hence the company name) they became famous for their gearboxes. After starting in business in Thomas Street, Aston in 1910 with ten staff, the Moss Gear Company gained experience in aircraft component manufacture that put them in a strong position as WWI broke out. In 1927 they moved to an 11 acre works near Castle Bromwich Aerodrome that is now part of the Erdington Industrial Park producing gearboxes, drive shafts and rear axles. The company lives on as FPW Axles but is now based in Accrington.

The Moss gearbox and axle.

E G Wrigley
Formed by Edward Wrigley in 1898 the company manufactured gearboxes, and rear axles, progressing to complete chassis and, eventually, cars (see **Wrigley**). They started in Aston but moved to larger premises in Foundry Lane, Soho in 1902. The company was taken over by William Morris in 1924 (see **Morris-Commercial**).

A 1920 E G Wrigley advert.

FUEL SYSTEM

Cox
The Cox Carburetters Ltd. produced a device called the 'Atmos Economiser' and 'Atmos' carburettors, as fitted on the 1923 Austin Seven Boulogne Racers, from their works in Lower Essex Street. They moved to new premises in Bradford Street and later to Knowle during WWII.

BEARINGS

British Timken
The Electric Ordnance and Accessories company was another Vickers company set up in 1901 and was responsible for producing 10-12hp two-cylinder, five seater cars briefly in 1908 and later, around the time of WWI (see **Stellite**). Its works in Cheston Road, off Rocky Lane in Aston produced a range of accessories, amongst them Timken tapered roller bearings under licence from America. During WWII production moved to a 'shadow factory' in Northampton and, in 2002 to works in Poland.

WHEELS

Warland Dual Rim
Early tyres were a problem, being less durable than modern tyres and running on uneven roads littered with horse-shoe nails, it wouldn't be unusual to have to change tyres a number of times during a journey.

Once removable wheels appeared the spare dealt with the first puncture, but what if you had a second? The Warland Dual Rim answered this by making tyre changes feasible on the roadside. Warne, Wright and Rowland (see **Rollo**) in collaboration with Frederick William Baker produced wheels from their Aston Works from 1911 and later from works in Coventry.

LUBRICATION

Best and Lloyd
Established in 1840, Best and Lloyd made brassware and electrical fittings at their premises in Handsworth but ventured into the car parts market with oil and air pressure gauges, lubricators, filler caps, oil pumps and direction indicators between the wars. They later returned to their core electrical business and survive to this day selling a range of light fittings from premises in Downing Street, Smethwick. Their 'Bestlite' designed in the 1930s and inspired by the Bauhaus design ethos is still in production today and sold through their Kings Road showrooms.

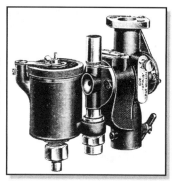
Cox 'Atmos' Carburettor.

Timken Bearings.

Warland Dual Rim.

Best and Lloyd advert.

Car Garages

The car manufacturers needed an outlet to sell their vehicles to the public and the public needed somewhere to have them repaired and maintained. From a very early stage, a new type of business appeared - the car garage.

These were the dealers and engineers who were the public face of the car industry and demonstrated an ability to survive that would allow them to outlast all of the pre-war marques.

The people that set up these businesses of necessity had extensive contacts within the industry and their names appear many times in the history of the marques. They also, commonly, had an interest in motor sport and appear in the results of many of the car races of the period.

The names of these companies are familiar today as nearly all still exist though they are, sadly, now mostly dealerships for foreign-built cars.

Thomas Startin

The company with the longest history has to be Thomas Startins. Thomas Startin was born in 1829 in Newcastle-under-Lyme and moved to Kings Norton and established a carriage building company in 1840. He acquired premises is Benacre Street and Vere Street on the site later occupied by Bristol Street Motors. He passed the business on to his son Frederick William Startin in the 1880s and they moved premises to the Victoria Works on the corner of Aston Road North and Holland Road. As cars appeared, Frederick Startin started to build car and van bodies. In 1923 the company won the

Thomas Startin works Aston Road North.

contract to coachbuild the Austin Seven van and thus started a long association with Austin (and later Rover) as a car dealership. In 1987 the company was bought by its Directors from the last living Startin family member and continues to this day, though no longer based in the City.

P J Evans

Percy James Evans, born in Birmingham in 1883, was a pioneer motorist and well known in motor manufacturing circles. He had started in business as a 'house furnisher' from premises on the corner of Stratford Road and Poplar Road, Sparkbrook before becoming a motor agent and opening Showrooms in the Roseberry Building in John Bright Street. This building has an important place in Birmingham's early motor industry as it was also the production base at various times for Heron (see **Heron**) and Mobile (see **Mobile**).

Percy J Evans in a racer.

He participated in, and won, TT races on the Isle of Man in his twenties and progressed to cars. Percy Evans was a keen motor racer but it was in an aeroplane accident flying back from the French Touring Car Grand Prix in 1922 that he was killed. His children were too young to take over the business so it was sold to his competitors Colonel Norman Steeley

Roseberry Building, John Bright Street.

PJ Evans showroom in 1913.

and Stanley Rodway, who steered the company.

In 1927 Bill Lyons, later Sir William Lyons, the founder of the Swallow Sidecar Company in Blackpool, was looking for a dealer in Birmingham to market his 'Swallow' version of the Austin Seven. He appointed P J Evans and the companies both grew. Swallow Sidecar became Jaguar at the beginning of the Second World War to remove the unfortunate associations with its SS branding. The company still operates but is now owned by Pendragon.

George Heath Motors

George Frederick Heath was born in Shirley in 1877 to William Heath, a gardener. George worked with his father as a gardener until his father's death and then got a job as a postman in 1894. He built racing cycles and took part in international shooting competitions. In about 1903 his career went in a new direction and he became a motor dealer, in partnership with a Mr Nicholls, with premises at 49 John Bright Street. He became involved with W T Willows (see **West**) in building airships in Handsworth and using them to advertise his garage business and continued trading, just along the street from P J Evans, until just after the First World War when the Rootes brothers, William and Reginald, bought the business as part of a larger expansion plan. The dealership continued in business in Birmingham until recently. George Heath died in Birmingham in 1934.

George Heath at the TT races.

Colliers

Richard Hamilton Collier was born in Chesterton in Cambridgeshire the son of a banker's clerk and became an engineer who commanded the Aircraft Repair Depot at St. Omer in France during the First World War having attained the rank of Colonel. On his return from duty he set up an engineering works in

KEEP YOUR

SWIFT

ON THE ROAD

Don't scrap your Swift Car. Keep it in confidence, for the Swift Service is to continue and will be better than ever.

Successors to Swift of Coventry Ltd., we are now the sole manufacturers and distributors of Swift replacements made from the original jigs and specifications. Refer to your present agent, who will confirm that your interests are in good hands—but if you have any difficulty write to us.

COLLIERS

CARRYING ON

R. H. COLLIER & CO. LTD.
(Successors to Swift of Coventry Ltd.)

COVENTRY ROAD, SOUTH YARDLEY, BIRMINGHAM, and at GREEN LANE, WOLVERHAMPTON.

'Phone: Acocks Green 1331 (4 lines).   'Grams: Colspar, Birmingham.

A Colliers advert from 1932.

South Yardley and repaired motor cars and, in 1926, started to sell cars.

Car building has always been a precarious occupation and companies were constantly going out of business making the finding of spare parts very difficult. Collier would buy the tools and jigs and produce the parts himself to replace those that were beyond repair. He purchased the assets of Crouch in Coventry in 1928, Clyno in Wolverhampton in 1929 and Swift of Coventry in 1931. R H Collier had served with William 'Max' Aitken, Lord Beaverbrook in WWI so Beaverbrook was aware of Collier's production facilities and commandeered them in the Second World War to manufacture aircraft components.

The company returned to selling cars after the war and is now a dealership for Fiat, Jaguar, Land Rover, Honda, Mazda, Citroen, Nissan and SEAT, employing over 300 people at three sites in Erdington, Acocks Green and Tamworth. RH Collier died in Birmingham in 1963.

Lowe and Wood

Charles Leonard Lowe and Joseph Daniel Wood had a showroom at 76-77 Broad Street from which they sold cars. In 1913 they became a dealership for Saxon cars imported from America. The business was run by Arthur Thistlewood from Wolverhampton.

Patrick Motors

Patrick Motors were another company that started life as coachbuilders (see **Patrick Motors**). The business started in 1931 at premises on the Bristol Road and exhibited at the Olympia Motor Show. They became an Austin dealership, then a British Leyland dealership alongside selling cars from a number of small sports car manufacturers.

They withdrew from the motor trade in the eighties, closing their last Mercedes dealership in Solihull in 1999. They are now a property development company but still maintain a representative selection of vehicles from the Patrick Collection of historic motor vehicles, most of which was sold at auction in 2004.

Smallbone and Son

The oldest family run motor garage in Birmingham still operating from its original site in Selly Oak. The company was started by 1927 by Percy A J Smallbone and his son Harold. For a short time Harold worked on a car of his own design, the HPS (see **HPS**) but it didn't go into any sort of production.

Smallbone and Son garage in the thirties.

The Surviving Cars

After over seventy years you wouldn't expect there to be many surviving examples of the work of Birmingham's early car makers - but there are.

It is hard to believe that many of the cars seen on the road today will still be around in ten years time let alone in 2080 but many of the early cars are treasured vehicles that will probably outlive the car sat outside your house at the moment.

Of the surviving cars few will have lasted this long without restoration or maintenance having taken their toll on their originality, but it is probably the intent of most historic car owners to keep them as faithful as possible using original replacement parts if they are available.

It wasn't always this way. The stories that are told about collections of early vehicles meeting an untimely end in less enlightened times are hair raising and the appreciation of what we have got before it is too late is by no means guaranteed.

In 1953 the film 'Genevieve' played its part in kindling a more widespread appreciation of what early cars had to offer but it is interesting to note that the cars that starred in that film - a 1904 Darracq and a 1904 Spyker were only 49 years old when the film was made, the equivalent of making a film today featuring an E-type Jaguar or an early Mini.

The cars on the road today are highly evolved pieces of technology. What they can do and the smoothness with which they do it could only have been dreamt of in the early years of the last century.

But this is a double-edged sword. I well remember opening the bonnet of car in the mid-eighties and not being able to recognise anything there. The dense network of pipes, ducts and cables connected together components that no longer reflected their function. The engine was now 'managed' and cars had started to head in the direction they have reached today when an essential workshop tool is the laptop and diagnostic software - not making it very easy for someone in the second-hand or third-hand market to keep it on the road without either a great deal of money or a degree in electronics.

This does not bode well for the historic cars of the future. The cars at the prestige end of the market or the ones that stand out enough to attract the attention of affluent collectors will survive but what about all the others, the cars that put the prestige offerings in context?

They all have their part to play, they are all part of the 'gene-pool' allowing us to avoid making the same mistakes over and over again, but if they cannot be affordably maintained they will go the way of all the cars lost in the scrappage scheme of 2009/10.

Worldwide there are an estimated 600,000,000 cars on the road today, an astonishing number, and one that is expanding as the aspirations of the populations of India, China and others grow to include car ownership, so is there any reason to preserve cars?

Well, yes. The resources and energy that go into making cars are not completely recovered when a car is scrapped even with the best of modern recycling technology. Energy expended in destruction only adds to the energy used in the original creation so, once a car has been built, if it has a useful function, it pays to preserve it.

In the case of the early Birmingham cars many met that untimely end and most of the marques described in this book have no surviving examples. This is a pity because if the early electrically propelled cars, for instance, had been on the road for more of the intervening 100+ years maybe we wouldn't be having to re-invent them from a standing start. Electric car technology certainly doesn't demonstrate over a century of improvement. The distance they can travel between charges, in particular, hasn't improved a great deal.

The cars that have survived have a function. They are a historic record, a blast of nostalgia, a form of recreation and for some even a means of transport. The one thing that they all provide is amusement and we all need cheering up sometimes.

The Surviving Factory Buildings

Despite the best efforts of the Luftwaffe, the City planners, highway engineers and property developers there are still a remarkable number of the factories that used to produce the Birmingham marques still in existence - but they are an endangered species. Ironically, the development of a road system that can handle the volume of vehicles now on the road has caused the demise of a number of factories in the city centre, notably the inner ring road, which cut a swath through the gun quarter. The wholesale markets replaced a dense fabric of streets with large buildings that are, themselves, now under threat. Such is the fate of buildings in a constantly changing city like Birmingham.

Even when the factories have been redeveloped remnants of them can still be seen. The vast site at Longbridge has been razed to the ground but there are still some buildings dating from before WWI remaining.

Many buildings have been 'facaded' with their frontages retained whilst the main bulk of the building has been rebuilt to modern standards. Some, like the Rover building in Hay Hall Road, Tyseley, have been re-clad so that, though many parts of the building are still there, they can no longer be seen - at least from the outside.

Under the heading of each of the marques there is a small excerpt from the old Ordnance Survey maps to indicate broadly where the works stood. The street numbering has often changed over the years making identification difficult. However, these are considered the most likely candidate buildings from the information available.

The maps on these two pages show the distribution of the motor factories in the city centre and the Tyseley area where the greatest concentration of makers were based. The Longbridge works are not shown as their location is well known. Some of the outlying plants are also not indicated but can be found on the website *www.brasspot.com*.

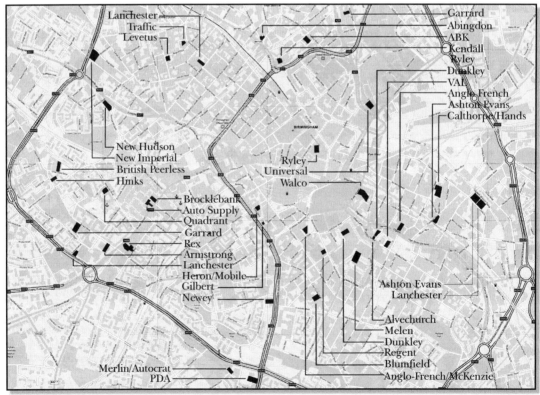

Motor Works in the central area.

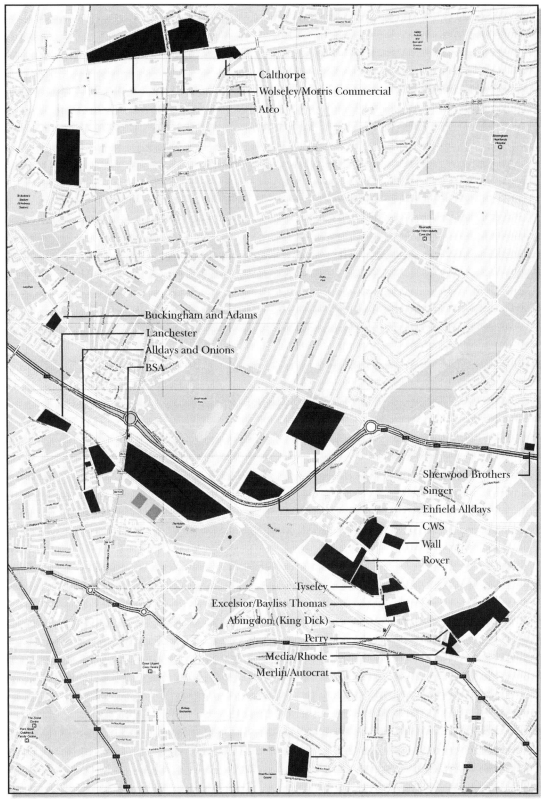

Motor works in the Bordesley/ Tyseley area.

207

Car Clubs and the Future

Pre-war examples of many of the Birmingham marques still exist. Some, like the Austin Seven, can be numbered in the thousands.

The way that most people experience them is in the many transport museums dotted around the country, but there are even more in private hands - they are just trickier to spot.

There are transport festivals, race events, shows at country houses and village fairs that give an opportunity to see the cars up close and talk to their owners... but how do you become an owner?

The first thing to do is join a Club.

It is a truism to state that car clubs are where the people who have the knowledge necessary to purchase and keep a pre-war car on the road gather. Many of the marques have Clubs specifically targeted at them. There are a large number of Austin marque clubs and even more Austin Seven Clubs, if you want to be even more specific. The number of Austin clubs reflects the number of surviving cars. In the case of the Austin Seven over 9000 are listed in the chassis register, but other marques fared less well and only single examples survive, so what do you do then?

There are a number of clubs that are not marque specific. Many are local and a few are international, notably the Vintage Sports Car Club and the Veteran Car Club. The depth of knowledge held within these Clubs and their archives is huge, so it would be odd not to join a Club and make use of it before heading into the world of historic motoring.

One big advantage that we now have is the internet, with sites like Ebay, Pre-war Car and Car and Classic making cars more available than ever before. But which one is a sensible purchase?
- ask the Club.

You have your new 'old' car and something drops off. Taking it to a modern garage will result in much head scratching and inappropriate application of modern technology so what do you do if you encounter a problem?
- ask the Club.

You have your car and it is roadworthy but you would like to do a little more with it than park it on the drive for the neighbours to admire. The media only usually advertise events when it is too late to register a car for it and a little notice is helpful so what can you do?
- ask the Club.

If nothing else, Clubs tend to have a higher concentration of people who have similar interests, the first step in meeting new people and another truism. By becoming involved in the historic vehicle world you are helping to preserve, in a roadworthy condition, fine examples of the car-builder's art and the chance to pass them on to future generations. The average age of historic car owners is high by the standards of most pastimes but the cars are there to be discovered by younger generations. Typically the younger enthusiasts have had that enthusiasm passed on down through the family along with heirlooms of a more mobile nature but there is a need to spread the net wider so that the knowledge can be passed on and the cars preserved.

Maybe it is time to join that Club?

Timeline of Birmingham Car Manufacturers

On the next page there is an illustration of each of the marques, put in order of appearance and arranged according to the length of time that they were each active.

Plotting the formation dates to create a chart and turning the chart upside down gives a graph of the level of activity in the industry, using this one measure. Though this doesn't give the complete picture, it does give a broad idea of what was going on.

The chart clearly shows the trends in car building and the effect of outside influences, such as legislation and conflict, on the rate of company formation.

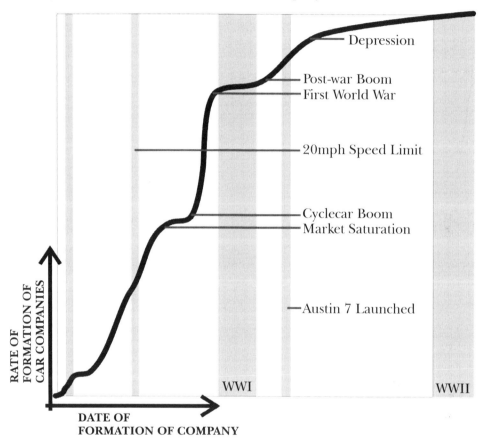

At the bottom left corner of the graph is the Emancipation Act of 1896 and the first opportunity to build cars that could legally be used on the roads of Britain. The start is a little bumpy but then there is a rapid growth in company formation that slows a little around 1903 before the increase in the speed limit to 20mph restores the growth rate. Around 1906 the rate again slows as the early-adopters market is saturated but then the cyclecar finds a new mass-market leading to massive boom in marque formation.

The First World War brings everything to a halt but the immediate post-war period sees another, short-lived boom before the economic depression starts to have an effect. The consolidation of car marques leading to fewer, larger companies is indicated by the gradual flattening-off of the graph as the Second World War approaches.

What this graph doesn't show, and can be seen from the illustration overleaf, is that the longer-lasting marques tend to be formed during the periods when the growth rate of company formation slows. The companies that appear at those times seem to be less governed by the whims of the market.

Timeline of Birmingham Car Manufacturers

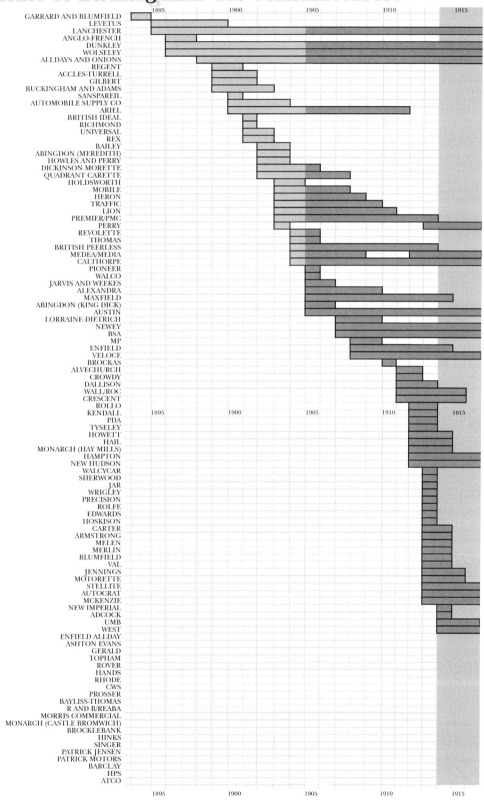

GARRARD AND BLUMFIELD
LEVETUS
LANCHESTER
ANGLO-FRENCH
DUNKLEY
WOLSELEY
ALLDAYS AND ONIONS
REGENT
ACCLES-TURRELL
GILBERT
BUCKINGHAM AND ADAMS
SANSPAREIL
AUTOMOBILE SUPPLY CO
ARIEL
BRITISH IDEAL
RICHMOND
UNIVERSAL
REX
BAILEY
ABINGDON (MEREDITH)
HOWLES AND PERRY
DICKINSON MORETTE
QUADRANT CARETTE
HOLDSWORTH
MOBILE
HERON
TRAFFIC
LION
PREMIER/PMC
PERRY
REVOLETTE
THOMAS
BRITISH PEERLESS
MEDEA/MEDIA
CALTHORPE
PIONEER
WALCO
JARVIS AND WEEKES
ALEXANDRA
MAXFIELD
ABINGDON (KING DICK)
AUSTIN
LORRAINE-DIETRICH
NEWEY
BSA
MP
ENFIELD
VELOCE
BROCKAS
ALVECHURCH
CROWDY
DALLISON
WALL/ROC
CRESCENT
ROLLO
KENDALL
PDA
TYSELEY
HOWETT
HAIL
MONARCH (HAY MILLS)
HAMPTON
NEW HUDSON
WALCYCAR
SHERWOOD
JAR
WRIGLEY
PRECISION
ROLFE
EDWARDS
HOSKISON
CARTER
ARMSTRONG
MELEN
MERLIN
BLUMFIELD
VAL
JENNINGS
MOTORETTE
STELLITE
AUTOCRAT
MCKENZIE
NEW IMPERIAL
ADCOCK
UMB
WEST
ENFIELD ALLDAY
ASHTON EVANS
GERALD
TOPHAM
ROVER
HANDS
RHODE
CWS
PROSSER
BAYLISS-THOMAS
R AND B/REABA
MORRIS COMMERCIAL
MONARCH (CASTLE BROMWICH)
BROCKLEBANK
HINKS
SINGER
PATRICK JENSEN
PATRICK MOTORS
BARCLAY
HPS
ATCO

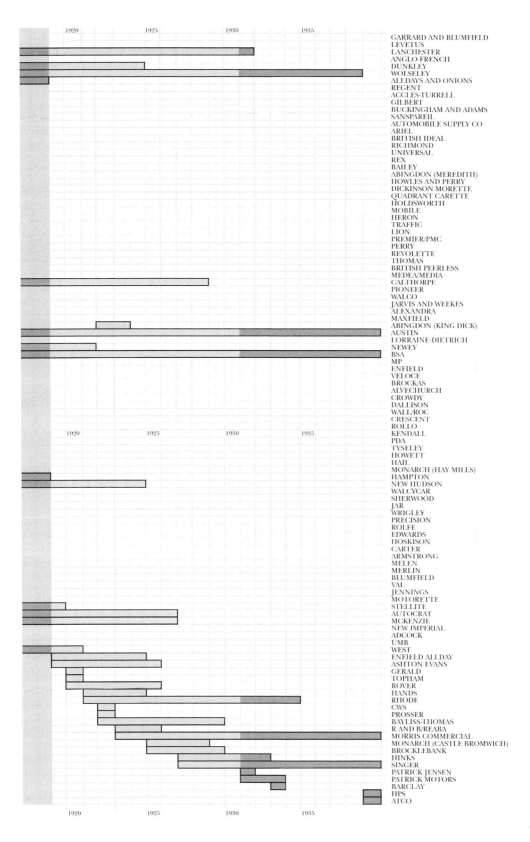

GARRARD AND BLUMFIELD
LEVETUS
LANCHESTER
ANGLO-FRENCH
DUNKLEY
WOLSELEY
ALLDAYS AND ONIONS
REGENT
ACCLES-TURRELL
GILBERT
BUCKINGHAM AND ADAMS
SANSPAREIL
AUTOMOBILE SUPPLY CO
ARIEL
BRITISH IDEAL
RICHMOND
UNIVERSAL
REX
BAILEY
ABINGDON (MEREDITH)
HOWLES AND PERRY
DICKINSON MORETTE
QUADRANT CARETTE
HOLDSWORTH
MOBILE
HERON
TRAFFIC
LION
PREMIER/PMC
PERRY
REVOLETTE
THOMAS
BRITISH PEERLESS
MEDEA/MEDIA
CALTHORPE
PIONEER
WALCO
JARVIS AND WEEKES
ALEXANDRA
MAXFIELD
ABINGDON (KING DICK)
AUSTIN
LORRAINE-DIETRICH
NEWEY
BSA
MP
ENFIELD
VELOCE
BROCKAS
ALVECHURCH
CROWDY
DALLISON
WALL/ROC
CRESCENT
ROLLO
KENDALL
PDA
TYSELEY
HOWETT
HAIL
MONARCH (HAY MILLS)
HAMPTON
NEW HUDSON
WALCYCAR
SHERWOOD
JAR
WRIGLEY
PRECISION
ROLFE
EDWARDS
HOSKISON
CARTER
ARMSTRONG
MELEN
MERLIN
BLUMFIELD
VAL
JENNINGS
MOTORETTE
STELLITE
AUTOCRAT
MCKENZIE
NEW IMPERIAL
ADCOCK
UMB
WEST
ENFIELD ALLDAY
ASHTON EVANS
GERALD
TOPHAM
ROVER
HANDS
RHODE
CWS
PROSSER
BAYLISS-THOMAS
R AND B/REABA
MORRIS COMMERCIAL
MONARCH (CASTLE BROMWICH)
BROCKLEBANK
HINKS
SINGER
PATRICK JENSEN
PATRICK MOTORS
BARCLAY
HPS
ATCO

211

Index

Index of People

Goodman, Eugene Frederick	1890-1970	Veloce
Goodman, Percy John	1884-1953	Veloce
Gothard, Joseph	1842-1914	Buckingham and Adams
Graham, Hubert Berger	1873-1944	MP
Hail, F N	?	Hail
Hamstead, Samuel	1881-?	UMB
Hands, George William	1871-1938	Calthorpe/Hands
Hawnt, William Montague	1874-1914	British Ideal
Hinks, Walter James	1872-?	Hinks
Horne, John James	1862-1938	Heron
Hoskison, Harry	1878-?	Hoskison
Hoskinson, Samuel	1881-1942	Hoskison
Howell, Ellen Elizabeth Anne	1886-1958	Merlin/Autocrat
Howles, Frank	1864-1933	Howles and Perry
Inshaw, John George	1855-1939	Rex
Jarvis, John Baxter	1879-1919	Jarvis and Weekes
Jennings, Arthur	1885-1918	Jennings
Jensen, Frank Alan	1906-1994	Patrick Jensen Motors
Jensen, Richard Arthur	1909-1977	Patrick Jensen Motors
Kendall, Fred Franks	1892-1955	Kendall
Lamplugh, Henry Arthur	1872-1937	Tyseley
Lanchester. Frederick	1868-1946	Lanchester
Lanchester, George Herbert	1874-1970	Lanchester
Lanchester, Frank	1871-1960	Lanchester
Leggatt, Franklin Warrenne	1883-1958	Armstrong
Leggatt, Frederick William	1844-1917	Armstrong
Levetus, Arthur	1877-1916	Levetus
Levetus, Edward Moses	1851-1898	Levetus
Levetus, Hymen	1849-1906	Levetus
L'Hollier, Leon Francoise	1847-1914	Anglo-French
Lintine, David Fridlander	1875-1941	Mobile
Lintine, Mark	1866-1955	Mobile
Lloyd, Albert	1857-?	Quadrant
Lloyd, Walter John	1853-1934	Quadrant
Lloyd, William Arthur	1855-1922	Walco
Lloyd, William Clayton	1862-1937	Revolette
Lord, Leonard Percy	1896-1967	Austin
Mabbutt, George Prosser	1849-1929	Abingdon (King Dick)
Mabbutt, Thomas	1830-1906	Abingdon (King Dick)
Maxfield, Alfred Pericles	1878-1964	Maxfield
McKenzie, Thomas Clyde	1867-1933	McKenzie/Rhode
Mead, Frederick William	1879-1966	Medea/Rhode
Melen, George Frederick	1868-1939	Melen
Melen, Henry Corfield	1870-1926	Melen
Meredith, Hubert Augustus	1874-1953	Abingdon (Meredith)
Meredith, John Child	1831-1898	Abingdon (Meredith)
Meredith, Ralph Child	1876-1932	Abingdon (Meredith)
Miller, Edward Alexandra	1854-1934	Crescent
Miller, Henry Taverner	1886-1960	Crescent
Milliship, Archibald James W	1878-1958	Lanchester/Jarvis and Weekes
Morris, William Richard	1877-1963	Morris Commercial
Newey, Edwin Gordon	1884-1927	Newey
Paddon, William	?	Hampton
Patrick, Albert Morton	1873-1951	Patrick/Patrick Jensen Motors
Patrick, Joseph Albert Morton	1911-1982	Patrick/Patrick Jensen Motors

Perry, Albert Thornton	1876-?	Howles and Perry
Phillips, John Alfred	1876-?	Rolfe
Pickering, Harold Cecil	1885-1953	PDA
Pilkington, Alfred Henry	1865-1934	Rex/Premier/PMC/Motorette
Pilkington, Arthur Abel	1862-1929	Rex
Pilkington, George	1860-1921	Rex
Pilkington, William	1857-1928	Rex/Premier/PMC/Motorette
Priest, William Alexander	1869-1942	Quadrant
Prosser, Edwin Thomas	1895-1960	Prosser
Pugh Charles Vernon	1869-1921	Lanchester/Atco
Reece, Joseph Henry	1869-1943	Regent
Renwick, William Somerville	1887-1962	Reaba
Richards, R W	?	Brocklebank
Richmond, Henry S	1877-?	Richmond
Rogers, Sir Hallewell	1864-1931	BSA
Rogers, William Ivy	1864-1935	Autocrat/Merlin
Rose, Henry Percival	1885-1972	Wall/Roc
Rowbotham, Walter	?	Levetus
Rowland, John David	1873-1937	Rollo
Ryley, John Albert	1861-1931	Ryley
Sangster, Charles Thomas Brock	1872-1935	Ariel
Sangster, John Young	1896-1977	Rover
Scarborough, John Thomas	1859-?	Automobile Supply Co
Shannessy, John Joseph	1869-1934	Buckingham and Adams
Sherwood, Albert E	1879-1965	Sherwood
Sherwood, Allen	1877-1952	Sherwood
Siddeley, John Davenport	1866-1953	Wolseley/Wolseley-Siddeley
Singer, George	1847-1909	Singer
Smallbone, Harold Percy	1915-1987	HPS
Smith, Arthur Joel	1880-1921	MP
Smith, John Milbrowe	1854-?	Lion
Smith, Robert Walker	1857-1933	Enfield
Tailby, Edward Mantle	1869-1932	Alldays and Onions
Taylor, Frederick Dudley Gerald	1891-1939	Gerald
Thomas, Walter Frederick	1872-1931	Thomas
Topham, Arthur	1887-1956	Topham
Tovey, George Edwin	1871-1946	Tovey
Turrell, Charles McRobie	1875-1923	Accles-Turrell
Walker, Reginald Eric	1883-1958	Monarch (Tyseley)
Wall, Arthur William	1873-1943	Wall/Roc
Warren, James	?	British Peerless
Warne, James Thomas	1829-1880	Rollo
Wathen, John Cornelius	1875-1936	Hoskison
Wathen, William Henry	1872-1967	Hoskison
Watkins, Valentine	1870-1955	V.A.L.
Weekes, Francis E.	1877-1948	Jarvis and Weekes
Weigel, Daniel Michel	1875-?	Crowdy
West, Enoch John	1864-1937	West
Whitehouse, Samuel Groves	1861-1930	Alexandra
Wilson, Edward Arthur	?	New Hudson
Wolseley, Frederick York	1837-1899	Wolseley
Wright, Alfred Cecil	1858-1920	Rollo
Wrigley, Edward Greenwood	1868-1941	Wrigley

Index of Marques

Hoskison	1913	139
Howett	1912-1914	126
Howles and Perry	1902-1903	67
HPS	1939	192
JAR	1913	134
Jarvis and Weekes	1905-1906	90
Jennings	1913-1915	148
Kendall	1912-1913	123
Lanchester	1895-1931	28
Levetus	1895-1899	25
Lion	1903-1910	75
Lorraine-Dietrich	1907-1909	101
Maxfield	1905-1914	92
McKenzie	1913-1926	154
Medea/Media	1904-1908, 1912-1916	83
Melen	1913-1914	142
Merlin	1913-1914	143
Mobile	1903-1907	72
Monarch (Castle Bromwich)	1925-1928	182
Monarch (Hay Mills)	1912-1914	127
Morris Commercial	1923-1968	180
Motorette	1913-1915	149
MP	1908-1909	107
New Hudson	1912-1924	130
New Imperial	1914	156
Newey	1907-1921	102
Patrick Jensen Motors	1931	189
Patrick Motors	1931-1933	190
PDA	1912-1913	124
Perry	1903, 1913-1916	78
Pioneer	1905	88
PMC	1909-1913	76
Precision	1913	136
Premier	1903-1908	76
Prosser	1922	177
Quadrant/Carette	1902-1908	69
R&B/Reaba	1923-1925	179
Regent	1899-1900	48
Revolette	1904-1905	80
Rex	1901-1902	62
Rhode	1921-1934	172
Richmond	1901	60
Roc	1911-1915	118
Rolfe	1913	137
Rollo	1912-1913	121
Rover	1920-1925	169
Sanspareil	1900	55
Sherwood	1913	133
Singer	1927-1939	185
Stellite	1913-1919	150

Thomas	1904-1905	81
Topham	1920	168
Traffic	1903-1909	74
Tyseley	1912-1913	125
UMB	1914-1916	158
Universal	1901-1902	61
VAL	1913-1914	147
Veloce	1908-1916	110
Walco	1905	89
Walcycar/Wall-Car/WallyCar	1913	132
Wall	1911-1915	118
West	1914-1920	159
Wolseley	1896-1904, 1910-1938	40
Wolseley-Siddeley	1905-1909	40
Wrigley	1913	135

If you are interested in finding out more about the pre-war Birmingham marques please go to the website associated with this book: **www.brasspot.com**
The website is a repository of all the information that would not fit into the book, and will be an ongoing source of updates and errata. It is free of charge to anyone who has a copy of this book. To access the website you will be required to answer a question, so keep the book to hand when you register.

Traffic (!) in New Street in the Twenties.

Bibliography and Further Reading

GENERAL

The Motorists's Companion
1936
John Prioleau

The Wonder Book of Motors
1926
Harry Golding

The Complete Catalogue of British Cars
1997
David Culshaw & Peter Horrobin

The Complete Encyclopaedia of Motor Cars
1968
G N Georgano

From Cyclecar to Microcar
1981
Michael Worthington-Williams

Veteran and Edwardian Motor cars
1955
D Scott-Moncrieff

The A-Z of Cars of the 1920s
1994
Nick Baldwin

The A-Z of Cars of the 1930s
1989
Michael Sedgwick & Mark Gillies

The Ilustrated Guide to Classic British Cars
2000
Graham Robson & Michael Ware

Great Car Collections of the World
1986
Edward Eves & Dan Burger

The Halcyon Days of Motoring
2006
A B Demaus

British Motoring - The Golden Age
2010
A B Demaus

When Motoring Was Fun
2008
Tom Tyler

The World's Automobiles
1931
G R Doyle

Cyclecars - An Anotated Index
2009
Stephen Kay

Automobile Treasures
1963
T R Nicholson

The Birth of the British Motor Car
1982
T R Nicholson

Automobiles of Great Britain
1972
Niall McCarthy

Veteran and Vintage Cars
1982
Peter Roberts

How to Build a Cyclecar
1913
Stanley Pontlarge

The Marques of Coventry
1990
Brian Long

The Light Car - A Technical History
1970
C F Caunter

Edwardian Cars
1955
Ernest F Carter

The Complete Motorist
1904
A B Filson Young

When Motoring Was Fun
2008
Tom Tyler

MARQUE SPECIFIC

The Austin Seven Source Book   Bryan Purves
1989
Alldays and Onions - A Brief History   Norman Painting
2002
The Real Wolseley - Adderley Park Works   Norman Painting
2002
Herbert Austin   Roy Church
1979
Rover - The First Ninety Years   Eric Dymock
1993
West Cars of Coventry 1904-1915   John Spicer
2005
Making Cars at Longbridge   Gillian Bardsley & Colin Corke
2006
The Lanchester Legacy   C.S.Clarke
1995

COACHBUILDING

A History of Coachbuilding   George A Oliver
1962
Coachbuilding - The Hand-Crafted Car Body   Jonathan Wood
2008

CAR CLUBS

Veterans of the Road   Elizabeth Nagle
1955
Light Car Journey   Tim Cork
2007
This Motoring   Stenson Cooke
1931

INDUSTRIAL HISTORY

Birmingham's Industrial Heritage 1900 - 2000   Ray Shill
2002
Workshop of the World   Ray Shill
2006

SOCIAL HISTORY

One Policeman's Story   Eric St Johnston
1978
One and All - An autobiography   Richard Tangye
1890
Philip Rodway - A Tale of Two Theatres   His Daughters
1934
A History of Birmingham   Chris Upton
1993

MAGAZINES AND PERIODICALS

Autocar   Published 1895 - present day.
The Automotor Journal   Published 1897 - 1908
The Motor   Published 1903 - 1988
Light Car and Cyclecar   Published 1912 - 1953
Old Motor   Published 1962 - 1982
The Automobile   Published 1982 - present day.